Managing Tomorrow's High-Performance Unions

Managing Tomorrow's High-Performance Unions

Thomas A. Hannigan

QUORUM BOOKS
Westport, Connecticut • London

331.87
H24m

Library of Congress Cataloging-in-Publication Data

Hannigan, Thomas A., 1935–
    Managing tomorrow's high-performance unions / Thomas A. Hannigan.
      p. cm.
    Includes bibliographical references and index.
    ISBN 1–56720–102–4 (alk. paper)
    1. Trade-unions—United States—Management. I. Title.
    HD6508.H245   1998
    331.87'068—dc21   97–15988

British Library Cataloguing in Publication Data is available.

Library of Congress Catalog Card Number: 97–15988
ISBN: 1–56720–102–4

First published in 1998

Quorum Books, 88 Post Road West, Westport, CT 06881
An imprint of Greenwood Publishing Group, Inc.

Printed in the United States of America

The paper used in this book complies with the
Permanent Paper Standard issued by the National
Information Standards Organization (Z39.48–1984).

10 9 8 7 6 5 4 3 2 1

Copyright Acknowledgment

Every reasonable effort has been made to trace the owners of copyright materials in this book, but in
some instances this has proven impossible. The editor and publisher will be glad to receive information leading to more complete acknowledgments in subsequent printings of the book, and in the
meantime extend their apologies for any omissions.

Contents

Preface

> Managing is a specific work. As such it requires specific skills. . . . No
> manager can expect to master all these skills. But every manager needs to
> understand what they are, what they can do for him, and what they require
> of him. Every manager needs basic literacy with respect to essential mana-
> gerial skills.
>
> Peter F. Drucker, *Management Tasks, Responsibilities, Practices*

Managing Tomorrow's High-Performance Unions is about an exciting new
style of management that will lead to recovery and revitalization of organized labor. It is concerned with developing the basic management literacy
and essential management skills for building tomorrow's high-performance
unions consistent with labor's culture and tradition. It is a two-front response to managing union organizations in a hostile, complex, and turbulent
environment and to labor's new and expanded role in a shared-fate, participatory-management environment. It is aimed at present and future union
officers—elected, appointed, and hopeful—who are called upon to make
everyday decisions that ultimately determine the destiny of America's unions. Its primary objective is to help them become more inspiring leaders,
better managers, more effective workers' representatives in the new American workplace.

Labor's natural aversion to management and budgeting appears to be a
major obstacle to the efficient operation of unions. Of the two, budgeting is
probably the more unpopular and difficult to accept. However, some form
of measuring performance is absolutely essential for successful management. Thus, this book focuses on the allocation of resources among nine
basic union functions and on the evaluation of results rather than budget
policies and practices. No matter how large or wealthy an organization is, its

resources are finite and must be allocated efficiently to achieve desired results. Resource allocation and results evaluation are the primary means that nonprofit organizations use to measure performance.

It can be argued that resource allocation and results evaluation are just other forms of budgeting. However, to union officers there is a simple, but critical, distinction. Resource allocation and results evaluation are part of a union officer's daily activities, while budgeting is done for them by their accountants. Likewise, management is also an important part of a union leader's daily routine. Thus, *Managing Tomorrow's High-Performance Unions* hopes to promote acceptance of management concepts, principles, and techniques by presenting them as familiar, daily union activities.

Since management is not a very popular word in labor's world, it is helpful to understand an important distinction. Management can refer to either the function of managing or the class of people who manage organizations. Management, as a class, triggers images of suspicion, exploitation, and conflict for most union leaders. Consequently, union leaders probably have a greater aversion to the word "management" when it refers to the class rather than the function. To note this distinction, in this text, whenever "management" refers to the class, it will be seen as an uppercase Management. Accordingly, organized Labor will always be in the uppercase.

To further minimize negative emotions, a clear understanding of the meaning of the words "manage," "manager," and "management" is helpful. Managing is to have charge or responsibility for; to handle, direct, govern, or control; or to conduct business and commercial affairs of an organization. A manager is a person charged with the direction and control of an organization or a person who controls and allocates resources and expenditures. Management, as a class, refers to the person or persons controlling and directing the affairs of an organization. The three levels of Management are strategic, tactical, and operational. However, management also refers to the function of managing. The four basic management functions are planning, organizing, directing, and controlling.

Obviously, the words "manage," "manager," and "management" refer to common, necessary activities. We are all managers. Everyone manages something. Religious leaders, other union leaders, friends, parents, and spouses are all managers. Some are good managers, and some are poor managers. Most are somewhere in between and, thus, can become better managers. Some managers are sensitive, while others are insensitive. Some managers are brilliant and creative while others are dull and unimaginative. People are not born with Management skills; they acquire them through experience and study. A college degree in business management or a masters of business administration (MBA) degree is not necessary to be an excellent manager. In fact, fewer than 20 percent of the chief executive officers of large corporations have business school degrees.[1] Sound Management decisions are a combination of intuition, experience, sensitivity, knowledge, and mostly hard work.

References to managers are embedded in the history of craft unions. From the very beginning, the business manager has been responsible for managing the business of the construction of local unions. Whether or not the word "manager" is part of the job title, all union officers and representatives have Management responsibilities. In this text, a union manager is an officer, man or woman, who is responsible for the effective and efficient operation of a union organization. Thus, union officers are leaders, workers' representatives, and managers, as seen in the figure below.

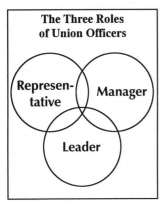

**The Three Roles
of Union Officers**

Represen-tative

Manager

Leader

It is clear that as workers' representatives, union officers are obligated to represent their members' interests, but there is often confusion between the roles of a leader and a manager. James MacGregor Burns, Pulitzer Prize-winning author, noted that the ultimate test of leadership is whether or not social change is intended. He believes that leaders promote social change, while managers are concerned with the efficient operation of their organization and do not consciously intend social change.[2] More simply put, good leaders must do the right things, while good managers must do things right. Union officers and representatives, as leaders, workers' representatives, and managers, are responsible for both doing the right thing and doing things right. Their record for doing the right thing is well documented. Now they must become high-performance managers—much more concerned with the efficient operation of their unions. High-performance managers provide their members and employees with the necessary information, skills, incentives, and responsibility to make decisions essential for innovation, quality improvement, and rapid response to change.

As a result of the AFL-CIO's report *Changing Situation of Workers and Their Unions*, there has been a recent surge of interest in developing management materials for Labor unions. However, the number of useful resources in this area is still very limited. Each year American businesses spend about $52 billion dollars on education and training, most of which is for managerial employees, while Management training and development are at the bottom of the AFL-CIO's priority list.[3] *Managing Tomorrow's High-Performance Unions* is an attempt to reverse this situation. Hopefully, unions and college-and university-based Labor education centers and the University and College Labor Education Association (UCLEA) will make a greater effort to collaborate with their business management colleagues to conduct research and develop materials for managing unions. Labor's survival as a major influential institution in the twenty-first century will require a drastic change in the prevailing assumption that Management development and training are of little or no value for union organizations.

To better understand the benefits of making Management development and training a high priority of unions, it is helpful to think in terms of new members. For example, if a large international union with $70 million in per capita receipts improved efficiency just 5 percent—$3.5 million—that would be the equivalent of over 36,000 new members. Even better: there was no cost involved in recruiting them, and there is no continuing cost for member support services. Similarly, total union income is estimated to be $5 billion: thus, a 5 percent efficiency improvement would be the equivalent of around 700,000 new members![4] An investment in Management development and training is a highly leveraged, safe investment. The savings would be reinvested in enabling technologies and other organization-building strategies. On the other hand, the likelihood of organizing 36,000 or 700,000 new members in today's hostile environment is totally unrealistic, and attempts to do so will be extraordinarily expensive and self destructive.

Managing Tomorrow's High-Performance Unions is not intended to be a comprehensive presentation of the nine basic union functions, nor is it intended to be a comprehensive presentation of the four basic management functions. In eight chapters it brings the basic union functions and the basic management functions together for the first time. Major subjects are summarized in a paragraph or two, sometimes a sentence or two. There are many lists, since lists are simple and easy to read and retain, and more important, they are a quick source of a lot of information. My objective is to save on words, splurge on information, and cover a lot of territory.

Ideally, it is best to read *Managing Tomorrow's High-Performance Unions* from the front to the back, but a reader with a special interest can read any section, in any order, and still benefit. It is a unique blend of practical, how-to-do-it tips and academic theory. There is something for every union leader with Management responsibilities. For readers interested in a more in-depth study in either the industrial relations or the management fields, there are many excellent works and an enormous amount of ongoing research in both areas. This text's bibliography is an excellent starting point.

Chapter 1, "Basic Union Functions," redefines a union, lists the nine basic union functions, and links the four basic management functions to the nine basic union functions.

Chapter 2, "The Union Environment," notes the importance of culture and tradition in managing unions and how the external environment influences the structure of a union. It concludes with a broad, general description of the union structure and governance.

Chapter 3, "Management for Union Leaders," starts with a brief history of management. It recognizes managers as professionals and Management's basic responsibilities. It then identifies the skills and disciplines of high-performance manager, and lists timesaving tips for working smart. This chapter also includes sections on resource allocation, managing nonprofit organizations, and managing consultants.

Chapter 4, "High-Performance Unions: Attributes of Excellence," is concerned with the qualities of excellent union organizations. Innovation is equated to excellence and is measured by performance drawn from an organization's unique competencies and qualities.

Chapter 5, "Communication—The Essence of Excellence," explains interpersonal and organizational communication, distinguishes between communication and information, describes the relationship of communication and management, notes the growing importance of contemporary communication practice theory, and identifies the most destructive communication barriers.

Chapter 6, "High-Performance Union Decision Makers," teaches that a manager is first and foremost a decision maker. The chapter covers decision theory, risk and probability, and risk and ethics. It explains the prescriptive, four-step decision model and identifies the reasons for faulty decisions. It also explains how risk and probability are critical to good decision making and how ethics are a guide for doing the right things.

In Chapter 7, "High-Performance Union Planners and Organizers," the planners section identifies the five key elements of planning and the hierarchy of organizational plans. It explains the eight-step high-performance union planning process and presents the 7-S framework as a diagnostic tool. The planners section also lists the core objectives and key strategies of high-performance unions. The organizers section is concerned with building an organization structure, and explains a four-step process that breaks it up horizontally, next breaks it up vertically, then puts it together, and finally fits people in.

In Chapter 8, "High-Performance Union Directors and Controllers," the directors section explains leadership and identifies the traits of successful leaders. It then covers motivation and teambuilding. The controllers section explains the control process and lists the various types of controls. It also covers budget systems and performance controls.

Managing Tomorrow's High-Performance Unions is primarily concerned with the basic union functions of administration, governance, and organization building and testifies to my confidence in the inherent excellence of unions and their enormous potential. It is primarily based on my four decades as a card-carrying member of the International Brotherhood of Electrical Workers (IBEW). Over this period I worked as an apprentice, journeyman electrician, foreman, director of the Research and Education Department, and assistant, administrative assistant, and executive assistant to the international secretary. My Management credentials include almost forty years as a student of management and twenty-two years as an actual practitioner at the operational, tactical, and strategic levels. My primary resources were my personal library, notes, clippings, and experiences.

Today, with employee involvement and worker participation, management is no longer the exclusive jurisdiction of managers. Thus, union leaders need a strong management background, not only to manage their unions more effectively and efficiently but, equally important, to more effectively represent their members in the new American workplace, where Labor and Management cooperate as *equal* partners to improve productivity and the quality of worklife in a shared-fate environment.

The strength of organized Labor is not measured by the number of members and percapita income generated but by the knowledge, skills, abilities, loyalty, and commitment of the union members in a high-performance union environment. Monday, 3 January 2000, the first workday of the next century, is only a few short years away. Now is the time for Labor to focus its energies, talents, and visions on the challenges and opportunities of the twenty-first century. Now is the time to develop a new commitment to Management training and development. *Managing Tomorrow's High-Performance Unions* is a first step; much more needs to be done; management concepts, principles, and techniques need to be adapted to the union environment, which requires much research and new forms of collaboration.

NOTES

1. John Dunlop, *The Management of Labor Unions* (Lexington, MA: Lexington Books, 1990), 17.
2. James MacGregor Burns, *Leadership* (New York: Harper & Row, 1978), 251.
3. Knight-Ridder, "Making Education Their Business," *Washington Post*, 17 Nov. 1996.
4. Aaron Bernstein, "Sweeney's Blitz," *Business Week*, 17 Feb. 1997, 56–62.

Acknowledgments

To Joseph D. Keenan, my early career role model, for his total dedication to his religion, his country, his union, and his uncanny knack for always doing the right thing.

To Ralph A. Leigon, my later career role model, for his remarkable patience, his talent for applying past experiences to present day situations, his unflappability in difficult situations, and his unique ability to collect information, make the right decisions, time their implementation, and delegate responsibility to get results.

To Virginia Beane, my special friend and secretary extraordinaire, who, before her untimely death, was so very helpful in editing early drafts.

To Tertia Sikora, my long-time friend and neighbor, who, to my good fortune, shared her publishing experience and creative keyboard skills.

Finally, and especially, to my precious wife Del for her sensitive understanding, loving patience, and confident support.

1

Basic Union Functions

> The union's task is to define the interests of workers in all sections in which their rights are concerned. The experience of history teaches that organizations of this type are an indispensable element of social life, especially in modern industrialized societies. . . . They are indeed advocates for the struggle for social justice, for the just rights of working people in accordance with their individual professions.
>
> It is characteristic of work that it first and foremost unites people. In this consists its social power: the power to build a community. In the final analysis, both those who work and those who manage . . . must in some way be united in this community.
>
> Pope John Paul II, *Encyclical on Human Work*

This chapter redefines a union organization, explains the nine basic union functions, and relates them to the four basic management functions. These subjects are covered only in sufficient depth to establish a basic relationship between management concepts, principles, and techniques, and the basic union functions. *Union Government and Organization* by James Wallihan was selected as the primary union reference because it was commissioned by the George Meany Center for Labor Studies pursuant to the U.S. Department of Labor contract. More important, it is one of the best books on union structure, administration, and governance functions available.

It is extremely important that union leaders recognize that Labor unions are nonprofit organizations and thus share many similarities with other nonprofit organizations. For example, Peter Drucker believes that the common mission of all nonprofit organizations is to satisfy the needs of the American people for self-realization, for living out their ideals, their beliefs, and their best opinions of themselves. The primary objective of nonprofit organizations, he contends, is to bring about change in individuals and in society and to provide community and common purposes. [1] Both Drucker's mission and objective are most appropriate for Labor unions.

Since there is much more information available on managing nonprofit organizations than there is on managing Labor unions, it is very helpful for unions to look for commonalities with other nonprofit organizations. However, it is also essential to keep in mind that in spite of many commonalities with other nonprofit organizations, unions are absolutely unique in that they are primarily conditioned on employment. So, in this book, we enter a unique and unexplored territory.

Life is becoming so very complicated that more and more people are searching for meaning and connection—the kind of support system that is found only in a community. Since communities are part of a larger whole, their success is measured by the community's relationship to the external environment. Communities just don't happen. Community building takes instigators, people willing to reach out to people and willing to share a common set of objectives. Suzanne Keller, a Princeton University sociology professor, sees community as "a sense your destiny is bound up with one another." In Labor's world, this sense is called "solidarity."

Amitai Etzioni, author of *The Spirit of Community*, explains that community includes two elements. The first involves being part of an interpersonal web, and the second is the moral voice that makes people better than they would be if they did not belong to the community. He sees community as a group of "like minded people" bound together by shared experiences, history, rituals, traditions, rules, and common values. Etzioni believes true community also enhances individual identity since it provides supportive relationships, tolerates differences among community members, and respects their viewpoints even when disagreeing with them.[2]

Etzioni's "community" is crucial to the future success of Labor unions. Workers are bound in unions as brothers and sisters in pursuit of individual improvement and social change. Since the Labor environment is a community of communities, high-performance union leaders understand how important the concept of community is to the future success of their union. They continually look for new ways unions can satisfy the needs of American workers for self-realization, for living out their ideas, their beliefs, and their best opinions of themselves. The American Federation of Labor-Congress of Industrial Organizations (AFL-CIO) recommendation that national unions add a new membership classification for associate members is an exciting new dimension with great potential for attracting new members and broadening the community of workers.

Wallihan defines a union as a continuous organization of employees that seeks to maintain and improve the terms and conditions of employment through collective bargaining and through other means. He notes that unions are unique in that they are voluntary organizations, have a dependence and conflict relationship with employers, and are democratic models.[3] However, in recognition of the growing importance of common purpose and community, this book defines the *new American union as a voluntary association of workers that represents their interests in the workplace, provides common purpose and community based on service to workers, and advocates social changes necessary to improve the lives of all workers*.

BASIC UNION FUNCTIONS

The fundamental reason for the existence of Labor unions is to represent the workers' interests and concerns, both in the workplace and in society. This representation process includes the following nine basic union functions:

- Collective bargaining
  - Contract negotiations
  - Contract administration
- Organizing
- Jurisdiction
- Administration
- Governance
- Political action
- Community action
- Organization building
  - Education and communication
  - Public relations
  - Leadership recruitment and development
- International affairs.[4]

These functions, from a Management perspective, can be thought of as systems or strategic areas.

Collective Bargaining

The first union function, collective bargaining, is an extremely complex process that begins after recognition of the union and covers all the aspects of work. Collective bargaining is Labor's defining distinction—its primary product, its reason for existence. Typically, it is divided into contract negotiations and contract administration. Contract negotiations include all activities related to wages, hours, and working conditions, while contract administration is concerned with the interpretation and implementation of the results of the negotiations.

Global competition is forcing American businesses to become more productive, which requires Labor-Management cooperation and employee participation. Labor-Management cooperation includes institutional processes and procedures that improve industrial relations and solve problems out-side, but consistent with, the traditional collective bargaining relationship. Employee participation refers to programs and policies that involve workers in discussions about improving the work environment and group perform-ance. Employee participation programs, which include quality of worklife (QWL), quality circles, and employee involvement, usually do not include any fundamental work reorganization. Employee participation programs are known as off-line participation.[5]

Since most employers are reluctant to redesign work to truly empower employees, unions must lead in the pursuit of new levels of Labor-Manage-ment cooperation and worker participation. The Greer, Margolis, Mitchell, Burns, & Associates Inc. (GMMB&A) report *Being Heard: Strategic Commu-nications Report and Recommendations*, found that a large majority of workers recognize the pressures of foreign competition, believe that unions are simplis-tically adversarial, and want unions to work collaboratively with Management to improve productivity.[6] Typical collaborative techniques include Labor-Man-agement councils, action councils, planning teams, action teams, and autono-mous work teams. Team systems look to improve work tasks and achieve or-ganizational goals through group problem solving and group responsibility. Team systems, which include job classification, job reduction, job enlarge-ment, job rotation, and reductions in direct supervision, involve work reor-ganization.[7]

The AFL-CIO's 1994 report *The New American Workplace: A Labor Per-spective* stresses the need for greater union participation in their employers' strategic decisions that affect their income, working conditions, and job secu-rity.[8] It identified four guidelines necessary for successful collective bargaining in the new Labor-Management partnership model. These guidelines require that Labor-Management partnerships be based on the need for mutual recog-nition and respect, inclusion of collective bargaining, the principle of equality, and the need to advance the interests of both parties.[9] Equally important, the organization of work must be structured to assure the union's ability to repre-sent the worker from the planning stage through the implementation stage. Even more important, these new Labor-Management partnerships must be founded on the free flow of information and mutual trust.

In all Labor-Management relationships there will always exist conflicting interests, as well as common interests. Integrative bargaining, the common interests, needs to be broadened, while distributive bargaining, the conflict-ing interests, needs to be narrowed. In spite of the broad consensus regard-ing the urgent need for Labor-Management cooperation, it is critical that both parties recognize that there will always be divergent interests. The em-ployers' need for flexibility and the employees' need for job security and a fair share of the increased productivity set many of these new Labor-Man-agement partnerships on an inevitable collision course. The common ground is the need to increase productivity and worker satisfaction in a shared-fate environment. The conflict is over how the profits from this increased productivity are shared. However, Labor-Management relations need not be antagonistic. In new Labor-Management partnerships, conflicts of interest are resolved in an atmosphere of respect, trust, and goodwill.[10]

Another major obstacle to successful Labor-Management partnerships is the Commission on the Future of Worker-Management Relations recommendation to repeal a six-decade-old tenet of federal law that guarantees workers an independent voice in cooperative committees set up by Management. This recommendation reverses the prevailing basic assumption that any legitimate Labor union must be completely independent of Management. If Congress passes legislation based on this recommendation, new competition for worker representation from intra-company unions (the old "company" unions) could further diminish the demand for traditional union representation. In addition, legalization of company unions may also trigger a major increase in decertifications. Local unions, dissatisfied with the national union's policies, programs, products, services, or per capita payments, could simply decertify and form an intra-company union—with the same officers and membership.

In hopes of decertification, hostile Management could promote dissatisfaction within unions. Management decertification strategies would, in most cases, intensify local union politics and generate internal union conflict. Such strategies are self-destructive because even the slightest perception that Management is actively instigating a decertification would absolutely destroy the mutual trust that is essential in all successful Labor-Management partnerships. Suspicion and mistrust are killer viruses in any partnership.

Since conflict and misunderstanding are natural in the workplace, a principal function of contract administration is to redress the grievances or complaints of both the worker and employer. Even where new Labor-Management partnerships restructure the workplace to enhance worker participation, the grievance system, which provides due process and assures justice in the workplace, will become an increasingly important consideration for joining unions. Grievances are often used to influence collective bargaining agendas and outcomes because grievance rates significantly increase just prior to negotiations. Hence, functional shop-floor bargaining often utilizes the grievance procedure as one element in the ongoing contest between unions and Management, with the end result being day-to-day accommodations. This type of functional bargaining is widespread and enduring.[11]

The decision to file a grievance is generally a function of job dissatisfaction and confidence in the effectiveness of the grievance system to satisfactorily resolve the problem. Employees are increasingly demanding due process rights on the job. In a nonunion environment, nonunion grievance procedures (NGP) and alternative dispute resolution (ADR) systems are the preferred Management response to halting employment-related lawsuits. However, a "trust gap" between employers and their nonunion workers is a serious problem.

Employment litigation is among the most significant industrial relations issues of the last decade. Employee-related lawsuits now outnumber personal injury lawsuits. This increase in employee litigation to resolve workplace problems is proof of a significant "trust gap." and NGPs are not seen by most employees as a viable option for solving workplace problems. The degree of trust is based on how the employee will be represented and whether or not there is a neutral decision maker. Very few employers will agree to use a neutral decision maker, because they are very reluctant to let an outsider set new policy or overturn existing policy. Most internal grievance systems merely permit representation by a peer or a human resources staff person, with appeal to a Management-appointed committee. Clearly, whenever the stakes are really high, neither alternative will produce a fair and objective outcome, nor are they likely to reduce the "trust gap."

In the union environment, there is little evidence that union employers or unions want to abandon, or even substantially modify, existing grievance and disciplinary procedures. Almost three-quarters of the collective bargaining agreements provide for some form of expedited grievance procedure. Expedited grievance procedures raise perceptions of the importance of grievance issues and increase the sense of equity of grievance settlements.[12] In recent years there has been renewed interest in grievance mediation. Personal experience has proven its effectiveness.

The shared-fate environment concept holds that Labor and Management either swim together or drown together. However, management initiatives overwhelm Labor. The list of Management strategies—schemes, in the eyes of some union people—includes total quality management, total employee involvement, results-focused groups, planning teams, quality-driven enterprise, quality action teams, value-added management, gainsharing, employee participation, integrative bargaining, distributive bargaining, reinventing, reengineering, downsizing, rightsizing, and so on. In regard to dispute resolution, there are arbitration, peer review, employee assistance plans, ADRs, NGPs, internal grievance programs, and mediation. To this Management potpourri, the complications associated with advanced enabling technologies must be added.

The AFL-CIO *New American Workplace* report notes: "Not enough has been done to provide them [union leaders] with useful information, instruction and assistance. The result has been that outside the national collective bargaining relationships, unions often have not been well enough prepared to respond to Management's proposals, let alone to take the initiative in seeking the reorganization of work." To remedy this situation, the AFL-CIO report suggests: "The federation should take the initiative in convening conferences and seminars for trade unionists to share their experiences, to teach and learn from each other. Most important, the federation should help unions identify paths to success so that the Labor movement can become more and more active in pushing our vision of a new model workplace."[13] Unfortunately, there is no consensus on what constitutes a new model workplace. Labor's vision of a new model workplace and Management's vision are, with few exceptions, dramatically different. You can bet Management dreams of union-free, intra-organization work groups.

Ironically, the AFL-CIO's belated recognition of the urgent need to train local union leaders will further intensify the internal struggle between organizing and servicing for increasingly scarce resources. It will also focus attention on the critical need for a comprehensive strategic management program. Unless unions immediately implement strategies, programs, and policies to train union officers and representatives to better understand management concepts, principles, and techniques, they will be increasingly dependent on outside expertise such as lawyers, academics, consultants, sociologists, historians, ethicists, and various other specialists. This demand for high-priced expertise is rapidly escalating when funds are more and more scarce.

The collective bargaining agreement is organized Labor's principal product. High-performance unions recognize this and are continually searching for innovative ways to improve the product. Since individualism is extremely important to American workers, union leaders should look for ways to individualize the collective bargaining agreement. Realistically, this new American workplace is at least ten years old, and many union leaders are far behind—in urgent need of management training and training in the application of advanced enabling technologies. Labor has the option to leapfrog over Management or be dragged behind it.

Organizing

Organizing includes all activities involving the recruitment of workers by unions. There are two basic approaches to organizing. The first is organizing the work, or "top down," and the second is organizing the worker, or "bottom up." The first approach generally applies to the skilled trades and involves efforts by the local union to persuade the employer to sign an agreement. The second approach generally applies to industrial workers and involves efforts by the national union to convince workers to join the union. In an industrial union, organizing is usually the responsibility of the national union or an intermediate body, while in a craft union organizing is generally the responsibility of the local union.

There is a critical relationship between organizing and collective bargaining. Unions that cannot organize are generally unions that cannot bargain effectively, because the increased nonunion competition forces the union employer to resist improvements in the collective bargaining agreement.[14] Hence, a drop in union membership is usually accompanied by a growing number of collective bargaining agreements that freeze or even reduce wages and benefits. As the differences between the union and nonunion employers diminish, unions cease to be perceived as organizations that can improve our members' lives. In effect, organizing is primarily a strategic function in support of collective bargaining.

Since 1965 AFL-CIO membership as a proportion of the American employed labor force (union density) has declined dramatically. Figure 1.1 shows this dramatic decline union density.

Figure 1.1
The Decline of AFL-CIO Density (percent)

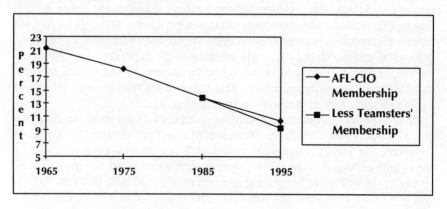

In response to this steadily escalating crisis, newly elected AFL-CIO president John J. Sweeney promised to "rebuild the Labor movement and to organize at a pace and scale unprecedented."[15] One of President Sweeney's first moves was to create a separate organizing department to coordinate and focus the federation's organizing activities. The new organizing department started with a $5 million budget, which will reach $20 million within several years.[16] The department promotes partnerships between the federation and affiliates and intends to focus on organizing industries and areas that were neglected in the past and to work aggressively with women and minorities. Multi-union drives, targeted industries, and increased local union organizing are seen as the key to success.[17] The Organizing Institute, which is responsible for the recruitment, training, and placement of organizers, supporting the local elected leaders task force, campaign consulting, and developing models for organizing programs and structures, is now under the new Organizing Department.

The new Organizing Department uses an expanded computer network to provide immediate access to organizing information. The network provides statistical and reference information, including representation and decertification filings, to help organizers. Information is available on union-busting trends and over 500 union busters. In the future, the system will provide first contract information.

Much of the AFL-CIO's optimism regarding organizing potential appears to be based on *Being Heard*, which found that by a 2 to 1 margin the public believes that unions have a role to play in society today, that unions strike only when forced to, and that unions give working people a voice in the political process.[18]

The AFL-CIO leadership is also excited about the potential of worker associations as another vehicle for establishing new relationships with workers. Worker associations are not involved in collective bargaining or other typical union activities. Instead, they provide help on a range of workplace issues such as pay equity, health care, job training, family leave, legal advice, language tutoring, and so on. Worker associations, now with a half-million members, are still another form of collective representation with great potential for increasing union membership.

Although not part of the AFL-CIO's organizing strategy, another potentially large source of new membership is those workers who signed authorization cards, but the union lost the election. Since Management usually interprets the signing of an authorization card as a sign of disloyalty, joining a union is a very courageous public act. The future of these courageous workers with the company is in great jeopardy. Thus, from an equity standpoint, they should never be abandoned by the organizing union as they have been in the past. Instead, as a reward for their public display of courage, high-performance unions welcome them with some form of associate membership. Associate memberships, nonmajority representation, individual membership, and nonunion grievance procedures (NGP) membership have enormous potential for union growth. The Union Privilege Benefits Program, with its many benefits, is a valuable organizing tool to attract these workers. High-performance unions amend their constitutions to provide new membership classifications and redesign the union's structure to properly represent them.

Flowing from these various forms of associate memberships, combined with traditional bargaining unit membership, is the concept of "lifetime" membership. In a lifetime member relationship, the union provides advice and various forms of assistance throughout the life of a member. This involves establishing an expanded membership database that starts when a worker joins a union or signs an authorization card and continues throughout retirement. The expanded membership database would include a detailed record of a worker's entire career, including various employers, assignments, training, and skill acquisition. It would help coordinate employer and local, state, and federal benefits. When a worker becomes unemployed, it would help the union provide job placement assistance. It would also increase member participation in union political and community action activities by identifying members' unique experiences, skills, and talents. Finally, a comprehensive member profile would provide direction and guidance for union policy. Lifetime membership has great potential for curtailing the staggering decline in union membership and influence.

Some national unions such as the Service Employees International Union (SEIU) have been very successful in organizing new members. The IBEW's innovative Construction Organizing Membership Education and Training (COMET) program has been so successful that it has become the model for all the building and construction trade unions.

Nevertheless, in spite of these success stories, the scale of Labor's organizing problems is overwhelming. Between 1993 and 1995 the AFL-CIO lost almost 300,000 members. The fact is that union membership as a percent of the workforce continues its downward path, and it is not likely to be reversed in the near or distant future. Twice before, after World War II and after the formation of the AFL-CIO, organizing was Labor's top priority, and both times it failed miserably.[19] The likelihood of success is further complicated in that organizing is not within the AFL-CIO's basic mission—union members cannot join the AFL-CIO. The federation's members are affiliated national and international unions.

To put in perspective, the scale of the organizing effort necessary just to maintain present membership, the International Brotherhood of Electrical Workers (IBEW), with over 700,000 members, would have to double its number of certification elections or double its win rate or double the size of the unit it wins for a net increase in about 3,000 members.[20] Projecting this situation for other AFL-CIO affiliates, it is almost impossible for the AFL-CIO to even maintain its present membership. In addition, the diversion of resources to support an organizing program of this size would severely undermine the other eight union functions.

Most workers join unions because they see unions as a means to improve their lives and/or because they are dissatisfied with their present work situation. To improve their lives, the first and most frequent reason workers say they would join a union is referred to as instrumentality and is concerned with Labor's primary mission. The next several paragraphs deal with the impact of the new organizing priority on union instrumentality.

The *AFL-CIO News* reported that the new Organizing Department's other role will be stimulating debate about resources and structural changes needed to increase organizing.[21] In resource allocation debates, risk should always be a major consideration, and organizing is an extremely risky venture even in a friendly environment. The probability of failure is extremely high, and the impact of failure is disaster because the service organization will have been irreparably weakened.

This top-priority commitment to creating an "organizing culture" has already intensified the ongoing, internal struggle with the "servicing culture" for increasingly scarce resources. This intensified conflict could be very harmful to the administration and operations of the federation, its affiliated national unions, and their local unions. For example, pressure on the national unions' field staff to allocate more of their time and energy to organizing is another potential source of tension and conflict. The field staff's primary responsibility was to provide services to the local unions. They were recruited for their ability to service local union, and are comfortable with this responsibility.

In contrast, organizers are Labor's salespeople, and selling clearly requires a very different personality and an entirely new set of skills. Inevitably, national unions, dissatisfied with the continuing loss of members, increase the pressure on field representatives to organize. Field representatives, isolated, unhappy, unable to organize in a hostile environment, and under increasing pressure from local unions for more and better services, are in an extremely difficult situation. Some are so frustrated they are considering organizing their own union.

Accordingly, the IBEW research report, *Industrial Project, April 1992*, found that the issue of tensions between organizing and servicing responsibilities was dealt with only indirectly by organizing directors and AFL-CIO officials. It notes: "In union after union we heard of conflict between servicing and organizing. Members demand services and question the relevance of organizing to their concerns. Regional directors, local presidents, and business agents, responding to their political constituencies, are reluctant to reduce servicing. Many also fear new members. Most union staff are comfortable with servicing and uncomfortable with organizing. A consensus seems to be evolving that the only way to deal with this clash is to confront it head-on."[22] While the report is not clear what a head-on clash involves, its authors appear too eager for some sort of divisive action which will ultimately diminish instrumentality.

The decision to join a union is influenced by many factors such as job satisfaction, psychological stress, role ambiguity, Management style, fairness, education, age, attitudes toward unions, social influences and union actions. Thomas DeCotiis and Jean-Yves LeLouarn found that the there is no "type" of union person and concluded that the perception of "union instrumentality" was by far the most important determinant of voting behavior. They reported that when instrumentality was used as a criterion, in excess of 75 percent of the vote was accurately predicted.[23] Instrumentality means that the union is seen an agent or means to improve the worker's condition in life. If the worker perceives this to be true, he or she will be more likely to vote to join the union. A predictive union support model assumes that there is dissatisfaction in the workplace or that the worker has a particular, unsatisfied need either in the workplace or in the community. Thus, the workers are searching for the best instrumentality to resolve this conflict or satisfy their need.

Unfortunately, from an instrumentality perspective, the outlook for organizing is also not very encouraging. The 1988 Gallup and the 1991 Fingerhut/Powers polls revealed considerable skepticism about the capability of American unions and significant discontent among members regarding their union's performance. In the Gallup poll 52 percent of the respondents thought "unions have become too weak to protect their members." The Fingerhut/Powers poll found that 43 percent of the union member respondents rated union performance "only fair" or "poor," with only 23 percent rating it as excellent.[24]

Further, in a study released 5 December 1994, researchers Richard Freeman of Harvard University and Joel Rogers of the University of Wisconsin polled 2,408 workers to find out what they wanted in the workplace. Freeman and Rogers found that by a strong 3 to 1 margin, employees prefer an employee organization with which Management cooperated in discussing issues but had no power to make decisions, as opposed to an employee organization that had more power, but Management opposed. This finding was true for even union employees. The Freeman and Rogers study revealed that while 40 percent of employees interviewed said they would prefer to belong to a union, the overwhelming majority said they believed their best hope was in some form of nonunion, Labor-Management committee at their workplace. Freeman and Rogers believe that their survey reflected the realities of the workplace, in that Management was not apt to give workers a voice in workplace deliberations if it did not have control over the final committee decisions. "I read the data as people not being fools. They recognize that Management is dominant in the workplace," Rogers concluded.[25]

What Freeman and Rogers mistakenly see as a reality in the workplace is really a short-term aberration. Granted, employees are not fools; thus, it follows that in the long run, they will not tolerate manipulation. This imbalance of power described by Freeman and Rogers can only lead to frustration and conflict. The Freeman and Rogers findings are much more likely the result of job insecurity than the acceptance of Management's dominance. What workers really want is empowerment—real influence in the workplace. The only effective instrument for true influence in the workplace is a union.

The declining relevance of unions is further confirmed by the *Being Heard* finding that unions are frequently referred to as "dinosaurs."[26] *Being Heard* also noted that while most Americans are not hostile toward unions, their dominant sentiments are disappointment, indifference, and apathy.[27] It identified the growing number of part-time jobs, people losing good jobs and being forced to take low-paying ones, and the squeezing of the middle class as the top three economic problems of American workers. It then concludes that while this appears to be an ideal climate for unionizing, workers believe that today's economic conditions make it hard for unions to protect their members.[28]

Being Heard notes that the most disappointing finding was that even though workers believed unions have been good for their current members, they show little interest in joining unions. Furthermore, it found that only 34 percent of nonunion workers would join a union, while 47 percent would not. Even more serious, the report points out, is an NBC *News/Wall Street Journal* survey finding that only 34 percent (of the respondents) said unions helped the cause of working Americans, while 48 percent felt they (unions) actually hurt the cause. The magnitude of Labor's problems is shockingly evident in the *Being Heard* suggestion to avoid the use of the word "union" and its implication that the AFL-CIO could improve its image by changing its name to Working Americans United or the National Federation of Working Americans.[29] It concluded that unions must be perceived as being more effective representatives and responsive to their members in a way that advances the interests of workers and the nation.[30] Consequently, before organizing can be successful, unions need to implement strategies that make unions more effective instruments for improving the lives of workers.

To the extent that organizing relies on dissatisfaction (the second reason workers join), the outlook is also not very good. Labor studies expert Professor Anil Verma found that nonunion workers consistently assess employer treatment as fair. This perception of employer conduct has a major negative impact on voting to join a union. She concludes that ". . . it is unlikely that major growth in union ranks will come in the near future from disgruntled employees, who have been traumatized by vicious employer mistreatment."[31]

In view of these enormous obstacles, assigning organizing as the top-level priority appears to be a rather impetuous and dangerous reaction to declining union membership—impetuous because it is such an obvious reaction to declining membership and dangerous because it is an irreversible commitment to a very risky decision to reallocate so many resources to organizing when Labor has so many much more serious problems. A more responsible alternative would recognize that organizing is just one element of a comprehensive strategic management process. Thus, organizing should be formally aligned with the other eight union functions for attaining Labor's mission and core objectives.

A comprehensive organizing strategy involves participation of all interested parties in the allocation of resources among the nine union functions, working within existing organizing cultures, the development of strategic targeting mechanisms, the careful selection and training of member organizers, the development of innovative organizing strategies and tactics, and the development of new services to meet the needs of a more diversified membership. Local unions should assume primary responsibility for organizing, since all organizing is local. National unions should build high-performance local unions that attract nonunion workers, because they are effective and efficient "instrumentalities" for improving their lives in both the workplace and the community. The AFL-CIO should continue coordinating and assisting national unions.

Jurisdiction

The third union function, jurisdiction, includes all activities relating to a claim on, or grant of, the right to organize or represent a category of workers. There are three basic types of jurisdiction: territorial, trade, and industrial.[32] Jurisdiction involves a description of a union's environment, its governance, and its structure. Elements of jurisdiction and the environment are used in classifying unions as either craft or industrial.[33] Industrial unions represent workers on a plantwide or industrywide basis and are described as vertical organizations because the workers are employed at all levels of the occupational ladder. Craft unions represent workers of a particular skill or trade and are considered horizontal organizations.[34]

The 1955 AFL-CIO merger replaced the concept of "exclusive jurisdiction" with an "established bargaining relationship" as the basic principle governing the relationships among affiliates in regard to raiding local unions. Article XX of the AFL-CIO constitution provides for an outside umpire to determine whether or not an affiliate violated this provision by raiding an established collective bargaining relationship. The constitution also provides for outside mediation before the parties resort to the impartial umpire. Ultimately, the AFL-CIO Executive Council has the authority to review and overturn an umpire's decision. The AFL-CIO regulates competition among affiliates not only over established bargaining units but also over the organizing of unorganized units and unions outside the federation. Non-AFL-CIO bargaining relationships are not protected by "no-raid" provisions.

Jurisdiction is also an important consideration in union mergers. A union merger is a bonding of two or more trade unions to form a single organization. It is a process, not an event. Mergers involve internal union politics, local-national relations, representational effectiveness, union rivalries, and a host of other contentious issues. Amalgamation and absorption are two basic forms of union mergers. An amalgamation joins together two or more unions of equal size. An absorption is the merging of one union into a larger one. Absorptions are by far the most prevalent form of merger.[35]

The rationale for union mergers is to

- enhance bargaining and organizing power;
- achieve economies of scale;
- eliminate costly duplication of efforts;
- increase financial and administrative resources;
- achieve common objectives;
- increase political influence;
- improve staff experience and expertise;
- strengthen the strike fund;
- prevent raiding.

On the other hand, the argument against mergers includes

- the abandonment of culture and tradition;
- the loss of institutional identity;
- the loss of leadership status;
- the imposition of the absorbing union's policies, practices, and philosophies on the absorbed union;
- the capacity of leaders to manage a larger and more diverse organization;
- diminished leadership and member participation opportunities;
- diminished ability to represent the members;
- diminished quality of democracy.[36]

In the business world, synergy is an extremely important consideration business executives look for when considering a merger. Synergy is the effect in which the combined return of an organization's resources is greater than the sum of its components. More simply, it is as if two plus two magically equaled five. Regrettably, synergy is not a very important consideration in union mergers.

The AFL-CIO's present policy is to encourage and facilitate the merger of national unions. The federation generally approves mergers of affiliates whenever there is a broad community of interest. It appears the federation's objective is to reduce the number of affiliated national unions to twenty or thirty large unions. However, the decision whether or not to merge is complicated and confusing. Each merger situation is unique, and success is determined by the abilities, commitment, management expertise, and vision of the people involved.

A convincing argument can be made favoring the exact opposite strategy—decentralization. The *Being Heard* report notes that many Americans see unions as bureaucratic institutions with an agenda primarily driven by organizational needs. It points out the importance of large institutions being perceived as distant from ordinary people and notes that "for the public, big is bad and small is good." It then explains that this is why the AFL-CIO's 22 percent favorable rating is lower than unions in general (35 percent).[37]

The major problems with union mergers are the inability to manage a larger, more complex, and more diverse organization; possible intense cultural conflict; and reduced membership depth of participation (MDOP) and leadership depth of participation (LDOP). (The concepts of MDOP and LDOP are explained in Chapter 4.) MDOP and LDOP are based on the observation that there are more opportunities and fewer obstacles for members to participate in union activities in smaller unions. In addition, at least fifteen officers are lost whenever a union is absorbed in a merger. Clearly, mergers are shrinking the Labor movement. Consequently, the AFL-CIO should reconsider its present policy on mergers until there is a much better understanding of their impact on unions. For now, the AFL-CIO should approve only mergers that are absolutely necessary and clearly synergistic, enrich union democracy, and do not diminish the ability of the merged unions to represent their members.

Administration

The fourth union function is administration. Administration covers all activities required to support the organization. Several typical administration activities are public relations, media technology, education and training, international affairs, civil rights, information services, library services, office operations, accounting, investment, record keeping, dues collection, bonding, risk management, personnel management, data processing, and the administration of welfare benefits and pension plans. Each of these functions is part of a complex organizational system that requires a wide range of management and specialist expertise.

In most union organizations these administrative activities are the responsibility of the secretary or the secretary-treasurer. In many unions the need for professional expertise has grown so fast that the union's leadership was unprepared to deal with the management challenges resulting from this unprecedented growth.

The trend toward larger centralized unions creates new, complex administrative problems and destroys the rich culture and tradition of the Labor movement. Centralization can also diminish union democracy and limit the merged union's ability to respond to an extremely dynamic environment.

To slow this trend toward mergers and centralization, the AFL-CIO and large, high-performance national, intermediate, and local unions need to establish administrative and support centers (ASCs) to provide advanced enabling technologies, communication networks, and routine administrative and support services to smaller union organizations with which they share a community of interests. ASCs would separate typical operating functions, such as collective bargaining and organizing from administrative activities, such as accounting and investment, and support services, such as research and education. ASCs would achieve most of the previously noted justification for mergers, yet avoid the expense, conflict, tension, and heartbreak associated with them.

In some situations an existing intermediate body would function as an ASC for small local unions. In other situations, two or more small unions could maintain their separate identities by sharing an ASC. In still other situations, a large local union could adopt one or more neighboring, small local unions. At the national union level, large national unions could provide support to smaller national unions, or small national unions could pair up to complement their strengths and weaknesses. At the federation level, the AFL-CIO would encourage and coordinate the growth of ASCs, and in some cases it would, through its state federations and central Labor councils, actually provide administrative and support services. Even private organizations such as the Union Labor Life Insurance Company (ULLICO) and other service providers could establish an ASC relationship with union organizations.

With the support of ASCs, small union organizations could remain viable forces for representing workers and in the struggle for social change. These small unions would be charged on a break-even, fee-for-service basis by the ASC. An ASC is a win-win concept; the small union not only continues to exist as a separate organization but becomes more efficient and effective, and the large union organization has a new source of income. The ASC concept incorporates the positive aspects of a merger while avoiding its negative aspects.

The principal advantages that ASCs have over an absorption are that the small union organizations maintain their identities, thus preserving their rich culture and tradition. Even more important, their leadership and membership depth of participation is not diminished. Further, ASCs generate many positive synergy effects. For example, the large union organization benefits by spreading its administrative costs over a larger base and collects fees for service instead of per capita. ASCs have the advantage of scale, distribute overhead over a larger organization, and share information. The ASC concept undermines the argument that small unions are too inefficient to exist. In these troubled times, no existing union should be labeled too small to be viable. Unions need all their leaders and greater member participation.

The ASC concept is based on brothers and sisters helping brothers and sisters. It is a win-win proposition, while absorptions are primarily win-disappear propositions. Typically, the large union gains members, the small union disappears, and the entire Labor movement is forever diminished. Unfortunately, many times even the absorbing union loses because the expenses are unexpectedly high, the economies of scale nonexistent, the conflict too intense, and the Management is unable to effectively and efficiently operate the larger, more complex, and diverse organization.

Governance

The fifth union function, governance, is concerned with the details of electing officers, conducting meetings, and establishing policies necessary to operate a democratic union organization.[38] Democracy is a form of government whereby the people directly or indirectly participate in ruling an organization. In a union democracy, workers elect officers to represent them in governing their union and in relations with their employer.

The very first democratic government began in 508 B.C. when the people of Athens overthrew a tyrant and established a government of the people. For over 2,500 years, people throughout the world have fought and died to attain or preserve democracy. Today, like a raging forest fire, the spirit of democracy roars through Eastern Europe, Central Europe, Russia, and many other totalitarian governments.

Democracy is the very essence of Labor unionism! It is the driving force for establishing common purpose and for building a committed community of workers. Nothing is more important. Union democracy is the process that keeps union leaders responsive to the majority of the members and protects the rights of the minority. Union democracy recognizes the importance of the individual and is based on the principles of equality and justice. Without democracy, a union is just another exploiter of workers—a shell, a mirage, a shame.

Lip-service, shoulder-shrugging, manipulative democracy, characteristic of too many unions, is a malignant disease that slowly, but surely, is devouring "boss"-led unions. *Being Heard* concluded that the belief that unions are not fully democratic and are not accountable to their members is one of the most serious problems facing today's Labor movement. It notes that in the long run, this problem is far more damaging than the "corruption" charge.[39] In the past, unions, like industry, thrived on the outstanding leadership of dynamic, charismatic, autocratic "bosses." However, times change, and unions must change. If today were yesterday, many of today's union bosses would be as effective as their predecessors. But that is impossible. Yesterday's "boss" Management style will not work today. Democracy is government by persuasion, not by command. Today's high-performance union officers are coaches rather than bosses—they lead union teams, instead of telling their employees and the rank-and-file members what to do.

There are three widely applied measures of union democracy. The first, procedural, is concerned with union constitutional guarantees of the right to free expression, the right to fair elections, and equal access to running for office. The Landrum-Griffin Act is the federal government's procedural approach to assure union democracy. The second measure is the behavioral view that focuses on evidence of high participation, electoral competition, and leadership turnover. The third measure of democracy, the substantive measure, attempts to determine if union officers reflect the desires of the membership.[40]

While all three measures have certain advantages, the substantive measure seems to be the best. It simply involves asking the members whether or not they think their union is democratic. Their perception of union democracy is the critical determinant. Well-designed opinion surveys that determine members' perception of democracy in their local union are very effective Management tools for high-performance local union officers. If these periodic surveys reveal that the members see their local union as undemocratic, the top local union officer must determine if their perception is accurate or not. If their perception is accurate, the top local union officer must take immediate steps to improve the quality of democracy. If their perception is inaccurate, then the top local union officer must immediately implement educational programs to correct this misconception.

It is very important to realize that this education program is not a call for more and improved incumbent propaganda. Political propaganda will only make the "thems" even more cynical. If the top local union officer is unable or unwilling to assure full participatory democracy, then the national union's top officer must take appropriate action. If the national union will not take action, then the AFL-CIO must. In the new American union, there can be absolutely no compromising of Labor's total dedication to union democracy.

In unions, as in most voluntary organizations, democracy is extremely fragile and must be coddled, protected, and enthusiastically encouraged by top union officers. There is a direct link between the quality of democracy and the union's effectiveness. Initiatives that enrich democracy increase the union's effectiveness, while initiatives that weaken democracy decrease the union's effectiveness. In high-performance unions, members feel fully enfranchised, truly empowered. Their comments are considered, and their opinions are respected. Today, with numerous interests competing for a worker's free time, a rich union democracy is absolutely essential to involve present members and to attract loyal and committed new members.

Even though the roots of democracy are the rank and file, the quality of union democracy is determined by the top union officers. The *Being Heard* report emphasized: "Perhaps a worse indictment [of unions] is that many people—especially low-income working people—believe unions are not responsive to their members. They are seen as largely undemocratic bureaucracies that impose decisions on their members from the top down."[41]

Thus, high-performance union officers are keenly aware of the enormous importance of democracy to their union's future success. They do more than just tolerate differing views—they actually encourage them. High-performance union officers lock onto democracy as a Tomahawk missile locks onto its target. You just cannot shake them off.

Internal strife and conflict are too common and too intense. In some unions, the politics are knock-down-drag-out, life-and-death battles. Tactics include locking doors; turning off the sound system, lights, heat, or air-conditioning; intimidating speakers by surrounding them with sergeants-at-arms to "protect them"; stacking the microphones; and ultimately outright stealing votes. Sometimes the conflict is so intense the union is barely able to operate, and reconciliation is virtually impossible. James Carville, President Bill Clinton's top political consultant, replied, "It's the economy, stupid!" when asked the key to a successful political campaign. In Labor's case, the key to future success is, "It's the pronoun, stupid!" In too many unions, the prevailing self-destructive tradition is "us" versus "them" instead of "we." Dissenters are labeled "rebels" and are subject to sanctions that range from economic abuse to physical abuse. They are blacklisted, isolated, harassed with vague charges of violations of the national union's constitution or the local union's bylaws, denied equal access to job referral systems, given poor jobs or assignments, and so on. The primary effect of these actions is to discourage the participation of anyone who disagrees with the incumbents. The end result is that the "thems" drop out. They figure, who needs this? They have lots of better things to do than be hassled by their union leaders. What looks like a winning strategy for the incumbents is actually a tragedy.

To compound these problems, in some national unions, tradition requires that an incumbent officer's decisions and sanctions be upheld at each level of the appeal process regardless of how vindictive, petty, misguided, or self-serving they are. Enormous amounts of time, energy, and resources are expended crushing "rebel" members and destroying "renegade" local unions. Tragically, a reputation for undemocratic policies and practices spreads rapidly throughout the workforce, chilling member commitment and participation and ultimately strangling organizing efforts.

Democracy does not end at the door to the union office—the workplace of union employees. Member and nonmember union employees are also entitled to join or form unions in order to participate more effectively in all union decisions that critically affect any significant aspect of their lives. The same democratic rights that apply to employees of businesses apply with equal moral and binding force to employees of unions.

In regard to the election of national officers, union reformers who advocate direct membership election of national union officers are very much mistaken. Apparently, they do not fully understand the union political environment. The direct election of national officers would further undermine union democracy and maybe even destroy it. Incumbent officers have an almost insurmountable advantage in a direct election. They totally control all the union's publications and all other printed material. In addition, they attend most major union events, meetings, and conferences. Their picture and/or name is prominent on every piece of printed material. Thirty-six, forty-eight, or sixty monthly union journals, depending on the time between elections, are filled with their editorials and opinions. They are also seen with high government officials, politicians, celebrities, religious leaders, and even the president of the United States. Furthermore, they are frequently pictured receiving or presenting awards at testimonials, making speeches, and testifying before legislative bodies.

Nonincumbent candidates simply do not have the exposure, time, resources, or money to effectively challenge incumbent national union officers in a direct election. Further, the direct election process is extremely expensive, resource-draining, and time-consuming. Equally troublesome is the ever-present risk that outsiders, possibly even employers, could finance a challenger's campaign to acquire improper influence in union decisions. A pro-employer media attack could influence the defeat of a talented and dedicated national officer.

In spite of the so-called success of the Teamsters 1991 election, it is not a transferable, or even an appropriate model for other national unions, because federal supervision was necessary to assure a fair election and because of the enormous cost to the government, the candidates, and the union—the U.S. government spent over $20 million to oversee the 1996 election. Besides, only 28 percent of the total membership voted in 1991 and increased slightly to 35 percent in 1996 when the incumbent president Ronald Carey was reelected by a narrow 4 percent.[42] Even worse, the 1996 Teamsters election was voided, and Carey was disqualified from seeking reelection because of alleged improper campaign financing.

Realistically, most rank-and-file members simply lack the necessary information to make a good decision regarding who is best qualified to serve as national officers. In addition, only a small percentage of the members even bothers to vote in a direct election. As we shall see in the next chapter, the national union's primary customer is the local union—not the members. Consequently, the local union officers and leaders, who work closely with the national union and attend various union conferences and meetings, are best qualified to evaluate the performance of the national union's officers. True union democracy is rooted in the election of well-informed, competent, and dedicated delegates to represent them at the national convention.

National conventions are the cornerstones of union democracy. They amend the constitution, elect national union officers, and establish union strategies, policies, and programs. They also serve as publicity events to focus attention on union activities, as rituals to build support for the union, to revitalize and reenergize the union, to strengthen intra-union bonds, and to renew acquaintances. Dynamic change is another reason for more frequent conventions. Perfectly sound strategies, policies, and programs can become obsolete or irrelevant in a matter of a few months in today's turbulent environment. Given these many important benefits, high-performance national unions schedule constitutional conventions at least every four years and national state of the union conventions or conferences every two years to review performance and compliance with the actions of the constitutional convention and, if necessary, to update union strategies, policies, and programs.

Growing financial problems should not be used to justify the extension of the time between conventions or the reduction in the number of delegates or national officers. In fact, in some national unions, new offices should be created, and more delegates authorized. The AFL-CIO report *The Changing Situation of Workers and Their Unions* calls for increasing member participation in union activities. More frequent conventions, more officers, and more delegates provide more opportunities for meaningful participation at the union's highest political level. Union democracy should never be sacrificed in the name of economy. There are many other much less important areas in which to cut costs.

Many constitutions and bylaws are the result of decades of reactions to short-term problems of a particular period. As a result, there are many outdated references to threats to, or criticism of, unions. In some cases, sections are poorly written, sometimes intentionally and sometimes as the product of many committee compromises. Some articles are extremely difficult to interpret, and others do not even belong in the constitution. Therefore, high-performance national unions eliminate all outdated, unclear, irrelevant, and inappropriate provisions. They also review and amend their constitution and bylaws to eliminate all provisions that impinge, or even appear to impinge, on union democracy.

Most important, however, high-performance national unions amend their constitutions to empower delegates by requiring a secret ballot, the most sacred of all democratic values, for the election of national union officers. Most union conventions now require roll-call voting, which is a public act. Since the delegate's vote is public, many delegates vote for the incumbents out of fear that they and their local union could be subject to some form of retaliation or that they would jeopardize their chance of becoming a national union representative. Consequently, a secret ballot for all elections of national officers would be a dramatic leap toward full participatory union democracy.

Electronic voting systems to facilitate voting can also be used on all important convention issues. Today, for large national unions the failure to provide electronic voting systems for their conventions is inexcusable. There are many proven and affordable off-the-shelf, electronic voting software systems available, or the AFL-CIO could develop and provide at cost, upon request, a flexible electronic voting system available to affiliates that cannot afford their own system. However, it is important to point out that computer records of all votes can be an entirely new means of incumbent intimidation. Delegates will quickly realize that long after the convention is over the incumbent national officers will have a printed record of how they voted on every issue. Possibly, the arguments for delegate accountability will have to be reconsidered for certain issues in view of its potential impact on union democracy.

For small conventions, voting machines or some form of paper ballot are all that is necessary for a secret ballot. For large conventions, an electronic voting system, a widely used and mature technology, would maintain secrecy and expedite the voting process.

Another democratization initiative involves formally empowering executive councils as executive boards. Councils, while gradually acquiring more board-like authority, are in most cases considered primarily advisory panels whose actions are not binding on the top union officer. On the other hand, boards bear ultimate accountability for organizational operations and performance. An executive board's authority is exceeded only by the union meeting or the convention of delegates. As a first step in restructuring, the AFL-CIO should establish an eleven-person board of directors with a chair, vice chair, and a member for each of the nine basic union functions.

Standards are guides and control measures that establish acceptable behavior. High standards are necessary to establish a reputation for excellence, and reputation is the key to successful franchises. High standards and reasonable enforcement systems are the tools of high-performance managers. Imagine responsible franchisers like McDonalds, Choice Hotels, Hertz, KFC, Ford, and so on operating without standards and an enforcement system. In effect, the AFL-CIO is a national franchiser, and its national and global reputation is dependent on standards to which every affiliate agrees with and complies with. The AFL-CIO ethics committee would monitor compliance with standards that assure a rich union democracy is the defining characteristic of all affiliated national unions, and administer sanctions for those unions that fail to comply.

Political Action

The sixth function, political action, relates to all activities necessary to achieve Labor's political objectives. Labor's typical political activities include political education and preelection, election, and postelection activities. Preelection activities involve fund-raising, education, and expanding and maintaining Committee on Political Education (COPE) voting lists. Election action refers to candidate endorsement and preprimary and primary involvement, including the contribution of volunteer time and money. The main postelection activity is lobbying.[43] Political action is important because it gives union members a stronger voice in the political arena, which *Being Heard* noted was one of the two activities people liked most about unions.[44]

The hierarchy of Labor's political goals is union issues, employment issues, class issues, and social issues. Union issues typically involve legislation and laws regarding Labor-Management relations and the regulation of the internal affairs of unions. Employment issues include all the issues that are concerned with protecting workers or increasing employment opportunities. Class issues improve the welfare of all working people or a particular class of people such as young, old, minority, or handicapped. Societal issues are all issues that apply to most of the population.[45] Theoretically, the potential for popular support increases as you move from union issues to societal issues. However, this is not always true, especially within unions where many sensitive class and social issues are extremely divisive.

In regard to political goals, *Being Heard* suggests, "Unions should highlight activities that people believe are the proper province and focus of Labor unions, rather than ranging far afield." It further advised that "unions must stay focused on activities that the public sees as central to their mission" and "that it is crucial that the legislation have an identifiable connection to the workplace and to unions' mission of helping workers."[46] *Being Heard* points out that "a key task in promoting more positive attitudes toward Labor unions is to link the work unions do for members in the workplace and around employment-related issues to the promotion of the nation's well being."[47] It concludes, "It is crucial that the legislation have an identifiable connection to the workplace and to the unions' mission of helping workers."[48] The AFL-CIO's efforts to involve rank-and-file members in political campaigns, its extensive use of focus groups and polling of union members, and its focus on workers' issues are clearly linked to this advice.

Whenever a significant minority of union members oppose a so-called good or moral class or social issue, union leaders have an obligation to convince them that their position is consistent with Labor's primary objectives and basic values. If they are unable to persuade them, then they should defer any action until they can. Public opinion polls, focus groups, and expanded membership databases are the primary tools for determining members' position on various political issues. Thus, high-performance unions constantly seek their members' views and support only legislative positions that a clear majority of their members support. That unions are the voice of workers is a straightforward, simple principle. If leaders do not speak as they would speak, they are misleading everyone involved in the political process. First, unions lose their trust and respect; then they lose member support; and ultimately lose members. Most important, as representatives of workers, union leaders are morally obligated to voice their members' concerns, beliefs, and values. Moral obligations are covered in more detail in Chapter 5.

As for coalitions, it is well known that many of Labor's "friends" are "not there" on key union issues or, at best, provide only token support. In these tough times Labor cannot afford to support coalition activities that are not consistent with Labor's primary legislative objectives. To strengthen union solidarity, Labor should also avoid coalition relationships that are emotionally sensitive and divisive.

In rating politicians for COPE endorsements, all so-called pro-labor vote should not carry the same weight. How politicians vote on union and employment issues is much more important than how they vote on class and social issues. Historically, even some of Labor's best friends disappear on really tough votes on union issues.

In February 1996, President Sweeney announced "a political effort of unprecedented scale" and pledged $35 million for an issues-oriented Labor '96 national election campaign.[49] The twin missions of the Labor '96 campaign were to educate and mobilize workers on the key issues and to get out the vote. In regard to educating and mobilizing workers, Labor '96 redefined the national election-year debate on the issues of Social Security, Medicare, education, and minimum wage. In regard to getting out the vote, 2.3 million more union members voted in 1996 than in 1992. This meant that almost 1.5 million union members voted for the reelection of President Clinton. It also resulted in the defeat of eighteen targeted, antiunion Republican representatives. From this point of view, Labor '96 was a success. However, the Republicans retained control of both the House of Representatives and the Senate, and thus, there is much less chance for Labor law reform than there was before the election. In addition, because of the intensity of union efforts in targeted Republican campaigns, there is a much greater chance of anti-Labor legislation. From this point of view, Labor '96 was a disappointment.

The realignment within the Democratic Party is another disappointing trend for Labor. Even the big increase in African-American, Hispanic, and female Democratic voters is not enough to beat business interests very often. Democratic pollster Geoff Garin argues that union blue-collar workers are caught by "the politics of resentment." "They are people who feel economically disconnected, and as (President) Clinton embraces a new economic order of high skills and international competition, they feel the Democratic party has left them."[50]

Ironically, as Labor's political influence diminishes, its militancy increases. Labor resorts more frequently to its traditional political philosophy of "rewarding your friends and punishing your enemies." Labor's lobbying efforts escalate from reason to outright threats of political destruction for all politicians who vote against Labor. Striker replacement is an example of politics by threat. Defeat left Labor with serious political wounds, fewer friends, and more enemies—some, bitter enemies. Revenge tactics have caused irreparable harm—important elections were lost. Labor cannot lambaste politicians for months for failing to support key union issues and then, just before the election, turn around and endorse them. It also cannot draw a line in the sand and keep moving away from it. It is obvious that labor needs to review its political strategies and tactics.

Given the present political situation, Labor law reform is obviously a long-term objective. What appeared to be possible by 1996 will now probably take much longer. *Being Heard* targets "passage of Labor law reform as one key to the future success of unions and their ability to effectively represent working people in collective bargaining, politics and policy. . . . Therefore we [Hart Research] suggest the long-range plan focus during the next few years on achieving this fundamental reform."[51] Consequently, high-performance unions develop and implement a comprehensive strategic political action plan that targets the enactment of fundamental Labor law reform by the year 2000.

The intense use of enabling technologies to increase individual member participation is the vehicle to greater political influence—the new union politics of the twenty-first century. Thousands, maybe even tens of thousands, of members and retired members in elected and appointed government positions or possessing unique knowledge and skills would welcome the opportunity to participate in union political action activities. At present, in most cases, unions know absolutely nothing about them, and there is no formal way to involve them.

Time magazine, which can personalize the weekly voting records of each subscriber's elected U.S. congressional representatives, is an example of an enabling technology that could promote greater member participation. Obviously, union organizations can utilize this leading-edge enabling technology to personalize their newspaper, journals, and magazines for voting records and other subjects. High-performance union managers possess a working knowledge of leading-edge enabling technologies and are extremely innovative in identifying union applications. They use enabling technologies and expanded membership databases to build political action networks for highly effective direct-mail fund-raising, targeted political education programs, and lobbying activities.

Community Action

The seventh function, community action, includes all union activities related to providing service to the community. In some areas, unions provide a community service through alliances with human rights groups, consumer and environmental coalitions, and local community action organizations. In the past, coalitions resulting from community action appeared effective in achieving more broadly based support for unions.

In addition to coalition activities, union organizations directly sponsor numerous worthy causes. The AFL-CIO Building and Construction Trades Department (BCTD) annually promotes DAD's (Dads against Diabetes) Day to collect funds to find a cure for diabetes. The IBEW's "Union of Hearts and Minds" encourages local unions to become more active in community services. The AFL-CIO Department of Community Services handles over 500,000 requests for help a year. The AFL-CIO Red Cross blood drive totals more than 250,000 units annually, and unions are major contributors to the United Way. Throughout the country, unions are among the first groups to volunteer help whenever disaster strikes. This is just an extremely brief summary of the many types of contributions unions make to the community.

In spite of Labor's outstanding record of community service, much of the general public is unaware of Labor's many contributions. High-performance unions use enabling technologies and expanded membership databases to provide greater opportunity for their members to participate in community action activities both as providers and as recipients. However, it is important to note the *Being Heard*'s warning that "United Way contributions and support for good social issues are fine, but in the end the challenge is to convince people that unions are inherently, not incidentally, good for America."[52] Therefore, high-performance unions develop and implement state-of-the-art public relations programs designed to convince people that unions' community action activities are good for their community. They also work within a comprehensive strategic management program to properly align community action activities to achieve core union objectives.

Organization Building

The eighth function, organization building, is concerned with improving the performance of the union organization. Education and communication are the primary means to achieve the union's core objectives, to promote cohesiveness, and to strengthen commitment to the union and its core objectives.[53]

On the first workday of the next millennium, high-performance unions, driven by enabling technologies, will be very different organizations. An enabling technology is any asset, idea, or technology that will facilitate performance. The sum of all the enabling technologies that are presently owned by, or available to, Labor organizations and union members throughout the world is an awesome strategic resource. With this resource, Labor can build on experiences of businesses and other leading-edge organizations in applying advanced enabling technologies. As the first step toward the next century, the AFL-CIO should coordinate a worldwide survey of all union organizations to determine size and characteristics of their available enabling technologies. Unfortunately, too many top union leaders do not see advanced enabling technologies as an essential, high-priority strategic tool and are reluctant to make a major broad-based commitment.

Enabling technologies also permit high-performance unions to more effectively reach members with special skills or unique talents who are willing to share them with their union. Members, holding elected or appointed government positions, will have the opportunity to share information and use their influence to help their union. Personalized direct mailing programs, based on special demographic profiles, needs, issues, and interests, are effective tools for involving members in union activities, lobbying efforts, and fund-raising activities. The AFL-CIO, leveraged by the intense use of state-of-the-art enabling technology, could be a more efficient and effective political, economic, and social force, even though it represents a declining percentage of the workforce.

Enabling technologies have long been available to facilitate the free flow of information between union organizations and between members and union organizations. Labor's introduction into the world of electronic networks began in 1984 with the International Chemical and Energy Workers Federation's Global Communications System, which had limited success. Recently, several other national unions have set up private electronic forums and home pages for their local unions and members on LaborNET, the AFL-CIO's new, computer-based communications network. This is a start, but it is still a long way behind other leading-edge organizations.

Successful electronic networks start with a comprehensive strategic communications plan, have top-level support, and are positioned high in the organization structure. Unfortunately, most union electronic bulletin board systems (BBS) and networks are more like teckie-driven, low-priority, hobby-type operations. Information networks are typically the responsibility of the data-processing department, which is structurally the wrong place, because, typically, union data-processing departments are mainframe, back-office, factory operations, positioned low in the union organization structure. Network management needs to be at the strategic level. A Global Labor Communication Network (GLCN), which can take full advantage of the proposed information superhighway infrastructure (formally named the National Information Infrastructure), Internet, and various other global networks, requires a total commitment from the AFL-CIO to design and operate it.

GLCN would be a secure, cost-saving, high-capacity network, designed specifically for the needs of an increasingly important global Labor movement and patterned after major corporate, large, nonprofit institutions and major university networks. It would be fully supported by user fees; thus, there is no cost to the AFL-CIO. Users would include rank-and-file members, all local, national, and international Labor organizations, government agencies, union consultants, contractors, vendors, and Labor education schools, colleges, and universities. In short, all Labor's stakeholders have access to GLCN. Typical uses are teleconferencing, multimedia presentations, national and international telephone calls, transferring computer data and information, electronic messages, e-mail, BBSs, on-line services, groupware, direct telemarketing of union made products, corporate campaigns, and so on.

A new lifetime union membership category will force unions into developing expanded membership databases that recognize members as unique individuals. Since some experts contend that the average worker will have six to eight employers in a lifetime, high-performance unions will be more like the multi-employer craft unions. Thus, unions will need to track each member's education, training, and work experiences for retraining, relocation, and job placement. Unions will also be more involved in administering pension, health, and welfare benefits. Further, a more diverse membership will be more dependent on unions for lifestyle services, expediting government services, and personal advice.

High-performance national unions establish social research departments to identify the changing values, attitudes, opinions, and needs of members, union employees, and other stakeholders. Social research departments will be responsible for anticipating and identifying problems associated with representing a diverse workforce in times of turbulent change. Their mission is to recommend programs to resolve, or at least minimize, internal conflict and promote union solidarity. Working with expanded membership databases, modern polling techniques, and enabling technologies, they will be the union's primary listening device that links top union officers to the rank and file, union employees, and other stakeholders.

Since people build organizations, leadership recruitment and development are the most important components of organization building. People are the organization; without people there would not be an organization. The future of any organization is determined by the efforts, skills, dedication, and visions of its people at all levels of the organization.

A typical union leader's career begins with participation in local union activities. Through participation, he or she gains the necessary experience and confidence to assume greater union responsibilities and is recognized and gains supporters for his or her various contributions. In addition, active members better understand their union's culture and traditions. Typically, it takes years to be elected to the top local union office. Generally, the bigger the local union, the longer the time required. After becoming the top elected local union officer, it frequently takes another five to ten years before being hired as a national representative or elected to a regional office. This traditional "from the rank and file" career ladder has been extremely successful in providing strong leaders. However, many of tomorrow's union leaders will need an entirely new set of skills.

The intense demands of the endless political struggle up the "from the rank and file" career ladder do not allow most union leaders the time to acquire necessary management skills or develop a specific expertise. Union politics are very time-consuming and thus exclude over 95 percent of the union members from career opportunities with their national union or with the AFL-CIO. Former IBEW international secretary Joe Keenan, convinced that all the ability and talent necessary to run a national union are present within its rank and file, was dedicated to giving talented young members, with very little or no political experience, a "break" by hiring them as national representatives. He also believed that workers are the best representatives of workers. The success of his policy is well documented. However, its weakness was that Management development was primarily limited to informal, on-the-job training. A comprehensive, formal Management development program would have made an extremely successful program an extraordinary one.

Unfortunately, too many of today's Labor representatives have never been career rank-and-file members. They have never experienced that defining awareness of a lifetime as a worker driving a bus, assembling widgets, sewing, teaching, typing letters, stocking shelves, cutting meat, bending pipe and pulling wire, laying bricks, fighting fires or crime, and so on. There is no substitute for this defining experience, which establishes a person as an eternal worker. Eric Hoffer, the world-recognized stevedore/philosopher, observed, "Still the awareness of being an eternal worker colors one's attitude." This essence of being an eternal worker binds you to an occupational lifestyle that affects your basic values and establishes your identity. For example, I am, and will always be, a construction electrician who was also very fortunate to have had the privilege to be an IBEW national representative for over twenty-two years. The two occupations, for me, are simply inseparable. I could not be one without being the other.

This bonding is a defining characteristic of many of the most effective union officers and representatives. No amount of worker empathy, liberal sympathies, brilliance, or academic achievement can ever substitute for this very personal experience. Summertime or part-time work in a union environment is not a substitute. Consequently, high-performance unions will implement a new "find and develop" career ladder to supplement the traditional "from the rank and file" career ladder. This new outreach program formally identifies, recruits, and develops talented rank-and-file members and local union representatives and officers for positions as union managers and specialists. In this comprehensive Management development program, capable and motivated individuals acquire, over a period of four or five years, the necessary Management experience, knowledge and skills, or specialist expertise to become high-performance union managers and experts. This program would include selected assignments, relevant college courses, Labor education courses, executive exchange programs, and other various Management development programs. Its twin objectives are to minimize Labor's dependence on nonmembers for filling key middle and top union Management and specialists positions and to provide young, dedicated, and talented members new opportunities within the Labor movement. Thus, hard-earned union dues will be used to provide union members with exciting new career opportunities.

In September 1992, the trustees of the George Meany Center for Labor Studies (GMCLS) established the Institute for the Study of Labor Organizations (ISLO). Its mission is to foster research on union administration, structure, and organizational development. While research is an important element of any Management development program, much more needs to be done. There is an urgent need for an action-oriented organization for managing unions. Thus, a more appropriate name is the Institute for Managing Labor Organizations (IMLO). However, since there was no reference to the ISLO in the 1995 AFL-CIO Executive Council Convention Report, it probably has a much lower priority or possibly has been abolished.

The IMLO's new mission is to *adapt management concepts, principles, and techniques for the union environment, to train union leaders to be high-performance managers and administrative specialists who constantly use union resources in innovative ways to efficiently and effectively manage union organizations, and to be effective workers' representatives, as partners with Management, in the new American workplace.*

The institute's core objectives are to

- serve as a permanent consortium to encourage urgently needed collaboration between Labor, business, and other various relevant academic disciplines;
- design and implement Management development and specialist training programs for union organizations;
- encourage, coordinate, and conduct research on matters relevant to adapting management principles, concepts, and techniques for the union environment;
- design and manage a union manager and specialist identification, recruitment, and development program;
- prepare Management development materials and provide assistance to union organizations;
- develop standards of excellence that promote effectiveness and efficiency, enrich union democracy, encourage innovation, create self-respect, and instill pride in unions;
- assist union organizations in developing and implementing strategic management programs;
- assure a new ethical dimension to union decision making;
- serve as a forum or "think tank" to help anticipate the challenges of the future and prepare top union Management to resolve them.

In brief, this organization-building subsection proposes the following seven major new organization-building strategies:

- the intense utilization of advanced enabling technologies;
- a Global Labor Communication Network;
- lifetime membership;
- expanded membership databases;
- social research departments;
- a "find and develop" career ladder;
- an Institute for Managing Labor Organizations.

A successful IMLO is absolutely essential to the survival of American unions as an effective representative of American workers and major force for social justice. Unless unions are more effectively and efficiently managed and more sensitive to the needs of their members, they will continue their decline to the point of irrelevance.

International Affairs

Since the future of American unions is so tightly linked to the success of international trade union solidarity, I added a ninth function, international affairs, to Wallihan's eight basic union functions. Over 100 years ago, Samuel Gompers, the first president of the AFL, led Labor into the international affairs arena. The AFL-CIO is involved in foreign policy in three ways, by

- formulating policies on international economic, political, social, and security issues, with the objective of influencing the foreign policies of the United States;
- developing activities abroad to assist in the building and reconstruction of free trade unions, especially in Central and Eastern Europe and the developing nations of Africa, Asia, and Latin America, as a major contribution to the defense and expansion of free and democratic societies;
- developing relationships with other national and international Labor organizations, such as the International Confederation of Free Trade Unions (ICFTU) and the International Trade Secretariats (ITS).

The AFL-CIO believes that global Labor standards can provide the basis for simple social justice for workers and their families. It also believes that labor standards promote a more stable, predictable, and, therefore, more prosperous global trading system. For decades the AFL-CIO has struggled to convince the U.S. government to make global Labor standards an essential component of American foreign policy.

In 1988, the AFL-CIO finally persuaded the U.S. Congress that the guarantee of worker rights by their governments is a legitimate prerequisite for certain trade benefits. The Omnibus Trade Act lists internationally recognized worker rights as

- the right of association;
- the right to organize and bargain collectively;
- the prohibition on the use of any form of forced or compulsory labor;
- a minimum age for the employment of children;
- acceptable conditions of work with respect to minimum wages, hours of work, and occupational health and safety.

In 1994, at the urging of the AFL-CIO, the U.S. Senate unanimously approved ratification of the International Labor Organization's (ILO) Convention 150. The ILO's 175 conventions are the world's Labor laws and have the force of international treaties among countries that ratify them. Convention 150 provides a general framework for establishing an effective Labor-administration system for the participation of workers and employers and their organizations. The fundamental element of Convention 150 is tripartism—the involvement of Labor, business, and government—in the work of the ILO. Inexcusably, this is only the twelfth convention the United States has ratified.[54] (The ILO is covered in more detail in the "Structure and Governance" section of Chapter 2.)

In this ongoing struggle for global social justice, the AFL-CIO has earned international recognition and respect. Consequently, the federation is well positioned to meet the challenges of global competition and the growing influence of transnational corporations. The stakes are enormous. American workers are being sucked into the Third World's bottomless pit of human suffering and misery. Labor and America cannot afford to lose to a conspiracy of renegade Third World nations and unscrupulous transnational corporations.

One of President Sweeney's first actions was to change the AFL-CIO from a force committed to fighting communism to one that can respond to transnational corporations and international competition.[55] For starters, he merged the four foreign institutes into one, which will emphasize education on workers' issues.

President Sweeney observed that over 200 million children are working under deplorable conditions and noted, "The challenge of our time is to make sure that every man, woman, and, child can benefit and not suffer from new opportunities of global trade and advanced technologies," not to let international economic cooperation degenerate "into a race to the bottom."[56]

National and local unions need to become more involved in activities that promote global acceptance of basic human rights and trade union rights and increase global union solidarity. High-performance local unions form global councils on the GLCN to exchange information with local unions in other countries that represent workers in similar occupations, industries, or corporations. Many also electronically "adopt" Third World unions to directly provide various types of urgently needed advice and assistance. High-performance national unions establish or expand international affairs departments to encourage and coordinate local union involvement in international affairs. A redirected, reenergized AFL-CIO, supported with GLCN and the intense use of other new enabling technologies, is the best counterforce to the overwhelming power of transnational corporations.

LINKING BASIC UNION AND MANAGEMENT FUNCTIONS

The primary objective of this chapter is to link the nine basic union functions to the four basic management functions of planning, organizing, directing, and controlling in a union environment. The basic union functions have been covered in this chapter, the basic management functions are covered in Chapter 6 and Chapter 7, and the union environment, which influences structure, is covered in Chapter 2.

This linking process begins by restructuring unions to focus on the nine basic union functions so that the various union activities can be assigned to the appropriate function or functions and then related to the four basic management functions and union structure. The following three new Management tools were developed to facilitate this process. First, the basic union functions/basic management functions matrix (Figure 1.2) links the basic union functions to the basic management functions. Second, the union structure/basic management functions matrix (Figure 1.3) links, in the same manner, union departments to the basic management functions. Third, the basic union management cube (Figure 1.4) adds a third dimension to Figures 1.2 and 1.3 for a more comprehensive analysis.

Figure 1.2
The Basic Union Functions/Basic Management Functions Matrix

Basic Union Functions	Basic Management Functions				
	Planning	Organizing	Direction	Controlling	PERFORMANCE
Collective Bargaining	✔	✔	✔	✔	
Organizing	✔	✔	✔	✔	Achieve functional objectives
Jurisdiction	✔	✔	✔	✔	
Administration	✔	✔	✔	✔	
Governance	✔	✔	✔	✔	Achieve core objectives
Political Action	✔	✔	✔	✔	
Community Action	✔	✔	✔	✔	
Organization Building	✔	✔	✔	✔	Achieve union mission
International Affairs	✔	✔	✔	✔	

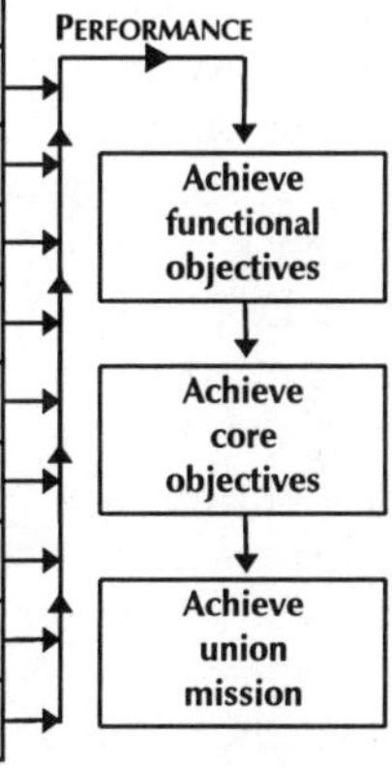

Figure 1.3
The Union Structure/Basic Management Functions Matrix

Union Structure	Basic Management Functions				
	Planning	Organizing	Direction	Controlling	PERFORMANCE
Industrial and Trade	✔	✔	✔	✔	
Grievance and Arbitration	✔	✔	✔	✔	Achieve department objectives
Accounting	✔	✔	✔	✔	
Organizing	✔	✔	✔	✔	Achieve core objectives
Membership Records	✔	✔	✔	✔	
Data Processing	✔	✔	✔	✔	
Research	✔	✔	✔	✔	Achieve union mission
Legislation	✔	✔	✔	✔	
International Affairs	✔	✔	✔	✔	

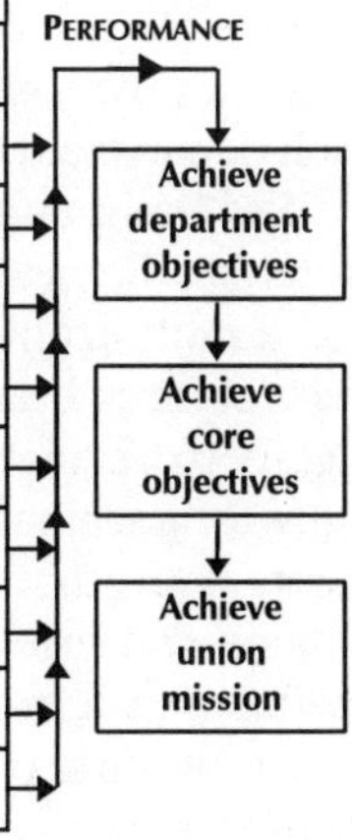

These new matrices are excellent planning tools. In Figure 1.2, the planning process starts by reviewing and, if necessary, revising the union's mission: next, core objectives are established for each basic function, then strategies are planned, organized, directed, and controlled to achieve these core objectives. For Figure 1.3, the planning process is the same except, here, core objectives are set for each union department. The emphasis swings from achieving departmental objectives to achieving the union's mission. Both require all union officers and directors to work together as a Management team to achieve the union's mission. The checks in Figure 1.2 and Figure 1.3 indicate that the basic management functions have been systematically applied to the basic union functions and to the union organizational structure. Checklists should be developed to facilitate the systematic application of management functions to union function and organizational structure.

The basic union functions/basic management functions matrix (Figure 1.2), or some variation of it, can serve as the foundation of the strategic planning process for all existing union organizations regardless of size. In large Labor organizations, a person, ideally an executive board or council member, could be assigned responsibility for one of the nine basic union functions. In small Labor organizations, a person could have responsibility for a cluster of several basic union functions. For example, political action and community action and possibly international affairs could be one responsibility cluster; other responsibility clusters could be administration, governance, and organization building; still another could be organizing and jurisdiction. The key points are, first, that someone is clearly responsible for achieving the mission and objectives for each basic union function and, second, that the four basic management functions are systematically applied to each and every basic union function.

The union structure/basic management functions matrix (Figure 1.3) is the most convenient planning tool. In this relationship there is no need to change the present union structure. Here the department director is clearly responsible for achieving the mission and objectives of his or her department and the four basic management functions are systematically applied to each department.

The basic union management cube (Figure 1.4) adds a third dimension to relate the nine basic union functions to the union's operating, support, and administrative departments. The cube is a strategic Management tool that requires little or no change in the existing organization structure, but high-performance unions restructure so there is a clear division of responsibility for each basic union function. Then they establish a structure, departments and other types of subunits, to support each basic union function's mission and core objectives. While this type of structural change is the most challenging, it can be the most rewarding.

On the first plane, the vertical axis is the nine basic union functions, and the depth axis is the four basic management functions. This plane also involves a systematic application of each management function to each basic union function. This is the same relationship as in Figure 1.2. On the second plane, the horizontal axis represents the existing departments, and the depth axis represents the four basic management functions. Here, department directors systematically apply the basic management functions to their operations. This involves thinking through the application of each management function to the operation of the department. This relationship is the same as in Figure 1.3. On the third plane, the new plane, the vertical axis represents the nine basic union functions, and the horizontal axis represents existing departments. This process requires a systematic resource allocation analysis of the existing union structure among the nine basic union functions. For this example, six typical national union departments were selected. On the department plane, the process of relating could be as simple as a yes or no for each basic function, or it could involve identifying the degree of effort required and weighting it on a scale of 1 to 10 or 1 to 100. The degree of effort is a measure of the resources consumed by a particular department. In this example, the research department provides a service for each of the nine basic union functions whereas the legislative department provides a service to only six of the nine basic union functions.

Figure 1.4
The Basic Union Management Cube

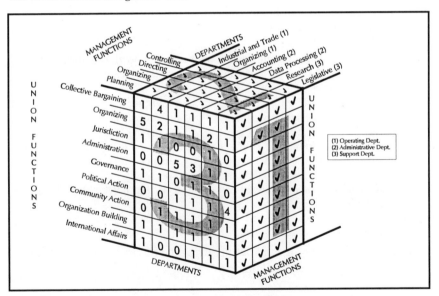

The basic union management cube also requires senior officers and directors to work as a team, to think in terms of the entire union, and to allocate resources in pursuit of the union's mission and its core objectives as opposed to individual department objectives. It gives officers an entirely new way of managing their union organizations. Assigning responsibility for the basic union functions, in effect, creates a "market" in which each executive board member, vice president, or assistant openly contends for available resources. This "market" concept is critical for effective and efficient resource allocation. This cube links the basic management functions, the basic union functions, and the union structure to help build and manage tomorrow's high-performance unions. It is the launch vehicle into the world of high-performance union management.

SUMMARY

This chapter explains the nine basic union functions and relates them to the four basic management functions. It also defines the new American union *as a voluntary association of workers that represents their interests in the workplace, provides common purpose and community based on service to workers, and advocates social changes necessary to improve the lives of all workers.*

Basic Union Functions

Collective Bargaining

Collective bargaining, Labor's primary product, is an extremely complex process that covers all aspects of work.

High-performance unions

- recognize that most American workers want unions to work collaboratively with Management in all strategic decisions that affect their income, working conditions, and job security;
- promote new Labor-Management partnerships and prepare union officers and representatives to be equal partners with Management in the new American workplace;
- recognize the importance of contract administration—due process and workplace justice—in new Labor-Management partnerships;
- expedite the existing grievance and mediation processes;
- continually search for innovative ways to improve and individualize the collective bargaining process.

Organizing

Organizing includes all activities involving the recruitment of workers.

High-performance national unions

- provide every worker with the courage to sign a union authorization card the opportunity for lifetime membership;
- build high-performance local unions that are effective and efficient "instrumentalities" for improving the lives of workers in both the workplace and the community;

- resolve the "organizing" versus "servicing" conflict by implementing a comprehensive strategic management program for allocating increasingly scarce resources among the nine basic union functions;
- recognize that in most cases worker dissatisfaction is unlikely to a major incentive for organizing.

High-performance local unions assume primary responsibility for organizing, high-performance national unions build high-performance local unions, and the new, high-performance AFL-CIO coordinates and assists affiliated national unions' organizing activities.

Jurisdiction
Jurisdiction includes all activities relating to a claim on, or grant of, the right to organize or represent a category of workers. It is also an important consideration in union mergers.

High-performance national unions

- reconsider present merger and centralization policies; and
- approve only mergers that are necessary and clearly synergistic, enrich union democracy, and do not diminish the ability of the merged unions to represent their members.

Administration
Administration covers all activities necessary to support the union.

High-performance national unions use ASCs, which provide advanced enabling technologies, communication networks, and routine administrative support services to small union organizations.

The AFL-CIO encourages and coordinates the growth of ASCs, and in some cases it would, through its state federations and central labor councils, actually provide administrative and support services.

Governance
Governance is concerned with the details of electing officers, conducting meetings, and establishing policies necessary to operate a democratic union organization.

High-performance unions

- implement changes in Management style and union structure to encourage the free flow of information;
- continually poll members to determine their perception of the quality of democracy in their union and take appropriate actions in response to the results of the polls;
- recognize that union democracy is extremely fragile and must be coddled, protected, and enthusiastically encouraged;
- recognize that even though the roots of democracy are the rank and file, the quality of union democracy is determined by the top national union officers;

- recognize that the right to belong to a union applies with equal moral and binding force to union employees;
- recognize that national union conventions are the cornerstones of union democracy.

High-performance national unions

- convene national constitutional conventions every four years to amend the constitution, elect national union officers, and establish union strategies, policies, and programs;
- convene national state of the union conventions or conferences every two years to review performance and compliance with the actions of the constitutional convention and, as necessary, revise union strategies, policies, and programs;
- review and amend constitutions and bylaws to improve clarity and to eliminate all provisions that impinge, or even appear to impinge, on union democracy;
- elect national union officers by secret ballot;
- use electronic systems to facilitate the convention voting process;
- empower executive councils as boards;
- set high standards to enrich union democracy and continuously monitor for compliance.

Political Action
Political action includes all activities necessary to achieve Labor's political activities
High-performance unions

- focus on legislation that has an identifiable connection to unions, the workplace, and to Labor's mission of helping all workers;
- continually poll their members to determine their position on political issues;
- continually evaluate their coalition relationships;
- rate politicians primarily on union and worker issues;
- use reason and diplomacy as their primary lobbying strategy;
- target enactment of Labor law reform in the year 2000;
- use expanded membership databases and enabling technologies to achieve Labor's political objectives.

Community Action
Community action includes all action related to providing service to the community.
High-performance unions

- use expanded membership databases and enabling technologies to provide greater opportunities for members to participate in community action programs;
- combine community action with creative public relations to convince people that unions are inherently good for America.

Organization Building

Organization building is concerned with the performance of union organizations.

High-performance unions

- use expanded membership databases and enabling technologies to increase member participation, promote open communication, and improve operational performance;
- use expand membership databases and enabling technologies to facilitate member training and job placement;
- establish social research departments to develop programs that identify members' needs, manage diversity, and help resolve inter-union and workplace conflict;
- establish "find and develop" career ladders to supplement the traditional "from the rank and file" career ladders;
- design structures that centralize the administrative and support functions but decentralize the union operations functions;
- implement Management and specialist development programs for all union officers and representatives.

The new, high-performance AFL-CIO

- has an expanded role in coordinating the application of enabling technologies;
- operates a GLCN specifically designed for the needs of American union organizations, their stakeholders, and an increasingly important global Labor movement;
- establishes the Institute for Managing Labor Organizations.

International Affairs

International affairs are tightly linked to the future success of American union and international trade union solidarity.

High-performance unions

- become more involved in international unionism;
- form global councils to exchange information on workers in similar occupations and industries or employed by the same transnational corporation;
- electronically "adopt" Third World unions to provide advice and various forms of assistance;
- increase global unions' solidarity.

Linking Basic Union and Management Functions

The primary objective of this chapter is to link the nine basic union functions to the four basic management functions within the union structure.

High-performance unions

- restructure to focus on the nine basic union functions;
- use the basic union functions/basic management functions matrix, the union structure/basic management functions matrix, and the basic union management

cube as strategic planning tools to link the basic management functions, the basic union functions, and the union structure to help build and manage tomorrow's high-performance unions.

NOTES

1. Peter F. Drucker, *Managing the Nonprofit Organization* (New York: Harper-Collins, 1990), xvii.

2. Susan Choen, "Community, an Impossible Dream" *Washington Post*, Magazine section, 31 July 1994, 27.

3. James Wallihan, *Union Government and Organization* (Washington, DC: BNA Books, 1985), 4–5.

4. Ibid., 14–16. I separated the administration and governance functions, and the political and community action functions into four separate functions and added international affairs.

5. David Lewin, Olivia S. Mitchell, and Peter D. Sherer, eds., *Research Frontiers in Industrial Relations and Human Resources* (Madison, WI: Industrial Relations Research Association Series, 1992); Harry C. Katz and Jeffery H. Keefe, "Collective Bargaining and Industrial Relations Outcomes: The Causes and Consequences of Diversity," 51.

6. *Being Heard: Strategic Communications Report and Recommendations*, prepared for the AFL-CIO by Greer, Margolis, Mitchell, Burns, & Associates (21 Mar. 1994), 15.

7. Lewin, Mitchel, and Sherer, *Research Frontiers*, 51.

8. *The New American Workplace: A Labor Perspective*, a report by the AFL-CIO Committee on the Evolution of Work (Washington, DC: AFL-CIO, 1994), 1.

9. Ibid., 11–12.

10. Ibid., 12.

11. Lewin, Mitchell, and Sherer, *Research Frontiers*, 47.

12. Ibid., 50.

13. *The New American Workplace*, 15.

14. Wallihan, *Union Government*, 51

15. Muriel H. Cooper, "Young Activists Deployed for Union Summer," *AFL-CIO News*, 10 June 1996, 1.

16. Muriel H. Cooper, "Organizing Program Seeks Innovation," *AFL-CIO News*, 11 Mar. 1996, 1.

17. Muriel H. Copper, "Organizing Wins Small Steps," *AFL-CIO News*, 20 May 1996, 12.

18. *Being Heard*, 35.

19. William Sarrin, "Is This Really Labor's Day?" *Washington Post*, Outlook, 1 Sept. 1996, 1.

20. *Industrial Project*, a research report prepared by Cornell University for the IBEW (April 1992), 11.

21. Cooper, "Organizing Wins Small Steps," 12.

22. *Industrial Project*, 143.

23. Thomas A. DeCotiis and Jean-Yves LeLouarn, "A Predictive Study of Voting Behavior in a Representation Election Using Union Instrumentality and Work Perceptions," *Organizational Behavior and Human Performance*, vol. 27, 1981, 103–118.

24. Bruce E. Kaufman and Morris M. Kleiner, eds., *Employee Representation Alternatives and Future Directions* (Madison, WI: Industrial Relations Research Association, 1993), 29.

25. Richard Freeman and Joel Rogers, "Worker Representation and Participation Survey: First Report" Dialogues, (Madison, WI: Industrial Relations Research Association, 1995), 1.

26. *Being Heard*, 12

27. Ibid., 11

28. Ibid., 12–13.

29. Ibid., 39.

30. Ibid., 40.

31. Anil Verma, "New Union Organizing: A Return to the Old Methods," *Proceeding of the 1989 Spring Meeting* (Madison, WI: Industrial Relations Research Association, 1989), 465–469.

32. Wallihan, *Union Government*, 63.

33. Ibid., 83.

34. Ibid., 7.

35. Gary N. Chaison, *When Unions Merge* (Lexington, MA: Lexington Books), 2.

36. Ibid., 24.

37. *Being Heard*, 16–17.

38. Wallihan, *Union Government*, 15.

39. *Being Heard*, 16.

40. Wallihan, *Union Government*, 213–215.

41. *Being Heard*, 25.

42. Martha Gruelle, "Reformers Win Tight Race against United Old Guard," *Labor Notes*, January 1997.

43. Wallihan, *Union Government*, 192–193.

44. *Being Heard*, 20.

45. Wallihan, *Union Government*, 182–185.

46. *Being Heard*, 21–22.

47. Ibid., 36.

48. Ibid., 22.

49. Michael Byrne, "Political Plan Raises Issues and Grass Roots," *AFL-CIO News*, 11 Mar. 1996, 1.

50. Thomas B. Edsall, "Democrats Face Another Identity Crisis," *Washington Post*, 21 May 1994, D1.

51. *Being Heard*, 42–43.

52. Ibid., 22.

53. Wallihan, *Union Government*, 15.

54. *ILO Washington Focus* (Washington, DC: International Labor Officer, Winter 1995), 1.

55. Frank Swoboda and Martha M. Hamilton, "Labor Looks to Grow from the Grass Roots," *Washington Post*, 18 Feb. 1996, H1.

56. David Kameras, "Sweeney Urges ILO to Seek Child Labor Ban," *AFL-CIO News*, 1 July 1996, 4.

2

The Union Environment

Without exception, the dominance and coherence of culture proved to be an essential quality of the excellent companies.

Thomas J. Peters and Robert H. Waterman, Jr., *In Search of Excellence*

It is not by consolidation, or concentration of powers, but by their distribution, that good government is effected.

Thomas Jefferson, *Autobiography*

This chapter explains how culture and tradition are major influences on the day-to-day behavior of people in organizations. It stresses the importance of continually adjusting the union's mission and objectives in a manner consistent with its culture and tradition. It then describes the environment's enormous influence on the union structure and explains the structure and governance of Labor unions.

CULTURE AND TRADITION

Culture includes everything ever created by man—material and nonmaterial. A culture is an integrated system of objects and practices that expresses a society's values, beliefs, sentiments, and attitudes that have evolved over generations and influence the behavior of its people. Culture is extremely important to people, and thus their behavior is emotional, not rational. Consequently, culture is not easily changed. The various levels of culture are national, professional, and organizational. It is omnipresent, and its influence on the functioning of an organization is strong. Understanding a culture helps Management establish constructive relations within the organization. It is important to be aware that the influence of culture is not always progressive and constructive.[1]

Sociologists divide culture into three categories. The first category includes all bodies of knowledge based on practice, experience, or reason. This includes such material objects as tools, machines, weapons, clothing, buildings, organizations, and so on. It also includes such nonmaterial objects such as crafts, skills, knowledge, logic, and so on. In the second category are such material objects as works of art, the symbols and vestments of ritual, and such nonmaterial things as forms of recreation, social conventions, and appreciation of fine arts. The third category contains all those things that exercise a control influence on the group members. This category includes such material things as patriotic emblems, the insignia of authority, and other such objects or symbols and such nonmaterial things as usages, moral standards, religious sanctions, and laws.

Tradition, a part of culture, involves the handing down of statements, beliefs, legends, customs, and so on, from generation to generation, mostly by word of mouth or by practice. Tradition also is not inherited, and to preserve it requires hard work. Tradition must be continually updated to fit the present situation.

Culture is a living thing, and like all living things it is continually growing and changing, but change is slow. The prime characteristics of culture are persistence and stability. Change is the result of new facts, new relations, discovery, and invention. However, change is frequently in the form of accident, such as a catastrophe or major intervention, rather than intent. Intended change is slow because its adoption disturbs the old relations or institutions. Another explanation for resistance to change is that the existing order function to the welfare of the incumbent decision makers.

To understand a culture, one must examine its human attitudes and values. A child is not born with culture. Cultural expectations are taught to the child by the family, the community, the formal education system, and other social, religious, economic, and political organizations. A knowledge of culture is essential to understanding how organizations work, since culture influences the day-to-day behavior of people in organizations and even the way in which they build organizations.[2]

Organizational culture is a set of beliefs about people, about society, and about organizational objectives, along with traditions of how people relate to each other. Each organization's culture is unique. Subcultures arise when their members interact with one another differently than with people in the culture at large. Occupations are cultures and subcultures within the workplace. Occupational ideology is an emotional set of beliefs that allows members of an occupation to make sense of their work environment. Culture forms are the means by which an occupation conveys its ideologies to its members and include rituals, ceremonies, symbols, mythmaking, and physical artifacts.

Occupations are useful in explaining how an organization works. They act as subcultures and arise in work organizations when workers in an occupation must cooperate with one another, but not with workers in other occupations. Managers and administrators are the most important occupational subculture because of their impact on other occupational subcultures. Conflicts are usually the result of the managerial subculture seeking more control of the work, while other occupational subcultures seek more autonomy. The tension between Management and the occupational subcultures is the result of the relative strengths of the occupational subcultures, and relief requires different types of accommodations. From the workers' perspective, unionized occupational subcultures are much more effective in resolving this tension than nonunionized occupational subcultures.

Occupational ideology is concerned with beliefs that help members of an occupation understand their work environment. Cultural forms are the means by which an occupation conveys its ideologies to its members. Analysis of occupational ideologies and cultural forms provides insight into how occupational subcultures influence organizational cultures.[3]

In today's increasingly dynamic and diverse society, the potential for conflict is always present and increasing. Since cultural differences often provoke conflict, it can be concluded that intolerance is universal. Conflict can be deceiving because what appear to be functional or structural problems often are actually cultural problems.

Since the essence of organizational culture ultimately is the people of the organization, Management's challenge is getting people to behave differently. Thus, it is important to concentrate on emotions and behaviors before building the new structure—information systems, compensation programs, and the decision-making process. When emotions and behavior change, then systems must be put in place to support the cultural change. Consequently, what really matters are the values of the top executive and how they create a strategic vision to provide meaning to the workers. Since the people are the essence of organizational culture, they should be always involved in any attempts to get them to behave differently.[4]

Several examples of union organizational culture are the

- union organization's mission;
- role of seniority and authority;
- importance of different Management positions and functions;
- treatment of people;
- role of women in union Management;
- selection criteria for union Management and specialist positions;
- organization of work and discipline;
- union Management and leadership style;
- decision-making process;
- circulation and sharing information;
- communication patterns;
- socialization patterns;
- ways of managing conflict;
- performance evaluation process;
- degree of identification with the union.[5]

Management experts see culture and tradition as a powerful Management tool. Richard Norman, author of *Management and Statesmanship*, explained that the "most crucial process going on in any company may be the continuing interpretation of historic events and the adjustment of the dominating business idea in that context." Andrew Pettigrew, a British strategic decision-making expert, believes the process of shaping culture is Management's prime role. "The [leader] not only creates the rational and tangible aspects of organizations, such as structures and technology, but also is the creator of the symbols, ideologies, language, beliefs, rituals, and myths."[6]

Pettigrew's statement regarding the role of leaders is clear, but Norman's requires some "adapting." In the union environment, the union's "dominating business idea" is its mission. Thus, Pettigrew's statement rephrased would read: the most crucial process in managing a union is the continuing adjustment of the union's mission and core objectives in a manner consistent with historic events.

If culture and tradition are extremely valuable Management resources for other organizations, they are even more so for union organizations. Unions, born out of the never-ending struggle for justice, human dignity, and human rights, have an incredibly rich and honorable heritage. Every union organization, no matter what size, has its heroes and heroines, its legends, myths, and stories, which provide shared values that could act as a unifying and directing force.

The AFL-CIO constitution recognizes the importance of culture and tradition. Its Preamble reads, "We seek the fulfillment of these hopes and aspirations through the democratic process within the framework of our constitutional government and *consistent with our institutions and traditions.* . . .With divine guidance, grateful for the *fine traditions of our past*, confident of meeting the challenges of the future, we proclaim this constitution." The George Meany Memorial Archives, dedicated to the preservation and dissemination of information about Labor's heritage, is another example of the AFL-CIO's recognition of the importance of culture and tradition.

Unfortunately, because of more urgent business, bitter internal political battles, jealousy, envy, insecurity, or just pure apathy, a great deal of our rich heritage is hidden, distorted, or lost forever. Too many Labor leaders simply see no value in preserving their union's culture and tradition. In other cases, the preservation of culture and tradition frequently results in a sanitizing, revisionist history that, in effect, destroys its major value—the truth. Equally troublesome, too many union leaders fail to recognize the practical utility of using culture and tradition as a Management tool.

On the other hand, high-performance union leaders use their culture and tradition to motivate and inspire their members and employees. The following are typical cultural and tradition-preserving activities:

- appointing union history committees;
- annual years-of-service milestone ceremonies linked to history—especially local history;

- collecting memorabilia, establishing heroes' and heroines' halls of fame, and Labor libraries in the local union headquarters;
- promoting union history displays in the workplace, hiring halls, civic centers, libraries, museums, sports arenas, shopping centers, schools, public parks, on electronic bulletin boards, and so on;
- naming days, parks, streets, schools, recreation centers, scholarships, golf outings, softball tournaments, bowling tournaments, days at the races, and picnics after local union heroes and heroines.

Change, complexity, and diversity force many cultural changes in the union environment. High-performance union leaders recognize that culture is extremely difficult to change and therefore adapt existing union culture to meet tomorrow's challenges. They also always try to minimize conflict in Labor-Management relations and join employers as equal partners within a shared-environment workplace. High-performance union leaders create a new, strategic vision of an inclusive culture with new guiding values and a new supporting structure for their members, employees, and stakeholders. Most important, they always adjust their mission and objectives in a manner consistent with their union's culture and tradition.

EXTERNAL ENVIRONMENT

The external environment and the efforts of union leaders to develop an effective organization determine the structure of a union. In *The External Control of Organizations: A Resource Dependence Perspective*, researchers Jeffrey Pfeffer and Gerald Salanick argue that to understand the behavior of an organization, it is necessary to understand the context of that behavior. "Organizations," they explain, "are inescapably bound up with the conditions of the environment. . . . All organizations engage in activities which have as their logical conclusion adjustment to the environment."[7] Today, this observation is of particular importance for unions because environmental conditions are becoming increasingly complex and rapidly changing.

The external environment of a union is the surroundings and forces beyond the control of the union organization that influence its structure and operations. Some of these forces are uniform, while others are variable. The uniform forces, those common for all union organizations, are economic, social, legal, technological, and political systems. Even though these uniform forces are common to all union organizations, changes in them will impact each union organization differently. For example, even in an economic depression some unions will gain membership, while most will lose membership. The variable forces, unique for each union organization, relate to the type of industry, markets, and employer; occupation/employment patterns; products/services; geographical area; and competition. Table 2.1, lists the typical environmental influences.

Table 2.1
Elements of the External Union Environment

Uniform Characteristics	
• The Economic System	• The Social System
• The Legal System	• Technical System
• The Political System	

Variable Characteristics	
Type of Industry, Markets, and Employers	**Occupation/Employment Patterns**
• Competitive or monopolistic • Concentrated or dispersed • Capitalization required for entry • Average firm size • Conglomerates, transnationals, or single firm • Local, regional, or national markets • Stable, seasonal, or other market fluctuations • Alternative sources of supply and production • Traditions and attitudes • Extent of hierarchy	• Degree of skill • Training requirements • Craft traditions • Tools • Casual, regular, or mixed • Method of entry • Form of compensation • Worker-supervisor ratio • Type of supervision • Uniform or variable working conditions • Union traditions • Employment level in the firm and industry
Product or Service	**Area**
• Fixed or transportable • Durable or nondurable standardized • Standardized or customized	• Area employment • Workforce mobility • Multi-employer organizations • Customs and traditions • Strength of unions

Source: Adapted from James Wallihan, *Union Government and Organization* (Washington, DC: BNA, 1985), 70.

The major external environmental forces on a typical local union are

- the local economic, social, legal, technical, and political systems;
- the national union;
- the employer's Management style;
- other unions in the area;
- area traditions.[8]

It is important to understand that the national union is considered an external environmental influence for the local union since the local union has virtually no control over the national union. If a local union does not comply with the directives of the national union, it is subject to various sanctions, including trusteeship. External environmental forces are also known as systems and are explained in more detail in Chapter 3.

Union organizations are continually adapting their structures to accommodate changes in their external environment. Wallihan identified the following four modes of organizational change:

- the piecemeal or evolutionary method;
- the formalization of an informal structure;
- imitation;
- conscious and comprehensive planning (strategic management).

Historically, union organizations have utilized all four modes with varying degrees of success. However, by far the most common mode of organizational change has been the evolutionary method, which is usually strongly influenced by the employer's structure.[9] While managed evolution is extremely important in keeping an organization adaptive, it is totally inadequate in today's turbulent times. In the past, when environmental change was much more stable, the evolutionary method was a very effective response. Today, in an extremely turbulent environment, with change taking place at a bewildering pace, strategic management is absolutely essential for survival.

Jack Fiorito, Cynthia L. Gramm, and Wallace E. Hendricks, collaborators in the paper "Union Structural Choices," point out that while the external environment is a major influence on organizational structures, it does not determine the structure of unions, because unions have significant discretion in their choice of objectives and organization structure. Objectives logically have a higher priority than organization structure since strategies are based on the objectives they are intended to achieve. Thus, structure follows as a function of strategy, and strategy and structure influence both organizational behavior and performance.[10]

The criterion for measuring organizational performance follows from organizational objectives and is measured by its effectiveness and efficiency. Effectiveness refers to whether the objectives are attained, and efficiency refers to the cost of attaining the objectives. Efficiency is fairly impartial, but effectiveness is very subjective. Measuring performance is further complicated because there is little agreement regarding what organizational effectiveness means and how to properly measure it. However, the following are five broadly agreed upon measures of union performance:

- financial performance;
- membership growth and union density;
- the economic status of union members or workers generally;

- members' and workers' attitudes toward unions, which include union commitment and union satisfaction;
- the political influence of unions.

Based on these measures, evidence, as a whole, indicates that the performance of American unions is down and in trouble. Union financial performance deteriorated in the 1970s; numerous studies document the decline of union membership; nonunion wage increases have exceeded those for union members in recent years; workers' perception of union effectiveness declined from 1977 to 1984; and political influence bottomed out in the 103d Congress. Fortunately, no two unions are alike, and since the external environment and structures of unions vary considerably, their performance also varies. Therefore, some unions are better prepared than others to meet the challenges of the future.

A critical, ongoing debate is whether performance or democracy is the best structural strategy to take unions into the twenty-first century. "Democrats" see union democracy as the primary cause of union effectiveness and contend that the current trend toward centralization and structuring has alienated union members. Decentralization, "democrats" contend, enhances member commitment, and they argue that member commitment is absolutely essential to union effectiveness. "Democrats" believe that, over the long term, centralization and the absence of an effective political process reduce union effectiveness.

On the other hand, "organizationalists," while not opposed to union democracy, stress the need for administrative solutions, including greater centralization and structuring. In recent years, there has been a clear trend toward centralization and increased structuring, with the AFL-CIO favoring administrative reforms (e.g., encouraging mergers and support for management, budget and planning techniques) and centrally orchestrated initiatives (e.g., coordinating organizing and bargaining, associated memberships, the "Union Yes" campaign, and corporate campaigns). The AFL-CIO is also assuming a greater role in what were previously considered national union responsibilities.[11]

Union centralization appears to be a global trend. For example, recent Australian legislation that requires a minimum of 1,000 members would eliminate roughly half of all Australian unions. Australia is also attempting to consolidate over 200 national unions into approximately 20 with a master plan designed to improve efficiency and effectiveness, as well as the overall functioning of the industrial relations system.[12] Unfortunately, like a great deal of legislation, the end result could be exactly the opposite of the intent. The true trade unionists will lose interest, leaving the 20 unions to the functionaries and bureaucrats who do not represent the workers. From an equity standpoint, it is extremely unlikely that legislators, in any advanced industrial nation, would ever even consider imposing minimum size requirements on small businesses based on the rationality of improved performance.

Centralization is not the same as structuring. Centralization is concerned with the location of control over organizational activities, while structuring deals with arranging units within the organization. For example, centralization can be measured by the national union's degree of control over the local union or by the national union's control of the distribution of union dues. In contrast, structuring involves the organization of union operations, formalization, and standardization. Specialized functional departments such as bargaining, research, and organizing measure structuring, not centralization. Structuring can be an effective tool to promote union decentralization.

Both structuring and centralization may conflict with the quality of union democracy, since both are part of the "administrative rationality," which is concerned with union performance. "Administrative rationality" can interfere with "representative rationality" which is concerned with objective formation or policy deliberation. Representative rationality is basically concerned with who and how decisions are made—union democracy.

While centralization, structuring, and democracy are totally separate concepts that theoretically do not influence each other, research studies indicate that the basic tensions that exist between the administrative rationality and the representative rationality often conflict with union democracy.[13] There are two striking features of the performance-versus-democracy debate. First, there is a tendency to link two distinct concepts: centralization (the point of control of decisions in the hierarchy) and democracy (who controls the decisions). Second, the debate has been, and continues to be, conducted in the virtual absence of usable research and information.[14]

Therefore, when making decisions, it is extremely important to willfully and consistently be aware of the separateness of centralization and democracy. For example, my proposed restructuring involves empowering union executive councils as executive boards and electing national officers by secret ballot. In this case, the location of control switches from one person, the national president, to five or more people, the executive board, thus enriching democracy. In addition, the secret ballot moves the location of control to the convention delegates and frees them from political pressure. My objective is to design structures that improve performance and empower members.

As to the second feature, the end results of centralization tend to be diminished union democracy, reduced environmental sensitivity, structural inflexibility, increased internal conflict, decreased opportunities for member participation, and potentially serious Management problems. This is a deadly combination for unions unless strategies are implemented to minimize the negative effects of past centralization, and ASCs are widely deployed to minimize the need for mergers and greater centralization. Consequently, until there is a body of evidence to the contrary, union democracy is vastly far more important than centralization. While this book is about the performance of unions—administrative rationality—its principal focus is on member empowerment through greater participation in objective formation and policy deliberation—representative rationality.

STRUCTURE AND GOVERNANCE

Structure is how the various units of organizations are arranged. Function refers to the basic purpose for which an organization is designed or exists and is concerned with mission, objectives, and strategies. Structure is the form or shape of an organization, and it always follows function. Process is concerned with the flow or action through which something takes place. Position, the content of the form, is concerned with the behavior of the people who make up the organization—with what they do and how they do it. Performance is concerned with organizational effectiveness and efficiency.[15] Function, structure, process, position (behavior), and performance are very important concepts in management theory. In this sequence, behavior and performance always follow structure. While this distinction is useful, behavior is sometimes included in structure because structure is no more than various patterns of behavior. Behavior interacts with particular environments to determine performance, which provides the primary criteria for judging the success of an organization.[16] Table 2.2 provides an example that traces the function of collective bargaining through this causal sequence.

Table 2.2
Function, Structure, Process, Position, and Performance

Function: Includes Mission, Objectives, and Strategies	Collective Bargaining
Structure:	Office of the President — Vice Presidents; Research Department; Industry Department; Coordinating Council; Local Unions
Process:	To provide the coordinating council and the chief union negotiator information on collective bargaining agreements with similar companies. 1) Collect the information, 2) select the information, 3) package the information, 4) deliver the information, 5) use the information.
Position (behavior):	• National President • Vice Presidents • Director of Research • Director of the Industry Department • Council Officers • Chief Union Negotiator • Agreement Analyst • Secretary
Performance (outcomes):	• Wage increase • Job security • Worker participation • New job classification • Retraining • Increased productivity • Greater workforce flexibility

The basic differences in union structures are the result of deliberate choices made in an attempt to build structures that best facilitate objective attainment. The two-dimensional union structure consists of the horizontal dimension, which applies to the external structure, and the vertical dimension, which applies to the internal structure. The horizontal dimension of union structure includes identity decisions that a union draws between itself and the external environment. These decisions involve setting boundaries for membership at the various tiers within the hierarchical structure. In general, the predominance of collective bargaining favors either industrial or occupational divisions, as opposed to regional divisions. The six-level vertical dimension, primarily concerned with the administrative rationality, includes the workplace, the local union, the intermediate union, the national union, the national federation, and the international federation.[17]

The first decision area, structuring, is concerned with such bureaucracy concepts as specialization, formalization, standardization, and so on. The second decision area is concerned with centralization—the point of control over the Labor organization's major activities. At one end of the range, control is centralized in the national union or federation level; at the other end, local unions retain almost complete authority.

High-performance unions continually seek the optimal structure for implementing strategies that involve external transactions. An optimal structure provides the best means of achieving a union organization's particular core objectives. Since vertical structures are influenced by various objective-strategy combinations, it follows that each union structure is unique.

The following three broad generalizations about choices of union structure will facilitate the analysis of variations in union structure:

- American unions traditionally give the highest priority to the attainment of workplace objectives through the strategy of collective bargaining.
- The distinguishing characteristic of American national unions has been the persistence of a spirit of local separatism and autonomy. Unions attempt to maximize the welfare of their members by decentralizing collective bargaining in order to give as much autonomy to local unions as it can without jeopardizing the interests of the larger body of members.
- Unions may have characteristics that make bureaucratic structures less important than in modern corporations because trust may minimize the need for formal organizational structure in achieving the union's objectives. In short, "solidarity" can be an attractive alternative to bureaucratic procedures.[18]

However, the election of John J. Sweeney as president of the AFL-CIO has dramatically changed priorities from collective bargaining to organizing. Clearly, this involves extensive restructuring. An enthusiastic Sweeney points out "We have to change every level of our structure. If we do, labor unions will grow."[19] Unfortunately, it is not that simple, since structure follows function—mission, objectives, and strategies—a mistake regarding function is a potential organizational disaster. Further, if change is to be accepted, it must be consistent with union culture and tradition. A much better approach would be to develop a comprehensive strategic management process that includes all the basic union functions and all stakeholders and implement it in a manner consistent with union culture and tradition.

In organizations, matters of function, structure, process, position, and performance are closely linked to matters of governance. Governance is the process of electing officers, conducting meetings that are necessary to set policy, and maintaining democracy in an organization, while government is an established framework of authority to decide what is binding on the activities of the people within its jurisdiction.[20] Robert Hoxie, VanDusen Kennedy, and Alice Cook have been leaders in classifying union structure and governance. Hoxie related union structure to the environment, Kennedy distinguished between the influence of the environment on factory unionism and nonfactory unionism, and Cook is noted for her elaboration of a dual governance in unions.

Kennedy identified two extreme types of environment and of union structure. He proposed that a nonfactory environment will result in a nonfactory union structure and that a factory environment will cause a factory structure. He further argued that not only were factory and nonfactory environments and structures associated, but each in turn produced distinctive patterns of behavior and ideology.

At the extremes of the continuum, the distinction between factory and nonfactory is clear, but as the middle is approached, the distinction is less clear, more complicated, and sometimes overlapping. Nonfactory unionism is not limited to the building trades, nor is factory unionism the same as the manufacturing industry. In fact, a few unions, such as those for professional athletes, do not fall within either classification.[21]

Cook teaches that the union structure is unique since it is made up of two governments—the internal union government and the collective bargaining government. The governing documents of the internal union government are the national union's constitution and the local union's bylaws, and union members are the citizens of the internal union government. The governing document of the collective bargaining government is the collective bargaining agreement, and the employees are the citizens. Table 2.3 identifies the characteristics of unions and relates them to the internal and collective bargaining governments of factory and nonfactory union structures.[22]

Union members, with multiple citizenship, have dual rights and responsibilities. A right is that power or privilege to which a person has just claim because of custom or law. All rights are derived from the purpose of the community in which they exist, but above all rights is the duty to the community. The most fundamental rights in a democratic community (a union) are the rights to free speech, to associate freely, to vote, and to run for office. Members' rights and responsibilities are found in the national union's constitution, the local union's bylaws, and the Labor-Management Reporting and Disclosure Act (LMRDA), plus various other federal, state, and local laws.

Table 2.3
Dual Union Government

Characteristics	Internal Factory & Nonfactory	Collective Bargaining Factory	Nonfactory
Task/Activities	• Meetings • Finances • Internal discipline	• Negotiations • Grievances	• Negotiations • Grievances • Job referral • Jurisdiction maintenance
Leadership	• President • Vice president • Financial secretary • Recording secretary • Executive board members	• Shop committee • Chief stewards • Stewards	• Business manager (BM) • Business representatives • Job stewards
Membership/ Citizenship	• Union members	• Bargaining unit employees	• Bargaining unit employees
Governing Document	• National constitution • Local union constitution and bylaws	• Collective bargaining agreement	• Collective bargaining agreement
Regulating Statute	• Labor-Management Reporting and Disclosure Act (Landrum-Griffin)	• National Labor Relations Act (NLRA or Taft-Hartley)	• National Labor Relations Act (NLRA or Taft-Hartley)
Comparable to other organizations?	Yes	No	No
Innovative	No	Yes	Yes

Source: Adapted from James Wallihan, *Union Government and Organization* (Washington, DC: BNA, 1985), 82.

Responsibilities are the obligations workers assume when they become union members. Basically, union members agree to abide by the constitution of the national union and the bylaws of the local union, support the objectives of both the national and local union, and pay dues. Unions can adopt and enforce reasonable rules defining members' responsibilities. Further, the union can restrain conduct by members that would interfere with the union in carrying out its contracts and other legal responsibilities. A union member sometimes must sacrifice his or her individual rights for the common good of the union.

The Workplace

Work is concerned with the creation or maintenance of wealth. It is a required activity as opposed to a preferred activity and provides remuneration for contribution. The workplace is the actual site where the work is performed; thus, work implies worker separation from where the worker wants to be. In the formal organization, the work is divided into a process of manageable tasks that can be performed by an employee. A position is the smallest organizational unit into which these tasks can be grouped. The informal organization of the workplace is characterized by informal networks, leaders, procedures, programs, customs, and occasional forms of resistance. In a craft situation, the workplace is generally in different locations, while in an industry situation it is in one location.[23]

The workplace is especially important because it plays such a major role in satisfying basic human needs. A. Maslow, an internationally respected American psychologist, classified human needs according to priority into the following five categories: physiological, safety/security, social, esteem, and self-actualization.

Physiological needs, the lowest level, includes the basic physical requirements, such as food, shelter, and clothing. Here, desirable job features are a convenient work location, an adequate salary, and comfortable work conditions. At the second level are the safety needs, which include the need to feel safe, secure, and protected. Workplace features at this level include health and welfare benefits, job security, and safe working conditions. The next level, social needs, is concerned with a worker's need to belong. Here the worker looks for friendly co-workers, acceptance by others, and organization-sponsored social activities. Unions can play an important role at this level. Esteem needs, the fourth level, relate to a worker's need to feel a sense of accomplishment. At this level, a worker needs recognition for performance, the admiration of others, and influence over others. Self-actualization needs, the highest level, cover a worker's need to fully develop his or her skills and talents. Workers need freedom for self-expression and creativity and the opportunity to maximize their abilities. Maslow's hierarchy is developed in more detail in Chapter 7.

As the government becomes more and more involved in satisfying the physiological and safety/security needs, categories where unions are especially effective, unions need to find new ways of meeting workers' social, esteem, and self-actualization needs. How well unions meet this challenge will determine their future. In addition to income and job security, today's workers need an organization that they can trust to protect their rights, and to provide special personal services and community. They also need to be recognized as unique individuals with the opportunity to develop their skills and talents to the fullest.

Job satisfaction from a Management perspective is also important because it has a direct bearing on turnover and business performance. Two insurance industry surveys of over 4,000 employees with a high level of customer contact "show clearly that Management practices and knowledge and skill building investments have a direct impact on a key indicator of business performance—the service capability of employees. The results show that job satisfaction is driven by the same factors affecting service capability." The more important job factors are necessary knowledge, information, authority, and training, performance rewards, availability of supervision, supervisory support for high-quality service, and supervisory latitude.[24]

The new high-performance workforce needs workers with greater reading and math skills than were required in the past. The Labor Department defines high-performance organizations as ones that provide workers with the necessary information, skills, incentives, and responsibility to make decisions essential for innovation, quality improvement, and rapid response to change. Not only do high-performance workers have different skills, but they assume different responsibilities from those in the old "job control workforce." A higher level of problem solving is involved in virtually all production jobs. Consequently, employers looking for workers with "an aptitude for learning" are having a very difficult time finding them. For example, Motorola estimated it had to interview 40,000 applicants to fill 4,000 jobs.[25]

In America, women make up 47 percent of the workforce, and two-thirds of all new union members are women. They are concentrated by sector and by the type of work they perform. Eighty percent of all women in the American workforce are in the following eight broad occupational categories: clerical workers, cashiers, nurses, nurses' aides, waitresses, elementary school teachers, sales workers, and child-care workers. The increased role of women as workers and homemakers challenges traditional work arrangements and raises demands for flexible working hours, job-sharing arrangements, child-care benefits, and parental leave. [26] The Bureau of Labor Statistics reported that 12.0 percent of all working women in the United States were union members, while 16.9 percent of all men belong to a union.

While the main impact of global competition is on the poor and unskilled, even the most highly skilled knowledge worker is not immune from intense global competition. A world of superelectronic networks will bring low-wage competition to the world's highest paid knowledge workers. Intel, for example, built a plant in Ireland because Irish computer engineers, systems analysts, and programmers work for less than California knowledge workers. Accordingly, in the future, these Irish knowledge workers could lose their jobs to knowledge workers in Bangladesh, Brazil, or Mexico. To save their jobs, American knowledge workers will be pressured to work for less, even as they become more productive. Transnational corporations will be just as ruthless in cutting the costs of their knowledge workforce as they were with their manufacturing workforce.[27]

Traditional industrial and Labor relations practices are under increasing pressure from the growing numbers of "contingent" and other nonstandard workers. The problem in this situation is how to balance employers' need for flexibility with workers' need for adequate income and job security. Employer flexibility programs include flextime, compressed weekends, job sharing, part-time schedules, telecommuting, and so on. There is also the problem that some of these arrangements often violate public laws, including labor protection and Labor relations statutes.

In the workplace, the union steward is the first and perhaps most vital contact between workers and their union. He or she may be the members' only contact with the union and, thus, the key to union democracy. The steward is also closely related to a variety of forms of member participation such as voting and attending meetings. Stewards belong to three, often conflicting, social systems: the departmental work group, the union, and the company. Stewards can be classified as either union-oriented or work-group-oriented. The union-oriented stewards are primarily concerned with local union officers and other union stewards, while work-group-oriented stewards have narrower interests and contacts and are less inclined to defer to overall union strategy. The work-group-oriented steward may more adequately represent members' interests, but the union-oriented steward may be crucial to overall union effectiveness. Here, again, there is a trade-off between democracy and union performance. Further, this distinction could be very important to effective shared-fate, participative-Management partnerships.[28]

While stewards have many responsibilities, their most important is the handling of grievances. Other duties include organizing; educating members about the union, their rights and responsibilities within the union, and the collective bargaining agreement; providing the liaison between local union officers and the rank-and-file members; and supporting community and political action activities. Many collective bargaining agreements provide the steward with "superseniority" to provide stability to employer downsizing strategies. Stewards also have a degree of immunity from discipline to be free to act and argue vigorously in support of the workers.

The steward, the one person in the union structure who usually is in daily contact with the worker, has to solve the elemental problem of governance— the relationship of the worker to authority. Authority for the worker in a union environment includes both the employer and the union. In the absence of a union, unrestricted formal authority remains with the employer.

Tragically, the workplace is becoming much more violent, and the steward is literally on the firing line. The National Institute of Occupational Safety and Health (NIOSH) reported 750 workplace homicides in 1992. This was 17 percent of all workplace deaths, a 5 percent increase over the rate for the 1980s. In addition, Northwestern National Life reports that 2 million workers were attacked, over 6 million were threatened with bodily harm, and some 16 million were harassed. Recent employee surveys indicate that increased violence is the result of the pressure of doing more with less, the stress of job conflict, and intimidating treatment by Management.[29] Stewards, well trained in conflict management and crisis management, can do much to identify and prevent violence before harm is done. They can also minimize damage once it exists.

As the new American workplace becomes more diverse, stewards are confronted by a wide range of entirely new challenges. For example, Muslims may want to dress as Muslims, they are required to pray five times a day, and their day of worship is Friday; Orthodox Jews must leave work in time for the weekly Sabbath rituals; Buddhism and other Oriental religions' beliefs and practices also can present unique problems in the workplace. Clearly, unions need strategies to accommodate the needs of people of various faiths in the workplace.[30] In view of the multiple roles of the union steward in a complex, diverse, and critically important workplace, high-performance unions conduct a wide range of steward training programs.

Democracy is the empowering characteristic fundamental to all new high-performance work systems. The AFL-CIO report *The New American Workplace: A Labor Perspective* stresses that only in a democratic system is the employee empowered with a real voice in determining the way work is conducted. The report notes that employees, as stakeholders, have a vital interest in the enterprise's strategic decisions, which ultimately determine how much work will be done, where it will be done, and who will do it. The report identifies five common principles of the new American workplace and lists four general guidelines necessary for successful Labor-Management partnerships. The five common principles are

- rejecting the traditional dichotomy between thinking and doing and between conception and execution;
- redesigning jobs to include a greater variety of skills and, more important, greater responsibility for the ultimate output of the organization;
- flatter Management structure to substitute for the traditional multi-layered hierarchy;
- workers' participation in decision making, through their unions, at all levels of the organization;
- Labor-Management negotiations to assure an equitable distribution of the rewards realized from the new work organization.

The four general partnership guidelines are mutual recognition and respect, collective bargaining, equality, and mutual interests.[31]

"Perhaps most important," *The New American Workplace* notes, "the new work systems require unions to embrace an expanded agenda and to assume an expanded role as representatives of workers in the full range of management decisions in which those workers are interested."[32]

Local Unions

Local unions are Labor organizations comprised of members within a particular jurisdiction chartered as a subordinate body of the national union. Their authority and responsibilities are prescribed by the union constitution. As noted earlier, the division of authority between the local union and the national union ranges from centralized to decentralized. Industrial locals tend to be more centralized, and craft locals tend to be more decentralized. The average size of a local union is 300 members; however, there are enormous variations in size and structure.[33] It is important to know that local unions control 70 percent of Labor's resources,[34] and local union dues pay for virtually all the activities of the intermediate, national, federation, and international union organizations. The functions, structure, and governance of a local union, the tasks of its leaders, and the role of its members vary according to its size, geographical scope, jurisdictional variety, and the number of different employers, bargaining units, and contracts.[35]

Local unions are the most important unit in the six-level union organization. In daily contact with both the employee and the employer, they are the "front line" in both Labor relations and community relations. Since local unions are the primary link to the community, the image of the national union and the entire Labor movement is influenced by the action of its members and leaders. Local unions are also the primary source of national officers and representatives since they serve as links to the higher levels of the union structure.

The primary governing body of the local union is the periodic membership meeting. The scheduling of this meeting is usually stated in the national union's constitution and the local union's bylaws. In most cases, it meets at least monthly. The order of business is usually a constitutional and bylaw provision. The executive board is generally the governing body between union meetings.

Collective bargaining, a core function of local unions, takes place within the following five major bargaining situations:

- local, single employer;
- local, multi-employer;
- corporatewide;
- local supplements;
- industrywide.[36]

In a local, single-employer situation, the local union negotiates with a single firm, while in a local union, multi-employer situation, the local union negotiates with all the union employers in a local market. In the corporatewide situation, one or more local unions negotiate with a large multi-facility employer. Local supplements are negotiated by the local union and local

Management in response to local issues after agreement is reached at the national level. This is referred to as "two-tier" bargaining. An industrywide agreement is with a major employer that sets an industrywide pattern.

In the collective bargaining process, the local union is responsible for both negotiating and administering the agreement. In an industrial (factory) union, internal governance and collective bargaining are basically one. The membership elects the officers and executive board, and the executive board appoints the various committees. In a craft (nonfactory) union, internal governance and collective bargaining government are separate. The membership elects the officers, including the executive board and the business manager. The officers and the executive board are responsible for the internal government, while the business manager is responsible for the collective bargaining agreement. Thus, the business manager appoints the business representatives and job stewards.[37]

New shared-fate, participative-Management relationships require that union representatives have a much better understanding of management concepts, principles, and techniques in order to be more effective partners. As it stands today, very few union representatives are adequately prepared to serve as equal partners with Management. The *New American Workplace* report notes, "In this area, we in the AFL-CIO have, regrettably, been insufficiently attentive to the needs of the trade union leaders who are on the firing line."[38] Since this admission there has been very little follow-up.

Mission-driven, value-based, high-performance local unions are more autonomous and, consequently, more able to respond to employer initiatives and better able to accommodate the needs of the individual worker. High-performance national unions conduct Management education and specialist training programs to prepare local union leaders to be better managers and to function as equal partners in the new American workplace. Ultimately, strong, autonomous, mission-driven, and democratic local unions are the key to success in organizing. As in the movie *Field of Dreams* about a baseball fan who believed that if he built a baseball field in his Iowa cornfield, Shoeless Joe Jackson and the ghosts of yesterday's great players will come to play on it, workers will come if Labor builds high-performance local unions.

Intermediate Unions

Intermediate unions are combinations of local unions within the same national union. The primary functions of intermediate unions are assisting in negotiations, grievance cases, and organizing. The secondary functions include assisting local union officers with internal governance and administrative matters and strengthening the organizational ties with the national union. The governance of intermediate unions has many variations. In most cases it is covered by a combination of the constitution and the intermediate union's bylaws.

Intermediate unions are also formed to cross geographical boundaries by occupation, common employer, and industry and to facilitate collective bargaining. They provide pooled resources and expertise to local unions that the national union cannot efficiently provide. Since few national unions have structures based solely on geographic, trade, or industrial dimensions, there are various overlapping divisions to accommodate unique needs. Other types of intermediate unions are involved in legislative activities and conduct educational programs. Frequently, intermediate bodies are organized on a statewide basis for legislative activities.

There are two basic types of intermediate unions. The first is a quasi-local union body that generally absorbs the functions of the local unions rather than supplement them. These bodies appear most often in local market situations that include several local unions in a metropolitan area. District councils, district lodges, and joint boards are examples of quasi-local union bodies.

The second type is the regional servicing and administrative unit that is concerned with assisting local unions in collective bargaining, organizing, contract administration, and internal governance. These units are frequently directed by a national union vice president and employ staff and national representatives to assist the locals. However, the locals still retain control over a wide range of activities.[39]

The IBEW has three main types of service and administrative intermediate unions. At the regional level, there is the vice presidential district servicing and administrative unit. For employers with one agreement, there are the telephone, manufacturing, railroad, and utility system councils. For employers with separate agreements for each local, there are the telephone, manufacturing, government, and utility coordinating councils.

High-performance intermediate unions serve as ASCs that provide small local unions with a constant stream of information and administrative services.

National Unions

National unions, the sovereign power within organized Labor, are self-governing combinations of local unions. In most cases, national unions are actually international unions because they have local unions in Canada. In this text, however, even union organizations with local unions in Canada or other countries or territories will always be referred to as national unions in order to minimize confusion when referencing the international union environment. The national union is administered by elected officers, appointed assistants, directors, international representatives, hired specialists, office workers, and other support workers. How these people are organized to perform the work depends on the union's size, financial resources, jurisdictional complexity, and the policies and styles of its leaders, past and present.

The supreme governing body of the national union is the convention assembly. Usually, the local unions elect delegates to the convention based on the size of the local union. Conventions amend constitutions, elect officers, determine per capita payments, hear final appeals on presidential decisions by locals and members, and approve broad statements of policy that are usually formulated by the national officers, their staffs, and convention committees. Conventions also serve as publicity events to focus attention on union activities, as rituals to build support and strengthen bonds, to reenergize and revitalize members, and as social occasions to renew acquaintanships.[40]

Some national unions have an executive board, while others have an executive council. The executive board or council is the primary governing body between conventions. In some national unions the executive board or council is elected at large, but in others it is elected by geographical districts. The executive board or council typically amends the constitution in certain emergency situations or when required by law, fills vacancies when an officer dies or retires, rules on judicial decisions, and approves pensions and welfare benefits. The executive council performs many of the same duties as an executive board, but generally it does not have the ultimate authority or responsibility of executive boards.

The principal functions of the national union include organizing, advising and assisting local unions, establishing uniform working conditions and pay levels, assuring that local unions comply with their agreements, and participating in the activities of the AFL-CIO. These responsibilities are assigned to departments, and the title of the department usually reflects the scope of its headquarters' function. In a typical national union structure, departments are classified as operating, support, and administrative. Included in the operating class are organizing, industrial and trade, corporate, and arbitration departments. Typical support departments are legislative, COPE, public relations, research, education, apprenticeship, community service, safety and health, International affairs, union label, and legal. Typical administrative departments are accounting, membership records, pensions, insurance, data processing, mailing, maintenance, and personnel.[41]

Many dimensions of the administrative operations of national unions are similar to those of other large nonunion organizations. However, in the area of collective bargaining, the resemblance to other organizations completely dissolves. Not only is this area uniquely union, but it is the dimension that is most adaptive to changes in the environment.[42]

National unions have generally been slow to adopt strategic management, budgeting, and other management concepts, principles, and techniques to cope with their many needs. As large organizations, however, they cannot escape the need to use these Management tools to benefit their members and employees. Strategic management involves selecting methods and technologies appropriate to the objectives, size, and available resources of the national union.[43] Management concepts, principles, techniques, and organization structure can be scaled to the needs of every union, regardless of size.

Table 2.4
The Four-Category Structure of the AFL-CIO

I. Governance
• **National Convention** (every two years)
• **General Board:** Usually the principal officer of each affiliated national union and affiliated departments.
• **Executive Council:** President, Secretary-Treasurer, Executive Vice President, Fifty-one Vice Presidents
• **Officers:** President, Secretary-Treasurer, and Executive Vice President.

II. Committee and Staff Departments	
Standing Committees:	**Headquarters Departments:**
• Civil Rights	• Accounting
• Community Services	• Building Management
• Economic Policy	• Civil and Human Rights
• Education	• Community Services
• International Affairs	• Corporate Affairs
• Legislation	- Center for strategic research
• Organizing	- Center for collective bargaining
• Political Education	- Center for workplace democracy
• Safety and Occupational Health	• Public Policy
• Social Policy	• Education
• Finance	• Facilities Management
• Strategic Approaches	• Field Services
• State and Central Bodies	• General Counsel
• Full Participation	• Information Services
• Workplace Democracy	• International Affairs
• Committee 2000	• Legislation
• Women Workers	• Occupational Health and Safety
• Constitution Review	• Organizing
• Article XX Review	• Personal
• Balanced Budget	• Political Action
• Ethical Practices	• Public Affairs
• Older and Retired Members	• Support Services
• Union Pension Funds	• Working Women

III. Trade and Industrial Departments	
• Building and Construction Trades	• Professional Employees
• Food and Allied Service Trades	• Public Employee
• Industrial Union	• Transportation
• Maritime Trades	• Union Label and Service Trades
• Metal Trades	

IV. State Federations and Central Labor Council
• State Federations (Fifty states and Puerto Rico)
• Central Labor Councils (607 committees)

The AFL-CIO

The AFL-CIO is a multi-union national federation with core functions of political action, public relations, inter-union coordination, dispute resolution, and international affairs. Several more recent functions are encouraging mergers and other forms of consolidation, expanding education programs, and increasing its support role in organizing and collective bargaining.

The federation is composed of two categories of union organizations. The first is the affiliated national unions that are not subordinate to the federation. The second is the subordinate bodies and includes directly affiliated local unions, state federations and central Labor bodies, and trade and industrial departments.

The structure of the AFL-CIO consists of the following four categories:

- Governance, concerned with the electoral and representational process at the national level.
- Committee and staff departments, organized to develop expertise in specific fields of activities and for administrative support.
- Trade and industrial departments, represent the various trades and industries.
- State federations and central Labor bodies, made up of local unions within a state, county, or city that choose to affiliate. [44]

This structure is seen in Table 2.4. The first category is concerned with the governance of the AFL-CIO. The biennial convention is the supreme governing body of the AFL-CIO. It elects officers, establishes policy, and resolves internal disputes. Between conventions the Executive Council is "authorized and empowered to take such action as may be necessary to carry out fully and adequately the decisions and instructions of the conventions and enforce the provisions in this constitution." In this sense, the AFL-CIO Executive Council has powers more like a board of directors than an executive council. The Executive Council is made up of the president, the secretary-treasurer, and the executive vice president of the AFL-CIO plus fifty-one vice presidents. In the past, the vice presidents were presidents of large, influential affiliated national unions. However, exceptions are made to provide more opportunities for women and minorities to serve on the Executive Council. The AFL-CIO's Twenty-First Constitutional Convention increased the Executive Council from thirty-three to fifty-one vice presidents to provide more opportunities to participate. There is also a general board that consists of all the members of the Executive Council plus the president or other principal officer of each affiliated national union not represented on the Executive Council, each trade and industrial department, and four regional representatives. The general board can be convened by the president of the federation or by the Executive Council to decide all policy questions referred to it by the Executive Council.

The second category includes the AFL-CIO's twenty-three standing committees and twenty staff departments. The president of the federation may appoint other committees and establish other headquarters departments as necessary. Staff departments are identified by their support and administrative functions.

The third category includes the AFL-CIO's nine trade and industrial departments, which represent national unions with common jurisdictional interests. The AFL-CIO Constitutional Convention or the AFL-CIO Executive Council may establish other such departments, but each department is responsible for its own financial affairs and may establish local councils. Usually, the presidents of the affiliated unions make up the executive board that determines policy and elects the principal officers. This is a structural category that is continually being revitalized as unions respond to changes in their environments.[45]

The fourth category is concerned with state federations and central Labor councils. The primary functions of central bodies are political representation, voter mobilization, education, public relations, community service programs, and assistance in organizing campaigns, strikes, and boycotts. There are fifty state federations, one commonwealth federation, and approximately 600 central Labor councils. Central Labor councils may be established by the AFL-CIO Executive Council on a city or other regional basis. A central Labor council is composed of locals of affiliated national unions, plus other union organizations affiliated with the federation. Affiliated national unions are required by the AFL-CIO constitution to instruct their local unions to join the central Labor councils.[46]

The present fifty-one member AFL-CIO Executive Council, with vast differences in power and influence among various vice presidents and a wide range of vested interests, is unwieldy, inefficient, and too easily influenced by large national unions. The AFL-CIO's structure is further complicated by twenty-three standing committees, twenty departments, three centers and nine trade and industrial departments. Current reorganizing efforts, which have increased the size of the Executive Council, the number of standing committees, and headquarters departments, have further weakened the AFL-CIO's structure. In response to previous structural weaknesses, President Sweeney, very early in his administration, established Committee 2000, which he chairs, with a mission to consider the structure and role of the AFL-CIO and its nine trade and industrial departments and to determine how best to integrate the work of the Labor movement.

International Federations

For over 100 years the AFL-CIO has been the leader in the struggle to help men and women of other countries attain universal worker rights, economic and social justice, individual liberty and self-respect, and peaceful relations both within and among nations. Solidarity with the workers of the world not only is the right thing to do but also benefits American workers. The AFL-CIO participates in international union activities as follows:

- the Trade Union Advisory Committee (TUAC) to the Organization for Economic Cooperation and Development (OECD);
- the International Labor Organization (ILO);
- the International Confederation of Free Trade Unions (ICFTU);
- the Inter-American Regional Organization of Workers (ORIT);
- International Trade Secretariats (ITS);
- the newly reorganized AFL-CIO's International Affairs Department.

TUAC consists of the representatives of trade unions in the twenty-four industrialized countries affiliated with OECD. Its major objective is to secure collective action to advance economic and social policies that emphasize economic growth, full employment, and fair labor standards in international trade.

The ILO, an agency of the United Nations founded 11 April 1919 by the Treaty of Versailles, is the only international tripartite organization where employers, governments, and union representatives negotiate international standards on rights and responsibilities pertaining to the workplace. These worldwide labor standards, referred to as conventions, are intended to improve the lives of workers, promote basic human rights, and provide research and assistance to needy countries. The ILO is the major forum for exposing labor rights violations. At the 82d session of the International Labor Conference, 2207 delegates from 160 countries approved a budget of $579.5 million for the 1996-97 biennium.[47]

The ICFTU, a democratic trade union confederation, represents 88 million workers in 100 countries. The functions of the ICFTU include developing common positions on international labor issues, assisting unions in the struggle against political repression, and coordinating assistance to trade union movements in the Third World. ORIT, headquartered in Caracas, Venezuela, is the ICFTU's regional organization for the Western Hemisphere.

ITSs are the equivalent of the AFL-CIO's trade and industrial departments and the International Affairs Department is working to improve cooperation and strengthen relations with ITSs.

The AFL-CIO International Affairs Department promotes human and trade union rights and assists in the development of free trade unions in the Third World, Central and Eastern Europe, and Russia. Its principal programs include education, organizing and research, trade union services, union-to-union activities, participant training, international visitors, voters' rights, and enforcement of international codes of conduct. Through bilateral relationships, the AFL-CIO participates in joint activities with free trade union movements from different parts of the world. These joint activities are aimed at reaching agreement with regard to the activities of the ICFTU, ILO, and TUAC in response to the mounting violations of trade union rights in many countries, particularly the totalitarian and dictatorial countries. Much work has also been done to secure economic cooperation in order to confront worldwide economic problems, energy problems, trade problems, and the activities of transnational corporations.

The AFL-CIO's mission is clear and inspiring, its record for protecting workers' rights is outstanding, and its commitment is unyielding. Thus, the AFL-CIO is well positioned to meet the challenges of global competition and the growing influence of transnational corporations.

SUMMARY

This chapter points out the importance of culture and tradition to managing unions, emphasizes the enormous influence of the environment on the union structure, and describes the structure and governance of Labor unions.

Culture and Tradition

Culture and tradition are major influences on the day-to-day behavior of people in organizations because they provide shared values that act as a unifying and directing force.

High-performance unions

- recognize the need to continually adjust their mission and objectives in a manner consistent with their culture and tradition;
- recognize that all cultural change must involve the people affected by it, including the employees and other stakeholders in the union;
- make extraordinary efforts to preserve their rich heritage and communicate it to members and the general public;
- use their culture and tradition to motivate and inspire their members and employees.

External Environment

All organizations are strongly influenced by their environment and, thus, constantly engage in activities that adjust to that environment. The environment consists of those external and internal forces that influence an organization's structure and operations.

High-performance unions

- continually adapt their structures to accommodate to changes in their external environment;
- choose objectives and strategies that improve organizational performance and enrich union democracy;
- empower executive councils as executive boards.

Structure and Governance

Structure is how the components of organizations are arranged, and governance is the process of electing officers, conducting meetings, and monitoring democracy. The six-level union organization structure, consists of the workplace, local unions, intermediate unions, national unions, the AFL-CIO and international federations. High-performance unions continually seek the optimal structure for implementing strategies to achieve their core objectives.

The Workplace
The workplace is concerned with the creation or maintenance of wealth, and it plays a major role in satisfying basic human needs. High-performance unions find new strategies for meeting workers' social, esteem, and self-actualization needs.

Local Unions
Local unions, the most important unit in the six-level union structure, are Labor organizations comprising members within a particular jurisdiction chartered as a subordinate body of the national union.

High-performance local unions

- prepare their officers and leaders to be effective representatives for negotiating and administering the collective bargaining agreement;
- conduct a wide range of steward training programs;
- apply the AFL-CIO's principles and guidelines for the new American workplace both as employers and as worker representatives;
- sponsor a wide range of training, education, and skill development programs to prepare their members for the challenges and opportunities of the new American workplace;
- establish a wide variety of special concern committees for members.

Intermediate Unions
Intermediate unions are combinations of local unions within the same national union. High-performance intermediate unions serve as ASCs that provide small local unions with a constant stream of information and administrative services.

National Unions
National unions, the sovereign power within organized Labor, are self-governing combinations of local unions.

High-performance national unions

- recognize that local unions are the most important unit in the six-level organization structure and build strong, autonomous, democratic, value-based, mission-driven local unions;
- adapt and implement management concepts, principles, and techniques to improve organizational effectiveness and efficiency;
- implement a broad range of new Management development and specialist training programs to prepare local union leaders to be better managers and to function as equal partners in the new American workplace;
- develop a comprehensive approach to steward training that includes such new subjects as member orientation, decision making, conflict, project, and diversity management, teambuilding, and basic management concepts, principles, and techniques.

The AFL-CIO

The AFL-CIO is a multi-union national federation with core functions of political action, public relations, inter-union coordination, dispute resolution, and international affairs.

The new, high-performance AFL-CIO

- establishes a new eleven-member executive board;
- refocuses its mission and restructures to meet the challenges of the twenty-first century;
- provides affiliated unions with more support and administrative services.

International Federations

For over 100 years the AFL-CIO has been a leader in the global struggle for workers' rights and social justice. The new, high-performance AFL-CIO implements strategies to meet the challenges of global competition and the influence of transnational corporations.

NOTES

1. Milan Kubr, ed., *Management Consulting* (Geneva, Switzerland: International Labour Organization, 1988), 81–87.

2. Alfred M. Lee, ed., *The Principles of Sociology* (New York: Barnes and Noble, 1964), 145–146.

3. John M. Lukasiewicz, "The Culture of Work," review of *Occupational Subcultures in the Workplace*, by Harrison M. Tice, *Monthly Labor Review* May 1944, 65.

4. Cindy Skrzyski, "Firms Balk at Changing Corporate Culture," Workplace, *Washington Post*, 23 July 1989.

5. Kubr, *Management*, 86–87.

6. Thomas J. Peters and Robert H. Waterman, Jr., *In Search of Excellence* (New York: Warner Books, 1982), 104.

7. Ibid., 116–117.

8. James Wallihan, *Union Government and Organization* (Washington, DC: BNA, 1985), 69–70.

9. Ibid., 236.

10. Goerge Strauss, Daniel G. Gallagher, and Jack Fiorito, eds., *The State of Unions* (Madison, WI: Industrial Relations Research Association, 1991); Jack Fiorito, Cynthia L. Gramm, and Wallace E. Hendricks, "Union Structural Choices," 105-137.

11. Fiorito, Gramm, and Hendricks, "Union," 128–131.

12. Ibid., 115.

13. Ibid., 112.

14. Ibid., 130–131.

15. Wallihan, *Union Government*, 72.

16. Fiorito, Gramm, and Hendricks, "Union," 127.

17. Ibid. Refers to five tiers instead of six, 113.

18. Ibid., 117–118.

19. Aaron Bernstein, "Sweeney's Blitz," *BusinessWeek*, Workplace, 17 Feb. 1997, 56–62.

20. Wallihan, *Union Government*, 15.

21. Ibid., 74–79.

22. Ibid., 82.

23. Ibid., 86–87.

24. Jeffrey Zornitsky, "Managing a Changing Labor Force: A New Look at Human Resources Management," *Proceeding of the Forty-Third Annual Meeting; December 28–29, 1990; Washington, DC* (Madison, WI: Industrial Research Relations Association, 1991), 19.

25. Frank Swoboda, "Losing a Numbers Game?," *Washington Post*, 15 May 1994.

26. Frank Swoboda, "Women Aspiring to Union Leadership Roles Find Limits There Too," Workplace, *Washington Post*, 14 Feb. 1993.

27. Michael Schrage, "The Data Highway May Be a Route for Exploring U.S. White-Collar Jobs," *Washington Post*, 23 Sept. 1994.

28. George Strauss, "Union Democracy," in Strauss, Gallagher, and Fiorito, *The State of Unions*, 216.

29. Herff Moore and Jack Kondrask, "Threat of Violence Demands HR Attention," *HR News*, 13, no. 3, Mar. 1994, 8.

30. Adelle Banks, "Faith and the Workplace Can Be an Uneasy Mix," *Washington Post*, 19 Mar. 1994.

31. *The New American Workplace: A Labor Perspective*, a report by the AFL-CIO Committee on the Evolution of Work (Washington, DC: AFL-CIO, 1994), 8–12.

32. Ibid., 15.

33. Wallihan, *Union Government*, 91.

34. Muriel H. Cooper, "Organizing Wins Small Steps," *AFL-CIO News*, 20 May 1996, 17.

35. Wallihan, *Union Government*, 91.

36. Ibid., 75.

37. Ibid., 97–107.

38. *The New American Workplace*, 15.

39. Wallihan, *Union Government*, 133–136.

40. Ibid., 112–113.

41. Ibid., 119.

42. Ibid., 128.

43. Ibid., 121.

44. Ibid., 156.

45. Ibid., 157–161.

46. Ibid., 163-164.

47. "ILO Widens Worker Protections, Adopts Budget for 1966–1967," *ILO Washington Focus*, 1.

3

Management for Union Leaders

The effective executive is, first of all, expected to get the right things done.
Peter F. Drucker, *The Effective Executive*

Character and intelligence. The poles your talent spins on, displaying your gifts. It isn't enough to be intelligent; you must also have the right character.
Baltasar Gracian, *The Art of Worldly Wisdom: A Pocket Oracle*

This chapter provides the reader with a brief overview of the various management concepts, principles, and techniques. It starts with the history of management, relates management to the manager, and explains resource allocation and several of the better-known management specialties. It continues with advice on managing nonprofit organizations, managing consultants and concludes with managing time.

HISTORY OF MANAGEMENT

Peter Drucker refers to managers as "craftsmen" who always strive for professional workmanship. As union leaders, we readily identify with craftsmanship and professional workmanship. Now we must learn and apply the various management concepts, principles, and techniques in order to provide better services to our members and establish better relationships with Labor's many stakeholders. Equally important, a better knowledge of management is essential in order to assume greater responsibility as equal partners with Management in a shared-fate environment.

In the past, union leaders acquired their knowledge of management by observing other managers, especially their employers, and by a random, piece-by-piece acquisition of management concepts, principles, and techniques. In our rapidly changing environment, this approach is no longer realistic. Hopefully, this chapter is the beginning of a formal Management development system for union leaders.

The roots of management can be seen throughout recorded history. The military conquests of Caesar and Alexander the Great, the engineering marvels of the great pyramid of Khufu, and the canal system of Mesopotamia are testimony to the Management abilities of the ancients. This section traces the development of management as a science and describes briefly the four basic schools of management: classical, behavioral, quantitative, and system-contingency.

Classical management theory began with the Industrial Revolution of the nineteenth century. The leaders of the classical school were Robert Owen, Charles Babbage, and Frederick W. Taylor. Robert Owen (1771–1858) was the manager of several cotton mills in Scotland during the early 1800s. He believed that employees' improved working and living conditions increased productivity and profits. He stressed that a manager's best investment was in workers, or the "vital machines," as he called them.

Charles Babbage (1792–1871), a British professor of mathematics, was an early advocate of the division of labor who believed that the application of scientific principles to the work process would increase productivity and lower costs. As an aside, there is a chain of computer retail stores named after Babbage.

Fredrick W. Taylor (1856–1915) was known for his pioneering work with time-and-motion studies and his differential rate system. His four basic principles are

- the development of a true science of management;
- the scientific selection of the worker;
- the scientific education and development of the worker;
- intimate, friendly cooperation between Management and Labor.

Taylor's work, while widely acclaimed, was severely criticized by Labor unions. In 1912, as the result of a strike at the Watertown Arsenal in Massachusetts, Taylor was subpoenaed by the U.S. Congress to explain his principles. He testified that even though Labor and Management shared a common interest in increasing productivity, his principles could not succeed without "a complete mental revolution" on the part of both Labor and Management. It is interesting to note that after eighty years, Taylor's words regarding the need for a "complete mental revolution" and Labor's and Management's common interest in productivity are identical arguments for today's various Management initiatives.

Henry L. Gantt (1861–1919), a collaborator with Taylor, modified Taylor's incentive system and advocated publicly rating an employee's work.

Frank B. Gilbreth (1886–1924) and Lillian Gilbreth (1878–1972) were a husband-and-wife team concerned with fatigue and motion studies. The Gilbreths developed a three-position plan for boosting morale and employee development.

Henri Fayol (1841–1925), a French mining engineer, is considered the founder of the classical management school because he was the first to systematize Management behavior. Fayol believed management was not a personal talent but a skill that could be taught. He developed many of the management concepts now taken for granted. He divided business operation into six activities:

- technical—producing products;
- commercial—buying resources and selling the product;
- financial—acquiring and using capital;
- security—protecting employees and property;
- accounting—counting and recording costs, profits, and liabilities;
- managerial—managing the organization.

He also defined managing in terms of five functions:

- planning—devising a course of action that permits the organization to achieve its objectives;
- organizing—organizing the resources of the organization to put the plans into effect;
- commanding—motivating the employees;
- coordinating—assuring that the resources and activities work harmoniously to achieve the desired aims;
- controlling—monitoring the plans to ensure they are being carried out properly. (A four-function management model combines "commanding" and "coordinating" into "directing.")

Fayol believed that management could be taught and applied to the home, the church, the military, and politics as well as to industry. To facilitate the teaching of management, Fayol developed the following fourteen management principles:

- the division of labor holds that the more people specialize, the more efficiently they can perform the work;
- authority is concerned with the ability to give orders;
- discipline involves respect for the rules and policies that govern the organization;
- unity of command means that each employee reports to only one person;
- unity of direction has one objective, one plan, and one manager;
- the interests of the organization take precedence over the interests of the individual through subordination of individual interest to the common good;
- remuneration requires that compensation be fair to both employees and employers;
- decentralization delegates enough authority to employees to do their jobs properly;

- hierarchy requires a clear line of authority that runs from the bottom to the top of the organization;
- order is concerned with materials and worker's being in the right place at the right time;
- equity requires managers to be friendly and fair to their subordinates;
- stability of staff teaches that high employee turnover is inefficient and should be minimized;
- initiative gives subordinates the freedom to conceive and carry out their plans, even when some mistakes result;
- esprit de corps holds that promoting team spirit will promote organizational unity.

By codifying these principles Fayol helped lay the foundation for management as a profession. He stressed the term "principles" as opposed to "rules" or "laws." Principles, he noted, ". . . avoid any idea of rigidity, as there is nothing rigid or absolute in administrative matters; everything is a matter of degree. The same principle is hardly ever applied twice in exactly the same way, because we have to allow for different and changing circumstances, for human beings who are equal, different, and changeable, and for many other variable elements. The principle too, is flexible, and can be adapted to meet every need; it is just a question of how to use them." This brilliant observation is as fresh and relevant today as it was almost 100 years ago.

Classical organizational theory has endured because it has helped identify major areas of concern to the working managers. Also, the assumption that certain managerial principles can be identified and taught has proven accurate. However, while classical organizational theory was appropriate when organizations were stable, and the environment was more predictable, it is much less useful when the organizational environment is extremely turbulent.

The classical school failed to recognize the difficulties and frustrations that resulted when workers did not follow predicted or rational patterns of behavior. This led to the behavioral school of management, which added the insights of sociology and psychology to classical organizational theory.

Hugo Munsterberg (1863–1916) added the tools of psychology to classical management. He believed the study of human behavior could help develop psychological techniques for motivating workers.

Elton Mayo (1880–1949) was the leader of the human relations movement. His study of human behavior at Western Electric's Hawthorne plant revealed that when workers get special attention, productivity is likely to improve regardless of the changes in working conditions. His follow-up study led to his most important finding: informal work groups have a great influence on productivity. Mayo concluded that Management must respond to the employee's need for recognition and social satisfaction in order to maximize productivity.

Mayo's work revealed that the work environment was also a social environment and that this social environment was important in determining the quality and quantity of the work. Therefore, managers began to focus on the group rather than the individual worker. Mayo's efforts stressed the importance of a manager's style and, thus, revolutionized Management training. However, their efforts did not completely describe the reasons for individual behavior in the workplace.

Behaviorists such as Chris Argyis, A. Maslow, Douglas McGregor, and others, trained in psychology, sociology, and anthropology, believed the "self-actualizing man" would more accurately explain the motivations of people. Maslow, as noted previously, established a hierarchy of needs to analyze individual motivations. At the bottom of his hierarchy are physical and safety needs. At the top are the ego and self-actualizing needs.

Later behavioral scientists recognized the shortcomings of the "self-actualizing man" approach and developed the "complex man" model of human motivation. This model recognizes that different people will react in different ways in the same situation and the same way in different situations. Behaviorists have made enormous contributions in understanding individual motivation, group behavior, interpersonal relations at work, and the importance of work to human beings. However, the human is such a complex being that much more work needs to be done.

The quantitative school was born in World War II. The British, with their survival at stake and confronted by complex war problems, formed operational research (OR) teams to solve such problems. OR teams, made up of mathematicians, physicists, and other scientists, applied the expertise of the various sciences to solving the problems. Impressed with the success of the British OR teams, the Americans also formed OR teams. After the war OR teams were used to solve the growing problems of industry caused by the rapid development and assimilation of complex, new industrial technologies.

The OR team constructs a comprehensive mathematical model containing all the variables necessary to simulate the situation. Using complex formulas and a computer, the values of the variables in the model are changed to simulate various situations. The decision makers thus have a range of computer-generated alternatives to help make their decision. The OR model technique, especially helpful in planning and control, is a well-established approach in most large organizations. Its shortcomings are with the people side of the organization, and thus, its contributions to organizing and directing are relatively limited.

The classical, behaviorist, and quantitative management schools offers different approaches to managing an organization. While each can be useful and appropriate for a given situation, management theorists now recognize the need for a broad conceptual framework that combines all these tools. There is a consensus that the system-contingency approach is the best way to integrate the three schools.[1]

A system is a group of elements, human and nonhuman, that is arranged in such a way that the elements as a whole move toward achieving some common objective. The organization is influenced by, and influences, its environment and, consequently, is constantly changing. The system management approach studies the whole situation and relationships, rather than the organizational segments. Typical business systems are management, operating, decision making, financial, personnel, legal, administration, and information.

The following are several key system concepts:

- Subsystems are the parts that make up the system. Each system may also be a subsystem of a larger whole.
- Synergy means the whole is greater than the sum of its parts.
- Open systems interact with their environment, while closed systems do not.
- System boundaries are the lines that separates the system from its environment. Closed systems have rigid boundaries, while open systems have more flexible boundaries.
- Flow refers to the system's inputs and outputs of information, material, and energy.
- Feedback, the key to system controls, is the information that is fed back so that progress or the lack of it can be assessed.

A union organization is a man-made system that has a dynamic interplay with its ever-changing environment, which includes members, employees, vendors, suppliers, society, and the government. It is a system of interrelated parts working together to accomplish a number of objectives, both those of the organization and those of individual participants. The hierarchy of systems that make up the union environment is seen in Figure 3.1.

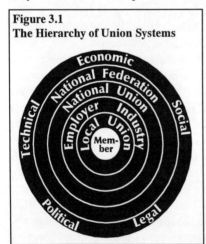

Figure 3.1
The Hierarchy of Union Systems

The outermost level includes economic, social, legal, technical, and political conditions. The second level is the national federation, and the third level is the national union. The fourth level is the employer and industry, and the fifth level is the local union. The sixth and innermost level is the employee-member level, where the greatest Labor-Management interaction takes place. Interaction between the fourth and fifth levels defines Labor-Management relationships.[2]

This system concept can be useful to union leaders as employers and as employee representatives because systems establish relationships within organizations, provide information to assist the decision-making process, and achieve organizational objectives. The foundation of the union system is the local union and its relationship to the environmental systems is seen in Figure 3.2. While each of the basic union functions can be considered a separate system, a common mistake many managers make is to stress one aspect of the organization at the expense of others. In contrast, the systems approach to management provides top-level managers with the overview necessary to balance the needs of the various parts of the organization.

In Figure 3.2, the local union is the center of the model. It is the primary contact with the member, firm, and community. The collective bargaining

Figure 3.2
A Dynamic Model for Union Management

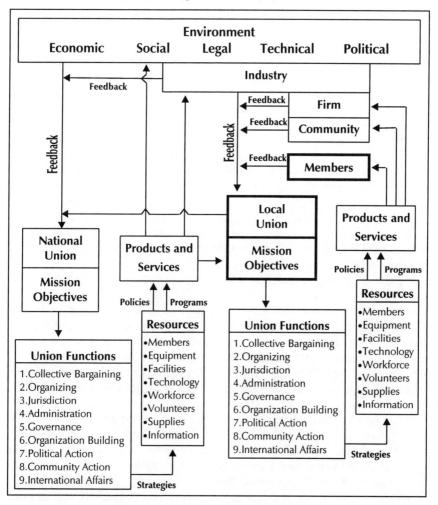

agreement, organized Labor's primary product, influences the worker, the firm, the industry, the community, and the environment. The upward arrows indicate the flow of products and services from the national union to the local union, the industry, the community, and the environment. The downward arrows indicate the flow of information (feedback) regarding the quality of these products and services. Based on this information, the officers of the national union establish objectives and implement strategies to produce products and services. This cycle is continuous, is ever-changing, and is always feeding back information to the decision makers.

The contingency approach recognizes that each situation is unique and complex. Regardless of the technique used, results will differ because situations differ. Hence, the manager's task is to try to identify which techniques will, in a particular situation, under particular circumstances, and at a particular time, best contribute to achieving organizational aims.[3]

For the last twenty-five years, the trend in management has been to become more and more specialized. This is seen in the development of such management specialties as total quality management (TQM), organizational development (OD), project management (PM), crisis management (CM), strategic management (SM), management by objectives (MBO), plus many other types. In addition, specialization continues to develop in the various traditional functional specialties such as human resource management, network management, administrative management, engineering management, sales management, marketing management, conflict management, and so on.

The underlying reasons for increased specialization are a dynamic environment, more complex organizations, and the need to be more competitive. Productivity, in this context, is defined to include both increased quantity and improved quality. Today's management buzzwords, "reinventing" and "reengineering," focus on the basic organizational mission and the best way of achieving the organization's core objectives. The leading rethinkers are David Osborne and Ted Gaebler, collaborators in writing *Reinventing Government*, and Michael Hammer and James Champy, co-authors of *Reengineering the Corporation*.

Traditionally, organized Labor opposed most Management initiatives. Labor countered Taylor's time-study experts and industrial engineers with time-study experts and industrial engineers of its own, and Labor has been countering most Management initiatives ever since. In most cases, Labor's resistance has benefited society, Management, and especially the workers by forcing the advocates of the various theories to reconsider and refine their original positions.

This very brief history of the development of the art and science of management reveals that most management theorists were primarily concerned with improving both productivity and the conditions of the workers. It points out that in industrial and Labor relations the core objectives, arguments, and basic positions of the parties have changed very little in the past 200 years. Almost everyone still agrees that increased productivity enriches our entire society and recognizes that conflicts inevitably arise in the distribution of the benefits of this increased productivity. Labor leaders, as workers' representatives, have always fought to protect member's jobs and to get a fair share of the greater riches.

Labor's problems are not with most Management initiatives that increase productivity but with the inequitable distribution of the increased wealth and the managers who abuse and exploit these initiatives. Greedy, unethical, and unprofessional managers should not blind Labor leaders to the urgent need to learn and apply management concepts, principles, and techniques in managing unions. High-performance managers, as craftsmen and professionals, are defined by outstanding character.

MANAGEMENT AND THE MANAGER

The Preface noted that management can refer to either a class or a function. Management, the function, is a multi-dimensional discipline based on a formal, systematic process for achieving organizational objectives efficiently and effectively. The practice of management, with its own concepts, principles, and techniques, is based on experience, knowledge, and responsibility. The ultimate purpose of management is to achieve organizational objectives with the least waste and greatest economy of resources. Managers are professionals with specific competencies who practice this discipline and perform four basic functions: planning, organizing, directing, and controlling. This section covers a manager's work and the skills and qualities necessary to do this work.

Peter Drucker explains that the tasks of Management are the reason for its existence, the determinants of its work, and the grounds of its authority and legitimacy.[4] He teaches that managers have two specific tasks:

- to create a true whole that is larger than the sum of its parts—a productive organization that turns out more than the resources put into it;
- to harmonize in every decision and action the requirements of the immediate and the long-term future.

The first task requires the manager to balance managing the organization, the worker and the work, and the organization in society. Decisions must always be sound in all three areas. Every decision must consider both the performance and results of the organization as a whole and the diverse activities needed to coordinate performance.

The second task requires the manager to balance two time dimensions—present and future. Managers must carefully consider the sacrifices they make today for the sake of tomorrow, since they are responsible for the performance of the organization in both time dimensions.[5] Drucker sees "management" in the last analysis as the substitution of thought for brawn and muscle, of knowledge for folkways and superstition, and of cooperation for force. It means the substitution of responsibility for obedience to rank and of the authority of performance for authority of power.[6]

Traditionally, a manager is defined as someone who is responsible for the work of others. Today this definition must be broadened to include the individual contributions of career professionals and specialists such as accountants, lawyers, computer technicians, economists, statisticians, and others, who frequently make decisions that have significant impact on performance and the results of the whole but are not responsible for managing the work of others.[7] Therefore, it is helpful to define a manager in the context of a "Management group."

Specialists and experts are considered managers when they take responsibility for leadership within their area of knowledge and expertise. It is their job to teach, raise new visions, show new opportunities, establish new horizons, and set new and more demanding standards. The only difference between managers and career professionals and specialists is that managers have people working for them, while professionals and experts usually do not. Both are held to the same standard of contribution, and thus, both are "Management" and "managers."[8]

Since the words "manager" and "executive" are frequently interchanged, it is helpful to distinguish between them. Managers, in addition to directing the work of others, are accountable for the success of programs, projects, and tasks. They also monitor and evaluate the performance of their unit and make appropriate corrections. In addition, they perform a broad range of duties and responsibilities necessary to achieve their objectives.

On the other hand, executives are charged with policy formulation and adaptation, including setting core objectives and the coordination of multiple functions. Executives have a significant role in shaping overall program policy and monitoring the effectiveness of subordinate managers in shaping their objectives and strategies to conform to organizational policy. Executives have leadership responsibilities that include setting the climate and tone of the organization, initiating changes in organizational philosophy, and generating advances in the state of the art of management.

As previously noted, union officers fill the roles of union leader, workers' representative, and manager. In this text, "manager" is always applied to union officers whether they function as a manager or an executive. Being a manager in a union environment is much more complicated than in a business or other nonprofit environment. There are frequent conflicts between their role as a manager and a leader. There are also conflicts between their manager and workers' representative roles. This is especially true in the union human resource area, where many union managers have great difficulty applying concepts, practices, and techniques and even greater difficulty practicing what they preach as workers' representatives.

Managers are, first and foremost, responsible for the well-being of the organization. This responsibility involves many personally difficult and unpopular decisions. The most difficult and unpopular decisions are people-related. When confronted with a tough personnel decision, objectivity, fairness, and consistency are the critical decision determinates. Managing also means taking hold of complex, ill-defined problems and converting them into organized, systematized solutions. Managers have to make rational decisions about products, people, and markets while allocating scarce resources efficiently.[9]

When it comes to identifying what a manager does, there are many different lists. Two were selected for this section to provide a broader insight into the thought process: Drucker's because of his reputation as the prominent leader in the field management and John T. Dunlop's, Harvard economist, former secretary of labor, chairman of the Clinton administration's Commission on the Future of Worker-Management Relations, and leading management expert, because he has worked closely with organized Labor throughout his career.

Drucker defines a manager's work as setting objectives, organizing work, motivating and communicating, measuring, and developing people:

- Setting objectives includes communicating them and determining the strategies necessary to reach them.
- Organizing work involves dividing work into activities, activities into jobs, and jobs into the organization structure. It also involves selecting the right people to manage the operation and do the work.
- Motivating and communicating refer to teambuilding and constant communication.
- Measuring includes setting standards and performance evaluation.
- Developing people includes programs to promote employee and manager growth and performance.

Dunlop sees a manager's work as analyzing the environment, setting objectives, selecting and developing people, shaping the organizational structure, negotiating and consensus building, and introducing innovation:

- Analyzing the environment involves perceiving and explaining the changing external environmental systems and specifying their impact on the organization.
- Setting objectives is concerned with allocating resources and maintaining internal cohesion and morale, which are vital to the mobilization of organizational effort.
- Selecting and developing people include training, educating, motivating, compensating, rewarding, and disciplining people.
- Shaping organizational structure is concerned with the levels of Management hierarchy, informal and formal lines of reporting, controls over money flows, relations with press and media, relations with governments, and interactions with other external groups.
- Negotiating and consensus building deals with internal organizational problems and external organizations and constituencies.
- Introducing innovation is concerned with managing change in the organization.[10]

The following is my list of ten basic responsibilities of union managers, which was compiled from Drucker's and Dunlop's lists plus other sources and personal experience:

- Determining the mission and core objectives of the union. Union managers are responsible for achieving the mission of the union. The mission of the union is its basic purpose, broadly defined as its role in society, and core objectives are the means to achieve the mission.

- Establishing and maintaining standards. Union managers are responsible for establishing and maintaining ethical and performance standards.
- Building the human organization. Union managers are responsible for selecting and developing high-performance workers, specialists, and managers.
- Dealing with crisis. Union managers must possess the skills and experience to respond to crisis and protect the members, employees, and union from danger.
- Making work productive and satisfying—Union managers are responsible for making work productive because the union achieves its objectives through the work of its people. They are responsible for making work satisfying because workers are people, and unlike any other resource, people have control over whether they work, how much work they will do, and how well they do it. Employees require responsibility, motivation, participation, satisfaction, incentives, rewards, status, and leadership.
- Managing social impacts and social responsibilities. Every union exists to serve its members, the community, and society. Thus, union managers are responsible for the quality of physical, human, and social environment of the workplace and the community.
- Allocating resources. Union managers are responsible for obtaining and allocating the resources necessary to achieve the union's mission and core objectives.
- Encouraging open communication. Union managers are responsible for providing a system of communication that encourages the free flow of information, both vertically and horizontally.
- Promoting the intense use of enabling technologies. Union managers are responsible for the intense use of enabling technologies to promote union communication and more effective and efficient union operations.
- Encouraging innovation. Innovation is the process of bringing any new, problem-solving idea into use. This process includes the generation, acceptance, and implementation of new ideas, processes, products, or services.

Clearly, management is a complex and demanding profession, and like all professions, Management has its superstars—its gold medal winners. These are the people who take ordinary organizations and turn them into extraordinary ones. These superstars share many qualities and skills. Here again, there are many lists; two were selected—Drucker's for the previous reason and Melvin Sorcher's, author of *Predicting Executive Success*, because it is especially appropriate for union managers.

Drucker teaches that all effective executives

- continually analyze how their time is spent and are quick to eliminate unproductive activities;
- judge themselves by results, not by time or effort expended on a certain task, and always ask themselves, What is expected of me?;
- build on strengths—their own and those of the people who work for them—focus on opportunity, not problems, and do not tolerate weaknesses;
- concentrate on a few major areas with the highest potential for achieving outstanding results, set priorities, and ignore everything else competing for their attention;
- make a few fundamental decisions rather than many less important ones.

Drucker believes these practices enable executives to be effective and concludes that while these practices are easy to grasp, they are not easy to master. He stresses they must be done over and over until they become a habit. Furthermore, Drucker notes that in his forty years of work as a consultant he never stumbled across a single "natural"—a manager who was born effective. However, he believes that if a manager is reasonably competent and highly conscientious, his or her chance for success is much greater than that of a brilliant colleague whose work is sloppy. He notes that effective managers thrive on all those unglamorous things that constitute hard work—the master key to success.[11]

Drucker also points out that while a manager's work can be systematically analyzed and learned, the single most important qualification is not genius, but character. Character must come with the manager. When honesty is compromised at the top, an organization can be destroyed. A survey of twenty-two senior executives supports Drucker's belief in the importance of character. When asked to identify reliable indicators of future executive success, they found that honesty and integrity, practical intelligence and street smarts, and the capacity to build teams were the top three qualifications.

Sorcher observed that all high performers

- demonstrate the ability to make things happen;
- exert an influence on the opinions and actions of others—an influence sometimes so subtle that it goes unnoticed;
- live up to their commitments;
- are steeped in organizational history;
- recognize and acknowledge their mistakes;
- express their views and perspectives in novel and interesting ways;
- possess penetrating insight into the nature of the organization or industry;
- have concrete ideas for positive change and organizational improvements.[12]

These lists demonstrate the wide range of management skills and qualities common to all high-performance managers. Each list approaches the subject somewhat differently, contains very useful observations, and provides an excellent overview of what it takes to be a high-performance manager.

However, in spite of all the time, effort, and money that go into management development, even the most successful managers make mistakes. Another survey of twenty-five top business executives identified typical mistakes, their consequences, and the reasons for making them. Typical mistakes were unwise business decisions (52 percent), unwise people decisions (28 percent), violation of policy (12 percent), and dishonesty (8 percent). The consequences of these mistakes were business losses (62 percent), damaged credibility (26 percent), and loss of job or business failure (8 percent). The reasons for these mistakes were poor business judgment (44 percent), desire to impress or to help someone, or to save the company (28 percent), arrogance (12 percent), negligence (12 percent), and greed (4 percent). The survey concluded that even with years of experience, senior executives make profound errors of judgment, for example, misplaced loyalty, unwise purchasing decisions, and outright negligence. However, after recognizing they made a mistake, senior executives tend to go through a three-phased reaction: shock, recovery, and learning. The major benefit here is that senior executives see mistakes as an opportunity to learn how to avoid future mistakes.[13]

In brief, management is a difficult and demanding profession, and no matter how brilliant or how well prepared, managers will make mistakes. Management development and training are an effort to limit the number of mistakes and minimize their impact.

RESOURCE ALLOCATION

One of a manager's most challenging responsibilities is to allocate resources. In this role, the manager decides how and to whom resources will be allocated. Since power and influence are measured by the amount of available resources, resource allocation is an extremely complicated and politically intense issue involving major shifts in power and influence.

In regard to resource allocation, it is important to distinguish between efficiency and effectiveness. Efficiency is concerned with doing things right and is a minimum condition for survival. It is the ability to achieve the union's core objectives with a minimum expenditure of resources. Effectiveness is concerned with doing the right thing—the foundation of success. It is about utilizing the union's resources to achieve its mission and core objectives. Efficiency deals with doing better what is already being done, while effectiveness is concerned with what combinations of resources are capable of producing extraordinary results. Efficiency is interested in the ordinary, while effectiveness is interested in the extraordinary. Most unions have been very effective, but, with very few exceptions, most unions need to become much more efficient.[14]

Resource allocation is governed by two fundamental economic propositions. The first is that resources are scarce relative to wants and desires and that the choice of objectives is limited by this physical scarcity. This proposition binds both the poorest and richest organizations. The second proposition is that resources have alternative uses to which they can be put. Productive resources have alternative uses and can be interchanged to produce different products and services. Not only do the resources have alternative uses, but the resources can, within limits, be substituted for one another. In addition, the composition of the final products or services is not fixed.[15]

Given available resources, the questions every union manager must ask are:

- What products and services shall we produce?
- How much of each product or service shall be produced or provided?
- How is this to take place?
- Who will benefit?
- Who is to do what?

To understand the importance of more efficient resource allocation, it is necessary to get some feel for the amount of resources involved. The AFL-CIO reported $65.4 million in per capita receipts on its 1995 LM2, Labor Organization Annual Report. Assume that better management and more intense use of enabling technologies can produce a savings of just 5 percent. This amounts to $3.3 million—the equivalent of 660,000 cost-free, new members with no service expenses. Obviously, organization building would be a much better use of scarce resources than organizing. Besides, there is almost no chance of organizing that many new members in the foreseeable future.

In the absence of information regarding the allocation resources among the nine basic union functions, guesstimates are necessary to develop examples of the trade-offs involved in resource allocation. It is important to be aware that the allocation of resources between the nine functions is a different mix at each of the five structural levels because each structural level has a different mission and core objectives.

Cost savings is not the only benefit of improved resource allocation. Greater efficiency improves organizational flexibility—the ability to switch resources from one function to another in response to environmental change—which increases effectiveness. Thus, while the potentially enormous monetary saving related to the more efficient resource allocation is important, the increased ability to achieve core objectives resulting from the more effective resource allocation is even more important.

Reporting for expenditures on a functional basis is critical to the efficient and effective management of unions. Union decision makers need to know how resources are being allocated among nine basic union functions if they are to make quality decisions. Planning without functional information is like a blind pilot steering a ship through a treacherous storm.

For a better understanding of the usefulness of functional reporting, it is necessary to make assumptions regarding the allocation of resources for a "typical" large national union. First assume that the top union officer of this large national union decides to follow the AFL-CIO's lead and makes organizing the union's number one objective. In this scenario, the resource-conversion process involves converting resources that were previously used to represent and service members into producing new members. This is an extremely complicated process that involves the transfer of various combinations of workforce, equipment, facilities, supplies, information, and technology from the other seven major union functions to the organizing and organization-building functions. There will be immediate losers and winners and, consequently, major swings in the center of power and influence. All sorts of complex interactions will take place. Since the basic character of the union undergoes major change, major, long-term risks are involved.

It is further assumed that there is no comprehensive strategic plan in place to allocate this major shift in resources, power, and influence, and thus their flow will be from the weakest functions to the strongest function. Figure 3.3, shows the dramatic shift of resources among the basic union functions as a percentage of total available dollars. Clearly, the winning functions in this internal struggle are organizing and organization building; the seven other functions are the losers. Only superbly managed organizations can successfully survive such a traumatic shift in resources.

Figure 3.3
Resource Reallocation among the Nine Basic Union Functions at the National Level to Support a Top-Level Organizing Priority

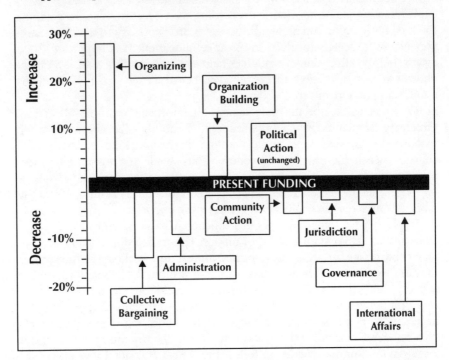

Local union leaders are faced with the dilemma of how to reallocate scarce resources to expand organizing programs and yet continue to represent and service their members. In these difficult times, reducing services could destroy or at least seriously harm the local union. Tragically, most of this change will be unanticipated and unplanned. Further, it is unclear if the good will outweigh the bad. Worse still, it is unclear if this major reallocation of resources will result in a long-term increase in membership. Even worse, there are no controls in place to terminate or reduce the project if a major shortfall becomes evident. More likely, as organizing targets are missed, more resources will be squandered in a futile effort to avoid embarrassing failure.

Clearly, there can be potentially serious problems if major resource allocation efforts are not part of a comprehensive strategic plan. This section is not meant to be a criticism of present organizing priority but is an argument for the need for a comprehensive strategic management process that provides informed choices regarding the efficient and effective allocation of scarce resources among the nine basic union functions.

MANAGING NONPROFIT ORGANIZATIONS

Much of this section is based on two excellent books, *Managing the Non-Profit Organization* by Peter Drucker and *Reinventing Government* by David Osborne and Ted Gaebler. *Managing the Non-Profit Organization* is the principal guide for nonprofit chief executive officers (CEOs), and *Reinventing Government* has been a major influence on the Clinton administration's reshaping of the federal government.

Drucker teaches that all nonprofit organizations have one thing in common—they change human beings. They exist to bring about change in individuals and society.[16] Osborne and Gaebler refer to nonprofit organizations as the "third sector" and they believe the words "voluntary" and "nonprofit" do not accurately describe the many organizations typically grouped into the nonprofit sector. Their "third sector" includes all organizations that are privately owned and controlled to meet public or social needs, as opposed to accumulating private wealth. They contend the "third sector" is society's preferred mechanism for delivering goods and services.[17]

Nonprofit or "third sector" organizations are distinguished from for-profit businesses by their

- basic mission;
- multiple constituencies;
- confusion between economic cause and moral cause;
- problems with measuring performance;
- need for standards;
- relationship with local organizations;
- need for information;
- dependence on trust;
- dependence on volunteers;
- conflict between compassion and competence.[18]

Obviously, unions are nonprofit, "third sector" organizations.

As previously noted, Drucker believes that all nonprofit organizations have a common mission—to satisfy the needs of the American people for self-realization and for living out their ideals, beliefs, and their best opinions of themselves. Since their products are changed human beings, nonprofits are human-change agents. In addition, he points out that nonprofits provide community and common purpose.

Effective nonprofits go beyond just satisfying needs—they create wants. Nonprofit managers need to continually reevaluate their mission and to think through whether it needs to be refocused because of the rapidly changing environment. They look outside the organization to see where the opportunities or needs are. While the mission is always long-term, actions are always short-term. Consequently, they must ask, "Are today's actions directly linked to achieving our mission?" They think through priorities and are results-oriented. They are sure the right results are being achieved and the right things are being done. Their primary objective is to raise the organization's mission, competence, and performance.[19]

Nonprofits cannot measure results the way businesses do, but there are some things that they can, and should, measure. Performance is the ultimate test of any organization. However, in nonprofits it is much more difficult to measure performance, since there is no convenient bottom line like business profits. For nonprofits, results start with the mission, and mission leads to very immediate and long-term objectives. In order to set objectives, performance must be defined for each of the nonprofit's basic functions. Nonprofits always need to set clear, specific objectives in terms of their service to members. When objectives are not clear or specific enough, success is much more difficult to achieve and harder to measure. Ultimately, a nonprofit has to judge itself by its performance in creating its mission, objectives, standards, values, commitment, and competence.[20]

Therefore, high-performance, nonprofit managers begin by defining the organization's mission in terms of the fundamental change their organization wants to make in society and in people. Then they set objectives and relate them to each of the organization's stakeholders. Performance in a nonprofit must be thoughtfully planned, and all stakeholders must agree on long-term, core objectives. For nonprofits, this is a much more difficult and demanding task, since they have more stakeholders than do business organizations.

The mission defines the results, and performance involves allocating available resources to achieve these results. Drucker believes that all nonprofits, including unions, should be judged by their performance "in creating vision, creating standards, creating values and commitment, and in creating human competence."[21] Since nonprofits are human-change agents, their results are always a change in people—their behavior, circumstances, visions, health, hopes, competencies, and capacity.

Thinking through the results in terms of the mission protects the nonprofit from squandering its resources because of confusion between moral and economic issues. In the union environment, it is frequently argued that moral causes always justify resources in spite of poor results. However, unions, like nonprofits, have the moral responsibility to invest resources, people, and money for the best results rather than squander them on being righteous. Since there are so many worthy causes, nonprofit organizations can no longer afford to continue projects that do not achieve desired results.[22]

In a mission-driven organization, the mission is the driving force behind everything. Mission-driven organizations free their members and employees from rules and regulations to pursue the mission with the most effective means available. Mission-driven organizations, when compared to rule-driven organizations, are more efficient, effective, innovative, and flexible and have higher morale.[23]

A confederation of local organizations forces the central organization to thoughtfully consider what is said and done. For people, especially volunteers, to take responsibility for performance, there must be clear, high, but attainable and uniform standards. High standards attract people to an organization, and clear standards are especially important to nonprofits that are a confederation of autonomous local organizations. Standards are essential for reconciling the need for local autonomy with the need for central conformity. Each local organization should have the power to make its own decisions consistent with appropriate centralized standards.

The control of these standards requires that the organization's top managers frequently visit various local organizations to understand their wants and needs. Equally important, they are always keenly aware that they are servants of the local organizations—not their bosses, but their conscience. On the other hand, local organizations must be equally aware that they represent the central organization.

As learning organizations, nonprofit must be information-based. Thus, it is critically important to build the nonprofit around information and communication systems instead of a bureaucratic system. Everyone in a nonprofit organization, from top to bottom, must take responsibility for sharing information. Information sharing involves two questions: 1, what information is needed to do the job—from whom, when, and how? and 2, what information do others need so that they can do their job—in what form and when? In an information-based organization everyone must take responsibility for informing their bosses and their colleagues and, above all, for educating them. Chapter 5, covers these subjects in more detail.

High-performance organizations are built on mutual trust. However, since nonprofit organizations depend on the contributions of volunteers, mutual trust is extremely more important for them than it is for a typical business. Trust means that people know what to expect from others—trust is mutual understanding. In a nonprofit organization, since everyone is dedicated to a common cause, confusion regarding core objectives can easily and quickly escalate to major problems. [24]

High-performance, nonprofit managers make it easy for workers to do their work, get results, and enjoy their work. Since productive and motivated workers require clear assignments, the responsibility for developing workplace plans and job descriptions should always be with the people who do the work. While emphasis on managing people should be on performance, evaluation should always be compassionate, since people work for nonprofits because they believe in the cause. Employees owe performance, and managers owe them compassion. Yet, whenever performance conflicts with compassion, performance should rule unless there are extenuating circumstances. A manager's ultimate responsibility is the well-being of the organization.[25] Motivation and performance evaluation are covered in more detail in Chapter 8, while workplace plans and job descriptions are covered in Chapter 7.

Drucker, in the preface of *Managing the Nonprofit Organization*, notes that nonprofits have a greater need for management because they do not have a convenient bottom line. They need very competent and focused managers to concentrate on their mission. He also points out that there is very little material specifically designed to help nonprofits with management and leadership problems.[26] For Labor unions there is even less help available. This is another reason that the Institute for Managing Labor Organizations is so extremely important.

Like other nonprofit organizations, Labor unions, human-change agents, need very competent managers who focus on their mission. While Labor unions share many similarities with nonprofit organizations, there are also some significant differences that require unique competencies for managing in a union environment. Hence, the Institute for Managing Labor Organizations should encourage research to identify these unique competencies. In the meantime, union officers should thoughtfully consider the many similarities unions share with other nonprofit organizations and how they can help them manage their organizations.

MANAGING CONSULTANTS

Unions, more than other organizations, use a wide variety of consulting services. In the future, as issues and organizations become more complex, and change becomes more dynamic, consultants will become an even greater influence in the management of union organizations. Today, unions rely on consultants for legal, accounting, financial, actuarial, technological expertise, public relations, membership opinion surveys, and media programs. Tomorrow, unions will look to consultants for help with behavioral science, specialty management, and strategic management. In brief, consultants' influence on unions, already extensive, will continue to grow.

Consultants are hired to help solve problems and provide special services and/or expertise. Typically, problems are either multi-functional or inter-disciplinary. Multi-functional problems are concerned with the basic union functions and focus on the interaction between the functions and problems involving more than one function. Inter-disciplinary problems typically involve technological, economic, financial, legal, motivational, political, and other activities.[27] The consultant's special services and expertise help organizations with decision making, policy development, operations management, and administration management.

The major benefits of consulting services are objective, diagnostic study and analysis, unbiased recommendations, and help in implementing change. Good consultants provide management experience, leadership ability, analytic skills, and prudent judgment. Another major advantage of hiring a consultant is the learning dimension that is the result of the close association of the client with the consultants.[28]

If you are thinking about hiring a consultant, you should

- learn about consulting and consultants;
- define your problem;
- define your objective;
- choose the consultant;
- develop a joint program;
- participate actively;
- involve the consultant in the implementation;
- monitor progress;
- evaluate the results and the consultant;
- beware of dependence on consultants.[29]

The qualities to look for in a consultant are

- intellectual ability;
- the ability to understand people and work with them;
- the ability to communicate, persuade, and motivate;
- intellectual and emotional maturity;
- personal drive and initiative;
- ethics and integrity;
- physical and mental health.[30]

Experience, integrity, and competency are the main criteria for selecting a consultant. The best way to find a consultant is through referral of satisfied clients or other consultants. For names of candidates, ask other union leaders and professional associations. You can also scan publications for related articles and contact the author for advice and recommendations. Make a list of prospective consultants and select the three most promising candidates. Limiting your list to three consultants encourages them to put full effort into their proposals.

Typical consulting assignments involve five phases: entry, diagnosis, action planning, implementation, and termination.

Entry includes

- first contacts with client;
- preliminary problem diagnosis;
- assignment proposal to client;
- consulting contract/letter of intent.

Diagnosis includes

- fact-finding;
- fact analysis and synthesis;
- detailed problem examination.

Action planning; includes

- developing solutions;
- evaluating alternatives;
- proposals to client;
- planning for implementation.

Implementation includes

- assisting with implementation;
- adjusting proposals;
- training.

Termination includes

- evaluation;
- final report;
- setting commitments;
- plans for follow-up;
- withdrawal.[31]

The consultant's job is to analyze the situation, identify options, explain the consequences of each option, and allow the client to make the decision. A well-managed consultant assignment starts with clear objectives and explicit proposals. It continues with the client's active involvement throughout the project and concludes with follow-through.

The client must sufficiently think through the situation to be able to accurately describe the objectives. Each objective should be in a few simple sentences stating exactly what is expected. This usually requires some preparation—the acquisition of a certain amount of knowledge by the union officer or senior staff representative assigned to oversee and coordinate the project. Knowledge levels flow from awareness, to familiarity, to understanding, to working, and ultimately to expertise. To properly manage the project, the project manager should at least be at the understanding level. Most of the time, to move from the awareness or familiar levels to the understanding level involves a period of preparation that includes scanning and study of related publications and background materials and discussions with all stakeholders. Adequate preparation is extremely important because both the client and the consultant must fully understand and fully agree on the objective of the project.

Closely related to the setting of objectives is identifying the criteria for achieving them. The project manager, together with staff and key stakeholders, should develop a list of criteria. It is also important to separate the need-to-know information from the nice-to-know information and, thus, establish clear parameters to facilitate drafting the consultant's proposal.

In most cases, detailed contracts are unnecessary and impractical because the principal purpose of a contract is to compel compliance. If your project is to be successful, you must trust and feel completely comfortable with your consultant. Compelling compliance in a consultant-client relationship is totally impractical because whenever the relationship deteriorates to this stage, it should be terminated.

A letter of intent is usually all that is needed. A letter of intent is a general description of the work to be performed and the fees to be paid. The letter of intent should include only those items that can be stipulated and should not be trusted to memory such as fees, costs, objectives, products or services, and schedules. As previously stressed, clear and mutually agreed upon objectives are critically important to the project's success. It should also include a statement that either party may terminate this agreement with thirty days' notice.

Always get a proposal. If the project is large, technical, or particularly complex, get three competitive proposals. Multiple proposals provide a great learning opportunity because they provide insight into the assignment from several different professional perspectives. To facilitate comparison of proposals, potential consultants should be given an explanation of the situation and the factors that influence it, the purpose and objectives of the assignment, and an estimate of expected benefits. Clients should provide all consultants who are invited to submit a proposal with a work specification form that includes

- a description of the problem;
- the objectives and expected results of the assignment;
- background and supporting information;
- a budget estimate or resource limit;
- a timetable with starting and completion dates, key stages and control dates;
- details regarding interim and final reporting dates;
- inputs to be provided by the client;
- any exclusions from the assignment;
- constraints and other factors likely to affect the assignment;
- client contact persons;
- a statement that the consultant is an adviser, not a decision maker;
- a statement that either party may terminate the agreement with thirty days' notice;
- a request for the consultant's references;
- a list of the firms invited to submit a proposal.[32]

A very comprehensive list like this is intended for large, complex projects. For smaller projects, or when the client is comfortable with the consultant, many steps can be omitted. Whenever more than one consultant is involved, it is critically important that the same submission form be sent to all bidders.

The proposal process is a great learning opportunity that can move the project manager from the understanding knowledge level to the working knowledge level. As a result of this new knowledge, it is common and appropriate to ask for minor changes in the proposal even after awarding it. These changes can reflect ideas from the other proposals. However, giving one consultant's proposal to another is an unfair advantage and could be subject to litigation. If major changes are necessary, ask that the proposal be resubmitted before accepting it.

Once the project starts, it is essential that the client stay actively involved. The project manager must maintain full awareness of the status of the work from the beginning to the conclusion of the project. It is important to stress that the project manager must always be a top-level union officer or senior staff. Unfortunately, too many union officers make the decision to undertake a project and assign responsibility to the middle management level. This common mistake immediately dooms the project to limited success—even failure.

Top-level involvement enables the client to identify and resolve unforeseen problems. The project manager should be personally involved with the work because it demonstrates the importance of the project, and provides valuable insights into the work process and more meaning to the results. Client involvement also provides greater insight into each party's operating style, which could lead to a better working relationship. The project manager should make certain progress reports are submitted as scheduled and contain the required information. The final report should be checked against the proposal to make certain that all agreed-upon objectives have been met and that the work has been performed. There should be no unresolved issues or questions about the work.

After completion of the project, the consultant should explain the findings and review the project. Both are important and integral parts of the assignment. The experience of the consultant is an important, unbiased resource when it is time to identify interpretations that are inconsistent with conclusions and recommendations. Further, both the client and the consultant should submit written assessments. Written assessments provide two important benefits. The first benefit is increased client competence for future projects. The client learns by reviewing what occurred throughout the project and identifies what might be done better the next time. The second benefit is that the consultant understands better the client's needs and operating preferences and, therefore, is positioned to perform at a higher level on the next assignment. Finally, the work of the consultant should be fully integrated as soon as possible into the operation of the union, with a union manager assigned full operational responsibility. With certain exceptions, a union should never become totally dependent on a consultant or hire the consultant to provide continuing services.

A common problem clients have with consultants is lack of communication over billing. Never accept a bill "for services rendered." The best solution to this problem is to always request a detailed monthly statement that includes the following: a description of the service, date the service was rendered, time spent on the service, amount charged for the service, expenses incurred, credits for payments made during the month, amount due or credit remaining, and period covered by the bill. If a billing problem cannot be resolved, an increasingly popular way of resolving consultant-client billing disputes is through arbitration instead of litigation. However, as noted previously, when client-consultant conflict reaches this level, with very few exceptions, the relationship should be terminated.

A closing warning of very special importance—consultants are in business to make money, and all too frequently this drive for the dollar overrides the consultants' ethical responsibilities to their clients. Consultants must be absolutely honest with the client when explaining the risks involved and the conditions the client must create and maintain. Examples of the risks involved are that the solution is innovative, but there is possible strong internal opposition or that there is a good chance the cost may be higher than predicted. Examples of conditions the client must create and maintain are high-level discipline in recording data or the transfer of members of senior Management.

Deplorably, to satisfy clients and ensure future assignments, some consultants tell their clients exactly what the clients expect or want to hear, regardless of whether or not it is good for the organization. This is a very expensive, intolerable, and destructive disservice because good decisions need objective and unbiased information. It is far better to have no information than to have subjective and biased information. Therefore, union leaders must make it explicitly clear at the outset of an assignment that the consultant is expected to perform according to professional ethics and that negative findings or undesirable recommendations will not interfere with future relations. Ultimately, the client always has the option to reject recommendations it feels are impractical or too disruptive.

Above all, professional consultants are always

- technically competent;
- conduct themselves as professionals in all matters and at all times;
- disclose conflicts of interest;
- respect the confidentiality of the client's proprietary information and business relationships;
- make it a policy to do top-quality work and deliver everything promised to the client;
- provide complete details regarding the progress of the assignment.

They never

- cover up or lie about mistakes;
- become involved in the client's organizational politics;

- accept an assignment that has a foregone conclusion;
- mislead the client;
- embarrass, compromise, or injure a client.

For unions, it is very important that consultants stress their commitment to confidentiality and disclosure of any potential conflict of interest, because business clients account for a large part of most management consultants' business. If either of these criteria is weak or missing, the consultant should be informed that unless the problem is immediately corrected, the consultant will not be considered for the project.

MANAGING TIME

Time is high-performance managers' scarcest resource, and unless it is managed, nothing else can be managed. Drucker listed time management as the first of five disciplines shared by all effective executives. Time is a unique resource. One cannot rent, buy, or otherwise obtain more time. It is a rapidly diminishing resource—minute by minute, day by day, week by week, month by month, year by year. Gone forever, never to return. Furthermore, there is no way to increase the supply of time. Yet everything we do requires time. All work uses up time. In brief, time is unique, irreplaceable, and essential.

In today's dynamic environment, it is increasingly important for managers to manage their time. Time management is a three-step process that includes

- recording time;
- managing time;
- consolidating time.

There are many ways to record time. Some high performers keep a daily log and analyze it weekly; others keep a log for three or four weeks twice a year. Some logs are maintained by the manager; others by the secretary. Some logs are handwritten; others are the result of computer software applications. Time use improves with time but requires constant vigilance to prevent it from drifting.

Managing time involves identifying nonproductive, time-wasting activities and getting rid of them. The following three questions are helpful in this step:

- What would happen if I didn't do this at all?
- What would happen if someone else did this?
- Am I wasting other people's time?

The most common time-wasters are

- lack of foresight;
- overstaffing;
- deficient organization;
- poor information.

Consolidating time involves setting "discretionary" time aside to do the really important tasks. Discretionary time is the time left over after all the necessary routine tasks are done. Even after extensive pruning, discretionary time will be very limited. Senior managers rarely have one-quarter of their time available for important matters. High performers also consolidate blocks of time so they can concentrate their efforts. Some high performers set aside one or two whole days a week; others set aside one or more hours each day.

You can improve your performance by improving your focus, organization, and process (FOP). Drucker believes that focus—single-minded concentration on one task at a time—is as close to the secret of high performance as there is. Organizing is the ability to arrange things efficiently and effectively. Process refers to your way of doing things.[33]

The following is a list of time management recommendations:

Focus

- Keep a log of your time, in fifteen-minute intervals, for one week. Enter every activity; evaluate and apply yourself where rewards are the greatest.
- Continually analyze how you are spending your time.
- Look ahead and set objectives. You should have short-term, middle-term, and long-term objectives. Remain flexible and alert so the future does not catch you unprepared.
- Establish a daily "quiet time" for creative thinking and planning. Shut the door, hold calls, do whatever it takes to have privacy.
- Invest your time in things that matter. Concentrate on the few major tasks with the highest potential for achieving outstanding results.
- Be honest regarding what task requires immediate attention.
- Consolidate blocks of time for major tasks. Continuous, uninterrupted blocks of time are essential.
- Break larger tasks into more manageable subtasks.
- Concentrate on one task at a time.
- Attack the most difficult task first.
- Complete the current task before moving to another one.
- Group related tasks.

Organize

- Take control of your desk! Keep items used most often within arm's reach. If you are right-handed, put the phone to your left so you can write. Keep other items such as calculators, staplers, a tickler file, Scotch tape dispenser, markers, pens, pencils, and so on to your right.
- Keep only work in progress on your desk.
- Always straighten your desk before you leave and the morning will be more productive.
- Use file folders marked "Action," "File," and "Reading."
- Arrange files alphabetically. Cross-index information on the outer front of the file folder. Keep recent papers to the front and mark a discard date.
- Each week cull your files and piles. If it is not necessary, throw it away.

- Start a "clip" file for useful articles and label file by topic.
- Discontinue publications you do not have time to read.
- Keep your calendar close at all times.
- Set aside a period of time each week to better organize your office.

Process

- Immediately write down everything that pops into your head.
- If the person you are calling is not available, leave a message for the person to return the call. Do not call again the same day.
- Return phone calls and answer correspondence at the same time each day.
- Keep letters and memos brief. State the reason for writing in the first sentence. Use the best paragraphs from past correspondence for future correspondence.
- Do not shuffle papers. Handle each piece of paper once. Then respond, refer, delegate, or throw it away.
- Use a 4 x 6 note card tickler file or a computer scheduler to keep track of meetings, activities, actions required, and due dates.
- Plan for the unexpected by building in extra time for major tasks.
- Tackle the toughest part of any task first.
- Buy extra time. Use forms, telematic equipment, software applications, specialists, and support services to conserve your time for work only you can do effectively.
- At the end of the workday, make a brief "to do" list for the next day. Prioritize each item and add everything that was not completed this day. No item should appear on the list more than two evenings in a row.
- Set "A," "B," and "C" priorities and try not to end your day doing an "A" priority.
- Develop a schedule that works for you.
- Delegate![34]

These time management recommendations will dramatically improve your performance. Start with the two or three suggestions from each category that you feel most comfortable with. Then add one suggestion from each category every week until most of them are fully integrated into your daily routine. The rewards will be enormous for both you and your union.

SUMMARY

History of Management

This very brief history of the development of the art and science of management reveals that most management theorists were primarily concerned with improving both productivity and the conditions of the workers. It points out that in industrial and Labor relations the core objectives, arguments, and basic positions of the parties have changed very little in almost 200 years. Almost everyone still agrees that increased productivity enriches our entire society and that conflicts inevitably arise in the distribution of the benefits of this increased productivity. Labor leaders, as workers' representatives, struggle to protect members' jobs and to get their fair share of the increased productivity.

Labor's problems are not with most Management initiatives that increase productivity but in the managers who abuse and exploit these initiatives. Unethical and unprofessional managers should not blind Labor leaders to the urgent need to become better managers.

High-performance unions adapt and implement management concepts, principles, and techniques.

Management and the Manager

Management is a complex and demanding profession based on a formal, systematic process for achieving objectives efficiently and effectively. Managers are, first and foremost, responsible for the well-being of their organization. This responsibility involves many personally difficult and unpopular decisions. When confronted with a tough personnel decision, the critical-decision determinants are objectivity, fairness, and consistency. Managing also means taking hold of complex, ill-defined problems and converting them into organized, systematized solutions. Managers have to make rational decisions about services and products, people, and markets while allocating scarce resources efficiently. This section identifies the responsibilities of union managers.

High-performance union managers

- recognize that their first and foremost responsibility is to their union;
- share a common trait—outstanding character.

Resource Allocation

Allocating resources is a manager's most challenging responsibility. Resource allocation is governed by the propositions of physical scarcity and alternative uses. But cost saving is not the only benefit of better resource allocation; greater efficiency improves organizational flexibility, which increases effectiveness.

High-performance unions use a comprehensive, strategic management process to allocate resources.

Managing Nonprofit Organizations

Labor unions, like other nonprofit organizations, are human-change agents with many similar strengths and weaknesses. Since nonprofits cannot measure performance the way businesses measure profits, they must measure results. Performance starts with the defining organization's mission in terms of the fundamental change it intends to make in society and people. Mission-driven, value-based organizations free their members and employees from rules and regulations to pursue the mission with the most effective means available.

High-performance unions are mission-driven, value-based organizations that make it easy for workers to do their work.

Managing Consultants

Unions more than other organizations use a wide variety of consulting services. Consultants are hired to help solve problems and provide special services and/or expertise. The major benefits of using consulting services are objective, diagnostic study and analysis, unbiased recommendations, and help in implementing change. Experience, integrity, and competency are the main criteria for selecting a consultant.

High-performance union leaders use a formal, systematic process for selecting a consultant defining and monitoring a project and implementing that consultant's recommendations.

Managing Time

Time is everyone's scarcest and most valuable resource. Everything requires time. Time is unique, irreplaceable, and essential. Time management is a three-step process that includes recording time, managing time, and consolidating time. Better time utilization can be achieved through focus, organize, and process (FOP). Focus is the single-minded concentration on one thing at a time, organize is the ability to arrange things efficiently and effectively, and process is the way things are done. This section contains time management recommendations.

High-performance union leaders are skillful time managers.

NOTES

1. Howard M. Carlisle, *Management: Concepts, Methods, and Applications* (Chicago: Science Research Associates, 1982), 30–51.

2. Harold Kerzner, *Project Management* (New York: Van Nostrand Reinhold, 1989), 67–69.

3. James A. F. Stoner, *Management* (Englewood Cliffs, NJ: Prentice-Hall, 1978), 32–55.

4. Peter F. Drucker, *Management Tasks, Responsibilities, Practices* (New York: Harper & Row, 1985), 37.

5. Ibid., 398–399.

6. Ibid., 454.

7. Peter F. Drucker, *The Effective Executive* (New York: Harper & Row, 1985), 8.

8. Drucker, *Management*, 396.

9. Harold J. Leavitt, "Corporate Pathfinders," *Washingtonian*, Apr. 1987.

10. John T. Dunlop, *The Management of Labor Unions* (Lexington, MA: Lexington Books, 1990), 10–12.

11. Peter F. Drucker, "Timeless Truths about Performing at Your Best," *Working Smart '87* (Stamford, CT: Learning International, 1987), 8–9.

12. "Most Likely to Succeed," *Working Smart '87*, 55.

13. "I Blew It!" *Working Smart '87*, 44–45.

14. Drucker, *Management*, 45–46.

15. Pearce Davis and Gerald J. Machett, *Modern Labor Economics* (New York: Ronald Press, 1954), 7.

16. Peter F. Drucker, *Managing the Nonprofit Organization* (New York: HarperCollins, 1990), xiii–xiv.

17. David Osborne and Ted Gaebler, *Reinventing Government* (New York: Plume, 1993), 44.

18. Source unknown.

19. Drucker, *Managing the Nonprofit Organization*, 45–49.

20. Ibid., 139-142.

21. Ibid., 112.

22. Ibid., 107–112.

23. Osborne and Gaebler, *Reinventing*, 113–124.

24. Drucker, *Managing the Nonprofit Organization*, 116.

25. Ibid., 182–183.

26. Ibid., xiv–xv.

27. Milan Kubr, ed., *Management Consulting* (Geneva, Switzerland: International Labour Organization, 1988), 214.

28. Ibid., 25.

29. Ibid., 503.

30. Ibid., 463.

31. Ibid., 14.

32. Milan Kubr, *How to Select and Use Consultants* (Geneva, Switzerland: International Labour Organization, 1993), 70.

33. Drucker, *Effective Executive*, 25–50.

34. These time management recommendations are a compilation of *Working Smart '87*, "Timeless Truths about Performing at Your Best" by Peter F. Drucker, and "Working Smarter, Not Harder; Personal Power; Effective Time Management," source unknown.

4

High-Performance Unions: Attributes of Excellence

Badness you can get easily, in quantity: the road is smooth and it lies close by. But in front of excellence the immortal gods have put sweat, and long and steep is the way to it, and rough at first. But when you come to the top, then it is easy, even though it is hard.

Hesiod, c. 700 B.C., *Works and Days*

With regard to excellence, it is not enough to know, but we must try to have and use it.

Aristotle, 384–322 B.C., *Nicomachean Ethics*

The above quotations, written over 2,000 years ago, are testimony to man's enduring reverence for excellence. Most people generally have a good feel for excellence and recognize it as something of very special worth or value. They refer to it frequently when describing the performance of athletes, writers, musicians, artists, crafters, doctors, and others. There is usually a consensus regarding excellent buildings, automobiles, paintings, movies, and books. However, excellence is much less clear when we refer to organizations. What qualities are common to all excellent organizations? How do we measure that extraspecial value or worth of an organization?

In Search of Excellence, by Thomas Peters and Robert Waterman, Jr., probably the best-known book on the subject of organizational excellence, is the result of the authors' comprehensive study of forty-three successful American companies. Their study identified eight attributes of excellence that were readily transferable to other organizations. While not all eight attributes were present or conspicuous to the same degree in these organizations, there was, however, a common intensity of commitment to those attributes that were present. Peters and Waterman argue that organizations are excellent because of a unique set of cultural attributes that distinguish them from other organizations. These cultural attributes are usually the inheritance of great leaders—usually the founders. Surprisingly, these same attributes are present, in varying degrees and combinations, in most unions. Furthermore, it is only logical that if ordinary unions were to intentionally build on these inherent attributes, they would become excellent unions. Thus, Labor's strength, its dominant values and rich culture and tradition, is the foundation for building tomorrow's unions.

Peters and Waterman's eight basic attributes of excellent organizations are that

- a bias for action means an organization prefers action over analysis;
- "close to the customer" refers to understanding the needs of the customer;
- autonomy and entrepreneurship involve creating an environment that provides sufficient autonomy for individuals to function as creative entrepreneurs;
- productivity through people is concerned with motivating all employees through various techniques to achieve consistently high-performance levels;
- "hands-on, value-driven" requires that senior executives be personally involved with the organization's essential mission;
- "stick to the knitting" means that an organization should primarily limit its activities to those it knows best;
- "simple form, lean staff" refers to a relatively flat organization structure with few staff employees;
- "simultaneous loose-tight properties" refers to creating an environment where central values are the basis of autonomy and control.[1]

BIAS FOR ACTION

Excellent companies employ various devices and techniques to encourage action. The four most common ones are organizational fluidity, chunking and hiving, experimenting, and simple systems.

- Organizational fluidity. This is a measure of how organizations respond to new issues. The "bureaucracy" or formal organization structure is designed to deal with routine business and thus has limited ability to respond to new issues. An "adhocracy" is an organizational form designed for quick action in response to new issues. Its main thrust is intense communications. Excellent companies are vast networks of informal, open communication. Factors that encourage intense communications are insistence on informality, open physical configurations, and regular, positive peer review. A principal feature of informality is "management by wandering about" (MBWA), or, simply, top managers getting out to meet the people.[2]
- Chunking and hiving. The purpose of chunking and hiving is to break things up to facilitate organizational fluidity and encourage action. Chunking breaks the organization into manageable work units, and hiving spins off new organizational teams. These techniques make large, complex organizations operate as small, simple ones. The small group is critical to excellent organizations. According to research, the optimal small group size is about seven people. The organization's basic building block is the section or department. The power of sec-

tions and departments is their flexibility. Project teams and profit centers are other frequently used chunking devices. The ad hoc task force, another effective chunking tool, is a small team of volunteers working within a set time frame to achieve a specific objective. Breaking a collective bargaining department into negotiations and administration departments is an example of hiving.

Peters and Waterman summed up chunking with four messages. First, ideas about cost efficiency and economies of scale lead to big bureaucracies that simply cannot perform. Second, excellent companies find numerous ways to break things up to encourage organizational fluidity and the efficient use of resources. Third, chunking will not work unless attitudes, climate, and culture encourage ad hoc behavior over bureaucratic behavior. Fourth, an ad hoc environment is only superficially unstructured because it is usually driven by ingrained cultural values.[3]

- Experimenting. The most important and visible sign of an action bias in excellent organizations is their willingness to try things out, to "experiment." In the business world there is no more important word than experiment. The alternative to experimenting is analysis. Experiments are an inexpensive form of learning and provide a strong user connection. Experiments should be numerous, and decisions to experiment (quick in) or to terminate an experiment (quick out) should be made swiftly. Since the beginning of an experiment is critically important to its success, managers should select doable projects and then build on success. Excellent organizations create an environment and set of attitudes that encourage experimentation.[4]
- Simple systems. A simple system is critical to success. Almost any system can be cleaned up and simplified. Excellent companies are also characterized by brief communications, fact-based decisions, a focus on critical numbers, and a few core objectives. If the core objectives are right, satisfactory results will follow.[5]

In regard to organizational fluidity, many unions are slow to respond when it comes to union administration, governance, and organization-building functions. In these areas change typically comes very slowly, and new technologies are usually first resisted and then severely restricted. Unions have a mixed record regarding communication. The typical union structure constrains vertical relationships and obstructs lateral communications. Yet unions typically have vast networks of informal communications that are usually discouraged by top union officers. Keenly aware of the value of information, too many top union officers tend to hoard and ration information on a need-to-know basis or as political currency. On the other hand, most top union officers are very informal, are on a first-name basis with local union officers and have a superb MBWA record. They attend a wide range of meetings, mingle with the delegates, and frequently visit job sites and plants. The physical configurations of facilities vary with each union organization, and the use of positive peer review is almost nonexistent.

Most local union organizations are typically small and naturally chunked. The jurisdiction function is a natural chunking mechanism since unions are granted jurisdiction by occupation, industry, employer, and region. Another chunking mechanism is the workplace. Here the union structure usually parallels the employer's structure. In the union environment, the chunking process includes social and sports clubs as well as special interest and activities groups.

While most unions have basically simple systems, they usually do not experiment or analyze before committing resources. They tend to have a very strong bias for action with very little analysis or experimentation. Hence, they could benefit from the four bias for action techniques, especially by encouraging open communications and the use of analysis and experiments before committing resources.

Peters and Waterman's strong bias for testing and experimenting and against planning and analysis and such Management devices as matrix management and management by objectives (MBO) is difficult to accept. To explain their biases, it is necessary to understand the period in which their work was done—1977 to 1980. This was the era of the conglomerate, when businesses were acquiring other businesses and centralizing operations to achieve economies of scale, and the business environment was much more stable. Matrix management, strategic planning, and MBO were new Management tools developed to manage these very complex, large organizations. In short, Peters and Waterman's criticism of these devices was an appropriate response to the excesses and failures of Management of that period.

In addition, Peters and Waterman apparently oversimplified and generalized to emphasize their points. Since the forty-three companies involved in the study were large, complex organizations, logic holds that if they did not have formal plans or planning departments, somebody somewhere in the organization had at least a five-year "scenario." If a few actually did not have a plan then, it is safe to assume that they have one now or are in serious trouble. Also, you can be sure that most of them utilized some form of matrix management, MBO, and other new Management strategies. In today's turbulent environment there is a need for analysis and planning, as well as structure and strategy.

CLOSE TO THE CUSTOMER

This attribute stresses that service, quality, and reliability are strategies aimed at customer loyalty and long-term revenue growth. Excellent organizations are obsessed with service and quality. They also practice nichemanship and listen very closely to their customers. Nichemanship is that special ability to recognize their organization's unique competencies for satisfying their customer's needs. Excellent companies, regardless of their business, consider themselves service organizations. Researcher Dinah Nemeroff identified three principal themes of all effective service orientations:

- an intensive, actively involved top Management;
- a remarkable people orientation;
- a high intensity of measurement and feedback.

Customer service always starts with top Management. A commitment to service begins with very powerful service themes that pervade the organization. Most excellent organizations hold that any failure is intolerable and overspend on service, quality, and reliability. Moreover, they recognize that every customer complaint requires an immediate response and commit their resources to satisfying the customer.

Excellent companies are clearly people-oriented and recognize that people service people. They also recognize that no part of an organization is untouched by the customer, and, thus, all personnel are held fully liable for customer satisfaction. Close-to-the-customer beliefs are backed by intensive training. This service-through-people theme is the distinguishing characteristic of excellent companies. They continually measure customer satisfaction and are always developing new incentive programs to reward employees for services to customers.[6]

An obsession with high-quality, reliable products and services is the paramount institutional goal of all excellent organizations. Growth and other goals are subordinated to quality and reliability. The commitment to quality also starts with top Management—they build quality objectives into all operations. All organizations make or provide something, but they differ in how much care goes into the product or the service. Successful companies have people in key positions who really care about the quality of their particular product or service. True service- and quality-oriented companies expect to do things right.[7]

Customer closeness involves finding a particular niche where the company does something better than any other company. Firms strong in nichemanship are skilled in technology manipulation, pricing, segmenting, and problem solving. In addition, they are willing to spend money to be recognized as special. Niche people are masters at applying sophisticated technologies to appropriate situations. They are superb at pricing mainly on value and are strong customer problem solvers. Spending to differentiate involves identifying particular areas that will distinguish one company from other companies.[8]

Listening to others is based on the belief that most real innovation comes from the market. Successful organizations understand the market by listening to, and understanding, the needs of their customers. They form partnerships with their customers and involve them in the development of the innovation. They also understand their competitors better than do other companies.

The principle of closeness to customers contributes to the success of an organization by providing necessary feedback to determine the customer's future needs. The better listeners are especially concerned with the front-edge customer who is years ahead of the typical customer. Moreover, close-ness to the customer also establishes a long-term bond with the customer that will provide sufficient revenue for future profit and growth.[9]

Unions also need to "customerize"—become more responsive to their members, employees, employers, and other stakeholders by treating them like *customers*. Note, the word "customer" is italicized to distinguish the *customer* of a union from the typical business customer. Customerization means ex-tending information systems and enabling technologies to the points of contact with the primary customers. It means staying very close to the customer. How does staying close to the customer apply in a union environment? Who are a union's customers? Unfortunately, the all-too-simple, common, and conven-ient reply is "the workers" or "the members." This convenient generalization is both confusing and misleading. Identifying a union's customers is much more difficult than it is for businesses. Like businesses, unions provide a wide variety of products and services for many markets and customers. Top union officers need to think in terms of products and services for "markets" and "*customers*."

The many external union customers include the employer, nonunion workers, public interest groups, retired members, academics, politicians, and the community in general. What products or services do unions provide these customers? How are resources allocated to provide these products and services?

Labor's primary external customer is the employer, and its primary product is the collective bargaining agreement—one of the most complex products ever conceived. All other products and services at each union or-ganizational level are in some way supportive of the collective bargaining process. The quality of collective bargaining agreements ranges from poor to excellent and from conservative to innovative. Like any other product, from toasters to tractors, customers remain loyal as long as they get top quality and full value. The union situation is further complicated because the employer is both the primary customer and the primary competitor. The typical employer probably opposed union recognition and, after recognition, is in constant competition with the union for the workers' loyalty.

The internal-customer model is the primary tool top managers use to in-stall a policy of customer satisfaction. This model views the organization as a chain of performance units. Each performance unit is an independent pro-ducer providing products and services for the next performance unit. The pri-mary performance units are those closest to the paying customer. This model applies to both work flow and the Management chain. Once in effect, yester-day's subordinates become today's customers, and new partnerships are formed. For example, pension departments are the *customers* of the invest-ment department, while all departments are the *customers* of the mail services department, and most departments, intermediate unions, and local unions are *customers* of the research department and information services department.

In the national union version of this model, the primary performance units are the local unions, and the paying *customers* are the union members. The other performance units in the *customer* chain are the intermediate unions, the national union, the AFL-CIO, and the international federations. Each is a *customer* of the next higher level. The local union's primary *customers* are the rank-and-file members. The intermediate unions' and national union's *customers* are the local unions. The AFL-CIO's and the international federations' *customers* are the affiliated national unions. Once the identity of the customer is established, then the markets, services, and products can be better defined, and customer satisfaction can be measured. This is an example of union nichemanship.

The linkage of structural levels, or *customer* levels, leads to the bottom line for all union activities—the rank-and-file member. At this level, it is critically important that top union officers be aware that the rank and file is not a herd of sheep. The fact is that every union member is a unique individual with his or her own needs and ambitions. Theoretically, these needs and ambitions are transferred by the local union through the various union organizational levels. Thus, the needs of the local union officers, the only directly elected representatives of the rank and file, are the primary market for intermediate unions and the national union. The local union officers' closeness to the rank and file validates their claim for products and services. Accordingly, the national officers' closeness to the local union officers confirms the type and quality of services and products provided by the national union.

The membership/leadership depth of participation (M/LDOP) models, Figure 4.1, are concerned with four categories of member participation: nonactivist, voting, activist, and leadership, and shows the impact of present centralization policies on each category.[10] The nonactivist category is made up of members who just pay their dues. The voting category refers to members who vote in the election of union officers and/or on the collective bargaining agreement. The activist category includes members who participate in a union activity such as running for a union office, attending union meetings, filing a grievance, bowling in the local union's league, working at the local union's Christmas party, staffing phone banks, and so on. The leadership category consists of all elected national and local union officers and national union and local union representatives (business agents). In general, there is an extraordinary degree of closeness and sensitivity within the union leadership and activist levels. Unfortunately, in most unions, there are little participation and a weak sense of community within the voting and nonactivist blocks, which include about 85 percent of the total union membership.

Figure 4.1
Membership/Leadership Depth of Participation Models

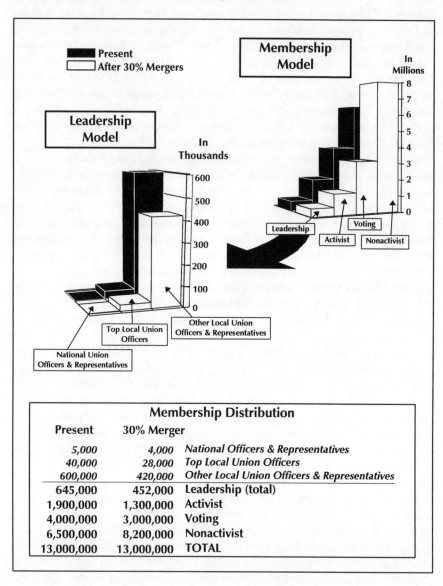

Membership Distribution		
Present	30% Merger	
5,000	4,000	*National Officers & Representatives*
40,000	28,000	*Top Local Union Officers*
600,000	420,000	*Other Local Union Officers & Representatives*
645,000	452,000	Leadership (total)
1,900,000	1,300,000	Activist
4,000,000	3,000,000	Voting
6,500,000	8,200,000	Nonactivist
13,000,000	13,000,000	TOTAL

The MDOP model compares the enormous voting and nonactivist members blocks to the much smaller leadership and activist blocks. While this graphic applies to the entire AFL-CIO, the MDOP model can be applied to even the smallest local union. The basic premise of the MDOP model is that unions become more effective as more members move from the nonactivist and voting categories to activist and leadership categories. Thus, the MDOP model is a measure of union effectiveness. Unfortunately, if unions continue their present merger policy, the leadership block will be dramatically reduced, especially the "other local union officers & representatives" block.

Michael E. Gordon, a widely recognized expert in the area of union commitment and participation, uses five measures of participation and four measures of commitment. His measures of participation are serving in elected office, voting, attendance at meetings, knowledge of the contract, and filing a grievance. His measures of union commitment are union loyalty, responsibility to the union, willingness to work for the union, and belief in unionism. Gordon found that the benefits a union provides are the most important basis for commitment and that loyalty is closely related to the members' attitudes about the local union and the local leader. His studies revealed that a strong predisposition toward unions at the time a member joined the union was an important influence on his or her future commitment to the union. Thus, both formal and informal efforts should be made to immerse individuals in the social and the business activities of the union as soon as they become members.

New strategies are also urgently needed to better understand the *customers*. The best way to determine if a product or service is what the *customer* wants is simply to ask them. Periodic membership survey and feedback techniques, expanded membership records, and demographic marketing information are examples of effective tools for listening to, and understanding, the primary *customers*.

The members' opinion of their local and national union is influenced by their perception of whether or not the union has their best interests at heart and the extent to which the local union officers are doing their jobs. Survey feedback techniques are practical means of collecting vital information from, and feeding it to, the members. Researchers Mitchell Fields and James Thacker found that merely surveying members improved their attitude toward unions and their opinion of the chief steward.[11]

In another study, Thomas Chacko found that members' perceptions of their union's performance and its responsiveness to their needs were significantly related to their participation in union activities. Members are more likely to participate if they perceive their union is effective in obtaining benefits for the membership. Member involvement also increased when shop stewards showed concern and consideration for the member as an individual. Chacko notes that to obtain better participation, unions have to emphasize noneconomic benefits that in the past have been downgraded.[12]

Expanded membership records, in addition to helping the local union leaders better understand their *customers*, can be a very useful resource for increasing member participation and bolstering political and community action activities. This information can be used to identify members with unique or special skills and talents or members who are elected and appointed public officials, community leaders, and activists. Newsletters, special mailings, or feature articles in the monthly publication could be designed to appeal to specific groups of members. Union journals could even be individually customized like special editions of *Time* magazine.

Many members support their union's objectives and would welcome an opportunity to be recognized and involved in union activities within their area of interest, expertise, or authority. For example, a national union or an intermediate union could convene special conferences of elected or appointed local government officials. David Osborne and Ted Gaebler, authors of *Reinventing Government*, estimate there are over 500,000 elected officials in the U.S. On a worst-case basis, it is fairly safe to assume that at least 5 percent are, or were, union members. Twenty-five thousand elected officials is a potentially enormous local political force. Directed mailing lists can also be a valuable resource for direct-mail fund-raising. Thus, even if union density continues to decline, unions will be richer, stronger, and much more influential because the remaining members will be better informed and more involved, committed, and active.

The leadership depth of participation (LDOP) model is an explosion of the leadership block of the MDOP model that subdivides it into three categories to facilitate the participation analysis. The first category is national unions' officers and representatives. The next category is the top elected officer of each local union, either the president or business manager. The third and largest category is the "other local union officers & representatives" category. This category is made up of vice presidents, financial secretaries, recording secretaries, treasurers, executive boards, examining boards, and business representatives. Even within the leadership block, there is a pressing need for innovative listening strategies. While there is an extraordinary closeness between the national union officers and representatives category and the top elected official category, a large percentage of the 600,000 "other local union officers & representatives" category has little or no contact with the national union.

In general, the size of these leadership categories is determined by the national union's constitution, the local union's bylaws, and the number of national and local unions. Constitutions and bylaws determine the number of officers. A typical local union has about fifteen elected officers. Note that the numbers used in the MDOP and LDOP models are projected guesstimates based on 13 million AFL-CIO members in 40,000 local unions. Guesstimates are sufficient to support my premise that centralization, especially mergers, is destroying opportunities for meaningful member participation and diminishing union democracy. Figure 4.1 shows that a 30 percent reduction in the number of unions would translate into the loss of 193,000 members in the leadership category, 600,000 members in the activist category, 1 million members in the voting category, while the nonactivist category increases by 1.7 million members. Mergers are like the black holes of deep space, absorbing the energy and vitality of organized Labor. Even in the light of better, less supportive information, the shape of the models would be basically unchanged.

The expanded membership records should include information on the people in this leadership block such as type, number, and length of offices held, conventions attended, and other union-related assignments and activities. Leadership opinion surveys need to be designed to determine the needs and views of other local union officers and representatives. A periodic leadership newsletter could provide information and advice specifically for local union officers. Likewise, a newsletter for convention delegates could be used to maintain the commitment generated by the convention and to report on the status of the actions endorsed by the convention. Through programs such as these, new two-way communication channels would be established between the national union and its primary *customers*—the elected officers and representatives of the local union.

Implementing a commitment to quality is a matter of taking concrete steps toward specific objectives and measuring performance. It starts with the top union officer, who must assign responsibilities to people who really care deeply about quality. However, even top officers may require some education regarding this new prospective. Implementers will need the support of the top officer as they bring the *customers'* voice into the union and translate it into performance at each link in the chain of operations. A quality operation is immediately evident to everyone.

Nichemanship for unions is much more limited than for businesses. Since a union's primary business is industrial relations, it does not have the option to decide which business it wants to be in. However, within this field there are many opportunities to identify niches, to develop unique competencies in technology manipulation, to allocate resources to achieve the greatest value, and to solve members' problems. There are also many strategies for distinguishing one union organization from other union organizations and for expanding union activities.

All the various "close to the customer" strategies involve education and communication. Peters and Waterman stressed that the key point of this wonderful commitment to the customer is that the winners seem to focus on revenue generation. Put more simply, closeness to customers is profitable for business and will be equally rewarding for unions. For unions, closeness to *customers* means new strength through greater member participation and union influence.

AUTONOMY AND ENTREPRENEURSHIP

Autonomy means independence or freedom, and an entrepreneur is a person who organizes, manages, and assumes responsibility. Excellent organizations permit greater autonomy far down into the organizational structure. They tolerate some disarray and disorder to bring about innovation. Rosabeth Kanter, author of *The Change Masters*, defines innovation as the process of bringing any new, problem-solving idea into use. The process includes the generation, acceptance, and implementation of new ideas, processes, products, or services. Innovation can be technical, social, or organizational. Furthermore, it can occur in any part of an organization and can involve creative use as well as an original invention. A wide variety of innovations is essential for an organization's economic survival.[13]

Innovation is the sum of all the minimoments leading to the "eureka" experience. Genius is those perfect crystals of time that Allen Lightman, author of *Einstein's Dreams*, calls the "Wild Magic." What being human is all about is that moment of genius, of inspiration, of which everyone is capable.[14] It thrives in some organizations and flounders in others. Innovation-suppressing organizations are classified as either innovation avoiders or unschooled in how to innovate. Both tend to set up similar barriers to innovation, such as

- the dominance of restrictive vertical relationships;
- poor lateral communications;
- limited tools and assistance.[15]

More specifically, Kanter has ten rules for stifling innovation:

- regard any new idea from below with suspicion;
- insist that people who need your approval to act first go through several levels of Management;
- have departments or individuals criticize each other's proposals;
- express your criticism freely and withhold praise;
- discourage people from letting you know when something is not working by treating the identification of problems as signs of failure;
- control everything carefully;
- make decisions to reorganize or change policies in secret and spring them on people unexpectedly;
- make sure that requests for information are fully justified and then make sure that it is not given out freely;
- assign to lower-level managers, in the name of delegation, responsibility for figuring out how to cut back, lay off, move people around, or otherwise implement the threatening decisions you have made. Then get them to do it quickly;
- above all, never forget that you, the boss, already know everything important about the business.[16]

Innovation-promoting organizations create a culture and structure that encourage change. While each highly innovative organization has its own unique environment, it also has a common pattern that distinguishes it from innovation suppressors. The integrative nature of the innovator's culture and structure is the common fabric of this pattern. In this environment managers can reach beyond the bounds of their jobs and, thus, collaborate with others to effect a higher level of performance.[17]

Innovative organizations usually have the following four features:

- broad job descriptions that are ambiguous, nonroutine, and change-directed;
- intersecting job territories;
- a culture of pride and a climate of success;
- incentives for initiative.

The first feature, broad job descriptions, recognizes that individuals are the source of innovation. Thus, innovative organizations provide a degree of freedom from top-level interference and vest more authority in a local group of people who are mutually dependent on each other. Innovation is initiated through top-down assignments that frequently ignore the formal organizational chart. Assignments identify the general, start the people in that direction, and let them decide how to get there.[18] In addition to independence from top Management, innovating organizations provide a relative interdependence among peers across functions with a highly integrative, rather than segmented, focus. This second feature, the intersecting of job territories, is promoted with various types of multi-disciplinary project teams. The third feature, a culture of pride and climate for success includes incentives for initiative, the fourth feature of innovative organizations. A culture of pride is found in companies that are people-centered and that look inside first for new ideas. A climate of success is the basis of a culture of pride. External prestige, due to success in the marketplace, promotes internal pride that stimulates individual self-esteem, which is directly related to peak performance. It also provides an emotional and value commitment between the person and the organization. An organizational culture in which innovation is mainstream rather than counterculture provides incentives for initiative by encouraging the development of "opinion leaders."[19]

Innovation flourishes in integrative organizations that are people-oriented, because people are the ultimate source of innovation. Kanter contends that the formal reward for individual performance does not play an important role in innovating organizations. Instead, they emphasize the investment in people and projects and provide incentives throughout the project, rather than payment for past services.[20]

Peters and Waterman identify excellent organizations as innovative organizations that are especially adroit at responding to change of any sort. This ability to respond to change is essential for the survival of an organization. Innovating organizations are built around the entrepreneurs—change masters who take an idea and bullheadedly push it to implementation.[21] They constantly use their resources in new ways to heighten both their efficiency and effectiveness. J. B. Say, nineteenth-century French economist, noted, "The entrepreneur [change master] shifts resources out of an area of lower yield and into an area of higher productivity and greater yield."[22]

The role of a change master is crucial to innovation, because he or she gets things done. In innovating organizations there are always special relationships involving the change master, since they do not emerge automatically. Change masters emerge when the culture and numerous physical supports encourage them, nurture them through difficult times, celebrate their success, and assist them through occasional failures. Innovative organizations all have some form of primary change master and some form of protection for them. Change masters take risks because the culture of the organization supports risk taking as a way of life.

Excellent organizations create a change master mythology, with role models and a structure of heroes and heroines that transfers the challenge of entrepreneurship onto unit or product managers. However, they also provide incredibly tight support systems that prop up the manager and assist him or her in getting the job done. They believe small is beautiful and employ various chunking techniques.

The cornerstone of the innovative process is communication. The five communication-fostering features are

- informality;
- intensity;
- physical support;
- forcing devices;
- controlling devices.

In excellent organizations, communication systems are characterized by people's casually getting together to talk about problems. Intense communication is no-holds-barred communication. The questions are blatant, the flow is free, and everyone is involved. Blackboards, computers, large tables, conference rooms, and campus settings are physical trappings that spur intense, informal communication. Recognition of excellence for innovation awards, new products, future projects, interdisciplinary activities, and special innovating departments are forcing devices. In an environment of intense, informal communications everyone knows how everything is going. This free flow of information serves as an extremely effective form of internal control.

Unions have an impressive record for innovation in many areas, especially in collective bargaining. The intensity of the Labor-Management struggle and the subtleties of the negotiating process are conducive to innovation. Unlike in the business environment, change masters in the union environment seem to emerge spontaneously in response to particular situations. Union change masters emerge because the democratic union heritage permits their emergence. Unfortunately, their emergence is usually not encouraged and frequently strongly discouraged. Fortunately, innovation takes place in spite of union structure, policies, and politics. Many unions are both innovation avoiders and unschooled in how to innovate. Examples of Kanter's ten rules for stifling innovation are the norm rather than the exception for far too many unions. Further, there are very few examples of unions' intentionally implementing policies or structural changes to encourage innovation.

In these hostile and turbulent times, innovation is the key to survival. Thus, unions need formal strategies to identify and develop change masters and to cultivate intense, open communication systems. Even though some unions have an impressive record for innovation in certain areas, there is an urgent need to be more innovative in other areas—especially in the union administration, governance, and organization-building functions. With more sweat, thought, structure, and persistence, an already impressive record can achieve excellence. Unions, founded on democratic principles, have a great natural advantage over business when it comes to innovation. Unfortunately, however, in too many unions there is a tradition of innovation-stifling, lip-service democracy.

PRODUCTIVITY THROUGH PEOPLE

This principle holds that performance is maximized through a genuine people orientation based on trust. Companies with genuine people orientation treat people as adults, as equal partners, and with respect and dignity. Excellent companies recognize that workers are their most important asset. They excel in their ability to achieve extraordinary results through ordinary people.

Excellent companies build upon the following three basic human needs:

- people need meaning;
- people need some control over decisions that affect their lives;
- people need positive reinforcement.

These companies also recognize that actions and behavior shape attitudes and beliefs rather than vice versa.

Lip service and gimmicks, the opposite of genuine people orientation inevitably result in disaster. In regard to lip service, without exception, companies say that people are their most important asset, yet in most there is no real commitment. In people-oriented companies, the caring is a core value and is embedded in the language. There is an unabashed hoopla in recognition of achievements, and people respond to it. Excellent companies are measurement-happy and performance-oriented. Control is based on high expectations and peer review. People like to perform against standards that they helped develop. They also like to be recognized and to compare themselves to others. The magic of high expectations is feeling needed.

Quality circles, job enlargement, job enrichment, organizational development, T-groups, conflict resolution, and managerial grids, when manipulated, are potential sources of disaster. The track record for gimmicks is littered with failures. The only way these types of programs are going to bring about fundamental change is with a real commitment to people and the total support of the entire top Management team. Excellent companies use these various programs, but their approach is entirely different. Lip service, manipulation, and gimmickry are not tolerated. They have a rich system of monetary incentives and an amazing variety of experimental incentive programs. They also recognize that any particular technique has a life expectancy of only a few years and, thus, are continually searching for new programs.

The common themes found in people-oriented organizations are language, an extended family environment, informality, open facilities, hoopla, training, information, and smallness. Excellent companies use a common language to upscale the status of employees. They include the entire family and do not follow a rigid chain of command. They also design open facilities to promote the flow of information. Various forms of hoopla, such as awards, newsletter recognition, employee of the month awards, and so on, are vehicles to recognize achievement. Training, such as sensitizing managers, also plays an important role in successful people-oriented organizations.

People naturally compare themselves to others, and this requires qualitative information. Qualitative information is the prime ingredient in the information-sharing process that triggers peer pressure—the most potent controlling force. General objectives and values are set, and information is added so workers know if the job is getting done. Recognition for achievement requires positive reinforcement through both monetary and nonmonetary incentives.

Smallness is a common factor in excellent organizations. Smallness is related to less layering and less structuring, which induce manageability and commitment and let the individual stand out. This basic principle contributes to the success of an organization by increasing productivity, creativity, and responsibility of its employees.[23]

In Peters and Waterman's business world, the term "people" refers to the managers and employees of the company. In the union world, the term "people" is divided into four groups: the member employee, the nonmember employee, the member/*customer*, and the combination of these three groups. The member employees, the first group, include all union officers, representatives as managers and operatives. The nonmember employees, the second group, include other operating, support, and administrative employees. Member and nonmember employees provide the services and products for the *customers*. The third group, the member/*customers*, refers to the union members as primary consumers of union products and services. The fourth group refers to the entire local union organization and is the intended reference unless indicated otherwise. For example, the local union is the *customer* of the national union, and the national union is the *customer* of the national federation and international Labor organizations.

In regard to the employee of the union group, union Management performance is frequently inconsistent. In some cases, their collective bargaining agreements with their employees are models for the industry. In others, they are inflexible, carelessly drafted, and the potential source of many serious problems. There are instances where the agreement is strictly adhered to, and others where it is conveniently and frequently ignored. On one hand, promotion, discipline, and discharge are implemented justly and sensitively in full compliance with due process, yet there are many examples where they have been arbitrary and capricious.

While there are many programs to inform union members about Labor's rich culture and heritage, typically, very little is done to educate employees of the union. Fortunately, the same programs used to teach members the union's history and culture can be an extremely useful tool for motivating union employees. Clearly, the same values that motivate union members need to be used to motivate union employees.

The business world, in many ways, is much simpler than the union world. There is usually a clear distinction between employees and customers. Union officers are not so fortunate because, as previously noted, the union world is much more complicated. Further complicating the situation, in most cases, the employees are also members of another union. Union-to-union collective bargaining is especially difficult and presents unique and very real challenges. Consequently, when adapting management concepts, principles, and techniques to the union environment, it is very important to distinguish between the various groups of "people."

HANDS-ON, VALUE-DRIVEN

Peters and Waterman were struck by the explicit attention that excellent companies paid to values and the way their leaders, through personal attention, persistence, and direct intervention, have created exciting organizations. Every excellent company they studied was very clear on what it stood for and took the process of shaping values very seriously. Institutional survival is a matter of maintaining values and a distinctive identity that is directly drawn from its primary mission.

"Hands-on" refers to the leader's role in instilling organizational values. These values are established by the personality of the leader. A value-shaping leader deals with both the highest level of abstractions and the lowest level of detail. Success is based on an obvious, sincere, sustained, personal commitment to these values, coupled with an extraordinary persistence to reinforcing these values. Clarifying the value system and breathing life into it are the greatest contributions a leader can make. However, the authors note that one individual leader is not sufficient; success requires the commitment of the entire top-level team.

Peters and Waterman observed that excellent companies had five common features that unify them despite having very different value systems. Obviously, unions have vastly different value systems than do businesses, but they can share the following features:

- values are almost always stated in qualitative terms;
- efforts to inspire people are aimed at the very bottom of the organization;
- an organizational commitment to seven dominant values;
- innovative people are at all levels of the organization;
- informal communication.

First, values are almost always qualitative as opposed to quantitative. Peters and Waterman found that poorly performing organizations did not have a clearly defined set of guiding beliefs, or their beliefs were ones that could only be quantified. Quantified beliefs, such as profits, sales, and growth, were measures that could motivate top-level managers but provided little motivation at the lower levels of the organization.

The second feature is an extension of the first. As noted in the previous paragraph, financial objectives do not motivate the lower levels of the organization. Effective value systems use qualitative values and objectives to inspire people from the bottom to the top of the organization.

The third feature is concerned with seven dominant values. Successful companies are concerned not only with the communication of values but with the content of those values. Peters and Waterman identified seven dominant values common to all excellent organizations:

- striving to be the best;
- attention to details;
- recognizing people as individuals;
- superior quality and service;
- innovation;
- informality;
- objectives of economic growth and profit. (In the union environment, democracy and community would be substituted for economic growth and profits.)

Every organization is a mixture of various important value contradictions, such as cost versus service, operations versus innovation, formality versus informality, a control orientation versus a people orientation. Excellent managers, guided by dominant values, can identify these contradictions and clearly make better choices.

The fourth feature involves the presence of innovative people throughout the organization. Excellent organizations recognize that even the best selection process is random and unpredictable and, thus, focus on creating an environment that encourages the development of innovative people.

Informal communication, the fifth common feature, is the very heart of most excellent organizations. It is characterized by the use of first names, managing by walking around, and the feeling of being one big family. An informal environment keeps communications moving and encourages maximum fluidity and flexibility.

Value-driven organizations succeed because their core values provide direction for the entire organization. Core values substitute judgment for rules and innovation for control and create an exciting environment.[24] Union values, dedicated to protecting workers' social and economic rights and improving their lives, are both moral and inspirational. In the area of the seven dominant values, union performance is strong in several areas but weak in others. Like most organizations, many unions pay lip service to being the best, but very few actually have formal programs in place to assure they are the best. The same can be said about details of execution, superior quality and service, and using values to motivate members and employees.

While a union's adversarial role in industrial relations promotes innovation, its extremely intense internal political environment constrains innovation. In brief, most unions are only as innovative as they need to be. However, given a comprehensive strategy to encourage innovation, unions possess the attributes to be among the most innovative of all types of organizations.

STICK TO THE KNITTING

This advice was in response to the wave of business failures related to the growth of conglomerates and mergers in the 1970s. It simply means that an organization should continue to do what it knows best how to do. Cultures that guide superior performance do so by emphasizing reasonably narrow competencies. Peters and Waterman give many examples of organizations that failed because they did not follow this advice. They note that even small acquisitions consume too much of top Management's time and contend this time could have been used more effectively in the mainline business. In addition, the dominant value system and the hands-on Management approach are in direct conflict with diversification strategies. In new and unfamiliar areas, Management loses its credibility and "feel" for the organization. Academic studies also reveal that unchanneled diversification is a losing proposition.

To survive, organizations must grow. Typically, organizational growth is achieved through acquisition or internal diversification. Excellent organizations grow through adaptation and stick very close to their knitting. They place more emphasis on specialization than diversification and prefer internal expansion to mergers or takeovers. However, a few excellent organizations thrived on growth through acquisition by buying small companies that do not change their character—the small-is-beautiful strategy. In short, they acquire and diversify in manageable steps by experimenting.[25]

At first glance, "stick to the knitting" does not appear relevant to unions, since union growth is either through organizing or through acquiring smaller unions with a community of interests, such as the same industry or similar occupations. Thus, unions are naturally inclined to stick to their knitting. However, a closer look reveals that this is not always true and that, in many cases, unions have much to gain by sticking to their knitting—avoiding mergers.

The "stick to the knitting" caution applies even to "mergers" of unions with a strong community of interests. In most cases, the overall strength and vitality of the Labor movement is diminished. The history of union mergers is unclear. Union mergers are especially risky and difficult, because they usually involve an intense clash of cultures. Tragically, a failed union merger is very difficult to identify, since there is no bottom line, no bankruptcy, no divestitures as in the business world. In the union world unsuccessful mergers of unions continue to co-exist—continually draining each union.

From a narrow prospective, a union's main business is industrial relations, and its principal product is the collective bargaining agreement. Whenever a union's resources are channeled into other activities, its primary business is directly diminished. Unfortunately, many unions have ventures outside their primary business, such as retirement homes, nonprofit housing, health care facilities, and various social programs which generally unsuccessful or have had only limited success.

Yet unions have actually been diversifying for ten years. With the growth of associate memberships and the related Union Privilege Benefits Program, unions are becoming true service organizations. For the first time, the member is truly the customer (note that "customer" is not italicized). This is a true innovation with enormous potential, but as in most new ventures there are many risks involved. Obviously, in this case, unions are not sticking to their knitting. When venturing from the familiar, the best advice is to remember that small is beautiful and to experiment.

The managers of the Union Privilege Benefits Program are responsible for overseeing many different types of service providers. These are areas in which they have limited experience and only limited control. Moreover, many service providers are not very knowledgeable about unions. Some may be condescending or even antiunion, but all are extremely eager to make money. This is an explosive combination that requires extreme caution and very close monitoring. Feedback systems are absolutely necessary to continuously collect members' opinions regarding the services provided, their quality, and suggestions for new services. In addition, the AFL-CIO agreement with Household International, Inc. that could generate up to $300 million in royalties based on credit card usage in the next five years is a potentially serious conflict of interest.[26] However, if scrupulously managed, the advantages of the AFL-CIO Union Privilege Benefits Program far outweigh its potential problems. Accordingly, national unions should make the necessary changes in their constitutions to take full advantage of this exciting new strategy.

SIMPLE FORM, LEAN STAFF

Stability and simplicity are the cornerstones of the organizational structure. Peters and Waterman, after thorough analysis, concluded there was a basic simplicity of form, which is stable and understandable to everybody, that is critical for solving the complexities of day-to-day operations. A clarity of values fuels the twin engines of stability and simplicity.

Excellent companies are very flexible in responding to the fast-changing environment. While they appear to be continually reorganizing, their basic form rarely changes. The simplicity in the basic structure actually facilitates organizational flexibility. The most common simple form, or basic building block, is the product or service division. Excellent companies reorganize more flexibly, frequently, and fluidly because they make better use of small divisions or other small units. They also make better use of temporary structural forms such as task forces and project teams.

Virtually every function in excellent companies is decentralized. They place a high value on pushing authority far down the organization and on preserving and maximizing practical autonomy for many people. Closely related to decentralization is the number of hierarchical levels in the organization. In the 1950s and 1960s management theory stressed that an effective span of Management was five to seven people. The Japanese, with a lot of help from U.S. management consultant W. Edwards Deming the father of total quality management (TQM), found this was not true. In fact, the biggest contrast between American and Japanese corporations is the number of middle Management levels. Hands-on management is much more effective when there are fewer people in the middle. This flattening of the traditional, hierarchical corporate pyramid is called corporate downsizing or rightsizing.

Peters and Waterman's studies of consolidation and centralization revealed that a lot of the efficiencies from the economies of scale were not real. New, larger, more complex organizations create inefficiencies that are not evident before consolidation. These inefficiencies are very difficult to eliminate because of conflicting value systems and inadequate controls. Unions considering mergers should pay particular attention to this finding.

Peters and Waterman believe in a lean staff, especially at the corporate level, as a companion to the simple structural form. These two features seem deeply intertwined and self-fulfilling. A simple organization requires fewer headquarters staff to keep things running. As a result they coined a rough "rule of 100," which means that seldom is there a need for more than 100 people in corporate headquarters.

The authors identified the strengths and weaknesses of the following five organizational structures:

- the *functional form* is efficient and does the basics well, but it is not creative or entrepreneurial and does not adapt quickly. Thus, it is apt to miss big chances;
- the *divisional form* can do the basics well and is more adaptive than the functional organization. However, the divisions invariably get too big and suffer all the problems of oversized functional organizations;
- the *matrix form* is in tune with today's realities but almost always ceases to be innovative. It has particular difficulties executing the basics and frequently degenerates into anarchy;
- the *adhocracy form* responds to multiple pressures without introducing a permanent bureaucracy. However, it too can become chaotic if all parties are always chasing temporary problems, and the basics are ignored;
- the *missionary form* provides stability via nonstructural means. If matched with plenty of experimentation within a value set, it can perform well. However, as is true of all dogma-based structures, it can become narrow-minded and rigid.

On the basis of these strengths and weaknesses Program, Peters and Waterman developed a hybrid alternative structure. This new organizational structure is a response to the need

- for efficiency around the basics—the stability pillar;
- for regular innovation—the entrepreneurial or innovation pillar;
- to break old habits—the habit-breaking pillar.

These three prime needs are the pillars of the new organizational structure. The stability pillar is based on maintaining a simple and consistent underlying form and on developing and maintaining broad, yet flexible, enduring values. Peters and Waterman believe the general underlying form should be the product-based division, because it is simpler, clearer, more direct, more tangible, and more honest. They admit a bias toward the division form and against the matrix. Flexible and enduring values are important because, broadly defined, organizational structure is basically a communication pattern.

The entrepreneurial or innovation pillar is built on "small is beautiful." Smallness is viewed as a requisite for continual adaptiveness. Other features of this pillar include the measuring system and the corporate staff. A simple form that does not require vast integrating systems operates effectively with simple measurement systems and smaller staffs. The measurement system provides the staff with information necessary to evaluate the performance of the organization.

The "habit-breaking" pillar involves a willingness to reorganize regularly in response to a rapidly changing environment. Reorganizing involves a willingness to

- break off divisions;
- shift product lines among divisions to take advantage of unique Management talents or the need for product realignment;
- bring top talent together on project teams to solve a special central organizational problem or to execute a central organizational strategy, always with the understanding that the project is temporary;
- reshuffle and reorganize frequently.

These "habit-breaking" structural techniques are remedies to the realities of today's complex, multi-dimensional environmental pressures. The authors contend that these three pillars taken together are a theoretical response to dynamic change and correspond closely to the management systems of many excellent organizations.[27]

Here again, the union experience is mixed as far as simple form, lean staff is concerned. The union structure, while relatively complex and somewhat difficult to understand, is fairly flat. Further, for each of the five levels, from the local union to the international federation, there is a basic simplicity of form that is relatively stable and understandable. The basic building block in the union structure is the national union, which can be considered the equivalent of a product division, and the local unions, the front line unit, are similar to the subdivisions. Union organizations have a history of reorganizing in response to corporate initiatives and social issues.

Union organizations generally do not have many levels of middle Management. For most large national unions, instead of the "rule of 100," a "rule of 10 to 50" is probably more appropriate. Today, after many years of declining membership, most unions already have fairly lean staffs. A typical union hierarchy has eight managerial levels: local union stewards, local union representatives, local union officers, national representatives, staff directors, assistants, regional officers, and national officers. While there are many job titles, there are only three basic classifications in the national union structure: nonmember employees, representatives, and officers. Furthermore, the union tradition of recruiting from the ranks effectively bonds organized Labor's dominant values to its simplicity of form.

Most unions are a combination of divisional, adhocracy, and missionary structures and have much to gain from Peters and Waterman's hybrid organization. The three prime-need pillars provide union officers with a useful guide to improve performance. The stability pillar stresses the need for simple form built on the basics and points out the importance of enduring values. Here the basics for building a union structure are the nine basic union functions. The entrepreneurial pillar emphasizes the advantages of small organizations, small staffs, and simple measurement systems. Most unions are extremely weak in applying measurement systems to evaluate performance. Performance evaluation for union decision makers is covered in Chapter 7.

Unions will probably benefit most from the "habit-breaking" pillar, because there are many old habits that need to be broken. Reorganizing simply involves a willingness to encourage change. It recognizes that individuals possess unique Management talents and that these talents must be brought together frequently, on a temporary basis, to solve pressing problems. This is done by taking union directors and representatives out of their department and assigning them to a project team or by putting the problem or product in their department. Either way, it breaks old habits and brings a new perspective to the decision-making process. However, all reorganization efforts should be part of a comprehensive strategic plan and not an ad hoc response to a particular problem.

SIMULTANEOUS LOOSE-TIGHT PROPERTIES

This attribute is mostly a summary attribute. It involves the balance of firm central direction (tight) with maximum individual autonomy (loose) driven by seven dominant values. Excellent companies are controlled by a remarkably tight culture involving rigidly shared common values. They emphasize regular, open communication that features very quick feedback. In effect, through intense communication, nothing gets very far out of line.

Successful companies excel in their ability to resolve contradictions or paradoxes, such as

- quality versus cost;
- effectiveness versus efficiency;
- execution versus autonomy;
- external versus internal;
- short versus long.

Excellent organizations always resolve the quality versus cost paradox by stressing quality. Quality is the most important word in these companies. It locks on doing the best for every customer with every product or service. Thus, quality fosters innovativeness, productivity, excitement, and an external focus. The compulsion to be "the best" affects every function of the company. High-performance unions emphasize top-quality services and products.

The effectiveness versus efficiency contradiction is resolved by "small is beautiful." Efficiency is traditionally related to large organizations and their assumed economies of scale. In contrast, effectiveness is identified with quality that is associated with small-scale enterprise. Excellent companies, however, have found that the small facility turns out to be the most efficient. Small-facility workers in constant communication and competition with their peers, are more productive than workers in the large facility. Thus, in the long run, both cost and efficiency follow the emphasis on quality and effectiveness. High-performance unions recognize that "small is beautiful" and implement a wide range of chunking and hiving techniques.

The solution to the execution versus autonomy contradiction involves discipline. Here, execution is associated with restrictive rules to control production, while autonomy is associated with the lack of rules and chaos. Autonomy in excellent organizations is a product of discipline based on a few shared values about what really counts. These shared values provide the framework for rules about discipline, details, and standards in which practical autonomy is routine. The nature of these rules is crucial. They must be positive as opposed to negative—underscoring building and expanding versus limiting and restraining. High-performance unions, are driven by a shared-value system based on providing quality service for their members.

The external versus internal paradox is resolved in excellent companies by focusing simultaneously on both sides of the contradiction. Externally, excellent companies are driven by their desire to provide quality, service, and innovative problem solving in support of their customers. This external focus, attention to the customer, is the tightest of all controls and the most stringent means of self-discipline. Internally, the crucial focus is on employees. Excellent companies emphasize quality and peer pressure. Quality is the responsibility of the individual worker, and service standards are self-monitored. Peer pressure is the toughest internal control. It is easy to fool your boss but hard to fool your peers. It is important to note that in the union environment the primary external customer is the employer, and the primary internal *customer* is the member.

Successful organizations thrive on internal competition, the family feeling, informality, fluidity and flexibility, and nonpolitical shifts of resources. They provide their employees with meaning as well as money. In brief, the organization provides the guiding beliefs and creates a sense of excitement, a sense of being part of the best, and a sense of producing something of quality and value. High-performance unions stress Labor's culture and tradition to guide and motivate their officers, representatives, non-member employees, and members.

The last of the contradictions is the short versus long. For excellent companies there is no contradiction. They are primarily concerned with the present and limit their planning to five years.[28] Unfortunately, in most cases, unions do not plan even a year ahead. They basically react to changes in their environment. Peters and Waterman's emphasis on the short versus the long has fallen victim to the test of time. Since *In Search of Excellence* was written, a persuasive body of evidence and collective wisdom establish the critical need for long-term planning. For most unions, the best short-term planning cycle is one year, the best midterm planning cycle is three to four years depending on the union's election cycle, and the best long-term planning cycle is double the short-term planning cycle, or six or eight years. Ideally, these planning cycles should be related to their national conventions.

NEW ATTRIBUTES

Two common themes, small is beautiful and intense, open communications, weave in and out of Peters and Waterman's eight attributes. These two themes are so important in the union environment that they must have equal weight with the other eight attributes.

Small Is Beautiful

Small organizations are easier to manage, and smallness is a critical element in promoting efficiency, effectiveness, creativity, community, solidarity, and communication. Smallness involves less layering and less structuring which induce manageability and commitment. Smallness lets the individual stand out and is a common factor in excellent organizations. This does not mean the large unions are unmanageable or ineffective and inefficient. Nor does it suggest that they be dismantled. It does mean that large, high-performance unions are decentralized and structured to operate as small unions. Decentralized, autonomous units enrich union democracy and empower members. Structuring includes chunking and hiving techniques such as creating committees, task forces, units, departments, and divisions.

Intense, Open Communication

Intense, open communication is so important that the entire next chapter is devoted to it.

SUMMARY

The purpose of this chapter is to identify and apply the attributes and values of excellent organizations to the union environment. The ten attributes and seven dominant values of excellent unions provide a clear guide for high-performance union leaders.

Bias for Action

The most common techniques for encouraging action are organizational fluidity, chunking and hiving, experimenting, and simplified systems.
High-performance unions

- encourage organizational fluidity;
- chunk and hive;
- analyze, plan, and experiment;
- simplify systems.

Close to the Customer

This attribute stresses service, quality, and reliability as strategies for union solidarity and growth.
High-performance unions

- are people-oriented;
- are obsessed with service, quality, and reliability;
- customerize;
- encourage member participation;
- develop new listening strategies;
- expand membership records; to better understand the *customer*;
- establish standards and measure performance;
- identify special niches;
- develop innovative enabling technology applications.

Autonomy and Entrepreneurship

Excellent unions permit a great deal of autonomy far down the organization to encourage innovation.
High-performance unions;

- identify and break down barriers to innovation;
- recognize that people and intense, open communication are essential for innovation;
- implement strategies and structural changes to encourage innovation.

Productivity through People

This attribute holds that performance is maximized through a genuine people orientation based on trust. High-performance unions are genuinely people-oriented.

Hands-on, Value-Driven

Excellent unions recognize the importance of shared values. Value-based organizations succeed because shared values provide direction to the entire organization. The seven dominant values of excellent unions are

- being the best;
- attention to details;
- reorganize people as individuals;
- superior quality and service;
- innovation;
- informality;
- democracy and community.

High-performance union leaders

- always state values in qualitative terms;
- inspire people at the lower levels of the union;
- are committed to the seven dominant union values of excellent unions;
- have innovative people at all levels of the union;
- have formal programs in place to assure it is the best.

Stick to the Knitting

Stick to the knitting means that a union should focus on what it does best—collective bargaining and industrial relations.
High-performance unions

- recognize that their primary product is the collective bargaining agreement;
- reconsider present merger policies;
- concentrate on the nine basic union functions.

Union Privilege and the AFL-CIO must carefully monitor vendors for performance and be keenly aware of potentially serious conflict of interest situations.

Simple Form, Lean Staff

A simple structural form and a lean staff are the cornerstones of successful organizations.

High-performance unions

- are built on the nine basic union functions and enduring union values;
- are decentralized for innovation and flexibility;
- have a small staff and use simple control systems;
- recognize that unique Management talents must be brought together frequently.

Simultaneous Loose-Tight Properties

This attribute is concerned with using shared union values to balance firm central direction (tight) with maximum individual autonomy (loose).
High-performance unions

- stress quality service and products;
- are value-based, customer-focused, and employee-oriented;
- provide their employees with meaning;
- have short-term, midterm, and long-term planning cycles.

New Attributes

Small Is Beautiful

Smallness is common attribute of excellent organizations. High-performance unions are structured to operate as small, mission-driven, value-based, autonomous, democratic unions.

Intense, Open Communication

Intense, open communication is the essence of excellence. High-performance unions promote intense, open communication.

Since *In Search of Excellence* was written in 1982, several of the companies have not done well, and other shortcomings are evident. It has been criticized as dated, too simplistic, too general, and ignoring obvious complications and exceptions. In spite of this, I was attracted to it because its attributes of excellence are, in varying degrees, inherent to union organizations, and it is obvious that unions that possess at least some of these attributes and dominant values will be much more successful than those that do not.

NOTES

1. Thomas J. Peters and Robert H. Waterman, Jr., *In Search of Excellence* (New York: Warner Books, 1982), 3–26.
2. Ibid., 121–125.
3. Ibid., 125–134.
4. Ibid., 134–150.
5. Ibid., 150–154.
6. Ibid., 157–171.

7. Ibid., 171–182.
8. Ibid., 182–196.
9. Ibid., 193–199.
10. The MDOP and LDOP models were developed on the following information, assumptions, and projections. AFL-CIO membership: 13,000,000 members and seventy-eight affiliates. The U.S. Department of Labor, *Register of Reporting Labor Organizations*, 1993 reports 41,097 active filers = 40,000 local unions. 273.

Assumption1: National Union Officers and Representatives   *National Union Officers*   • Each national union has 20 officers.   • Present—78 affiliates x 20 officers per affiliate = 1,560.   • After—55 affiliates x 20 officers per affiliate = 1,100.   *National Union Representative*   • Present—1 representative for every 4,000 members = 3,250 national union representatives.   • After—1 representative for every 5,000 members = 2,600 national union representatives.   *Total national union officers and representatives:*   • Present—3,250 national union representatives + 1,560 national union officers = 4,810 = **5,000.**   • After—2,600 national union representatives + 1,100 national union officers = 3,700 = **4,000.**
Assumption 2: Top Local Union Officers   • Present—40,000 local unions = **40,000** top local union officers.   • After—28,000 local unions = **28,000** top local union officers.
Assumption 3: Other Local Union Officers and Representatives   • Each local union has 15 other officers and representatives.   • Present—40,000 local unions x 15 other officers and representatives/local union = **600,000** other local union officers and representatives.   • After—28,000 local unions x 15 other officers and representatives/local union = **420,000** other local union officers and representatives.
Assumption 4: Activists   • Each local union officer and representative has 3 contacts who are willing the participate in union activities.   • Present—640,000 x 3 = 1,920,000 = **1,900,000** activists.   • After—448,000 x 3 = 1,344,000 = **1,300,000** activists.
Assumption 5: Voting   • Present—30% of 13.0 million AFL-CIO members vote in local union elections = 3,900,000 = **4,000,000** voting.   • After—25% of 13.0 million AFL-CIO members volt in local union elections = 3,250,000 = **3,000,000** voting.

11. Mitchell W. Fields and James W. Thacker, "The Impact of Survey Feedback upon Member Perceptions of the Union," *IRRA Spring Meeting* (Madison, WI: 1985), 477–483.
12. Thomas I. Chacko, "Member Participation in Union Activities: Perceptions of Union Priorities, Performance and Satisfaction," *The Journal of Labor Research* 6, no. 4 (Fall 1985), 363–373.

13. Rosabeth Moss Kanter, *The Change Masters* (New York: Simon & Schuster, 1983), 20–22.

14. Joel Garreau, "100 Percent Inspiration," *Washington Post*, 9 June 93.

15. Kanter, *The Change Masters*, 70–71.

16. Ibid., 101.

17. Ibid., 142–144.

18. Ibid., 144–146.

19. Ibid, 149–152.

20. Ibid., 152–154.

21. Peters and Waterman use "champion" as opposed to Kanter's "change master."

22. David Osborne and Ted Gaebler, *Reinventing Government* (New York: Plume, 1993), xix.

23. Peters and Waterman, *In Search,* 235–278.

24. Ibid., 279–291.

25. Ibid., 292–305.

26. "New Credit Card Offers Better Deal," *The AFL-CIO News*, 1 July 1996, 10,

27. Peters and Waterman, *In Search*, 306–317.

28. Ibid, 318–325.

5

Communication— The Essence of Excellence

In essentials unity, in action freedom, and in all things trust. And trust requires that dissent come out in the open and that it be seen as honest disagreement.

Aristotle (384–322 B.C.)

Good, the more communicated, more abundant.

John Milton (1608–74), *Paradise Lost*

Excellence is related directly to an organization's ability to communicate cultural values, to motivate, and to encourage innovation. Hence, effective communication, the essence of excellence, is the one attribute common to all excellent organizations. Communication is the exchange of information by symbolic messages that convey meaning between two or more people. Key points in this definition are that there must be least two people and that the message is symbolic and meaningful. Symbolic messages include body language, sounds, music, letters, and numbers, plus other symbols that convey meaning.

Communication at its lowest level involves awareness and comprehension. At its middle level, communication provokes interest, evaluation, and conviction. At its highest level, communication triggers action. Quality communication can strengthen commitment to the union, its core objectives, and values. It can also motivate, maintain cohesiveness, and permit members, union employees, and representatives to join with union officers in all important decisions that affect their lives.

Communication is classified as either interpersonal or organizational. Interpersonal communication is a person-to-person exchange of meaningful information, while organizational communication is a major subsystem of an organization that transmits information and conveys meaning to large numbers of people both within and outside the organization. Organizational communication includes formal and informal networks, local area networks, wide area networks, e-mail, magazines, memoranda, meetings, intercom systems, and so on.[1]

INTERPERSONAL COMMUNICATION

Interpersonal communication is communication between two persons or within a small group and includes the perception, attribution, motivation, personality, and the personal development of the message sender and receiver.[2] It imparts knowledge and conveys information by writing, speech, or other various signals. It also permits the exchange of ideas and opinions through shared symbols. Communication is a clearly understood message that furnishes information, influences, and motivates. It is useful to be aware that by adding an *s*, communication then refers to the act or process of communicating. Another useful subtlety—Management communication refers to the class, while communications management refers to the ability to convey values throughout an organization. Management communication is concerned with how managers convey messages, while communications management is concerned with the process of managing the communications system.

The communication process involves the sending and receiving of messages. Communication in its simplest form involves a sender, a message, and a receiver. If any one of these three elements is missing, communication cannot take place. If there is a speaker but no audience, there is no communication. Similarly, there is no communication when the receivers do not understand the language of the sender. The most common methods of communication are speaking and writing by the sender and listening and reading by the receiver. While most communication consists of speaking and listening, there are many other forms of communication.

Figure 5.1 is a detailed graphic of the communication process. The elements of this comprehensive communication model are:

- The sender is a person with needs and values and a reason or desire to initiate a communication.
- The message is the physical form that conveys meaning through one or more receiver's senses. In its simplest form, the physical form uses words and gestures that the receiver is familiar with. Familiarity is known as the "mutuality" of meaning between the sender and the receiver. The most common cause of misunderstanding is the lack of mutuality of meaning.
- The channel is the mode of transmission, which is often inseparable from the message. The channel must always be appropriate for the message. Several common methods are telephone, face-to-face conversation, meetings, memoranda, reports, teleconferences, facsimile, e-mail, and electronic bulletin boards.
- The receiver is the person whose senses—sight, hearing, touch, smell, and taste—perceive the sender's message. The process by which the receiver translates the message into meaningful information depends on the receiver's experiences and values.
- Noise is anything that interferes with, confuses, or distorts the sender's meaning.

- Feedback occurs when the receiver acknowledges the receipt of a message and provides the sender with information about the receiver's understanding of this message. Feedback is necessary to assure that the receiver understands the sender's meaning. It reverses the communication process to determine the reaction of the receiver. In feedback the receiver becomes the sender, and the sender the receiver.

Figure 5.1
A Typical Communications Model

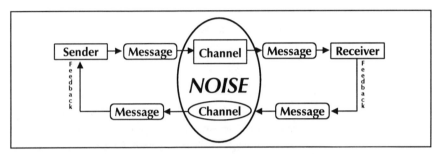

Nonlanguage communication, such as gestures, movements, material things, time, sounds, and space, influences the message's meaning. Nonlanguage communication can:

- repeat the verbal message;
- contradict the verbal message;
- substitute for the verbal message;
- complement the verbal message;
- accent the verbal message.

Nonlanguage communication is especially important since most employees are always trying to understand what their leaders really mean. They look for what is really important as opposed to what is marginally important. They are constantly "reading" or looking for the nonlanguage communication to provide a better understanding of the message. Effective senders, keenly aware of the importance of their nonlanguage communication, make sure it is consistent with spoken or written communication.

Spoken, face-to-face communication is Management's preferred channel of sending messages. Studies show that managers spend 66 to 80 percent of their total work time in this form of communication. Managers generally prefer spoken, face-to-face communication because it tends to be more complete, and permits the sender to judge the receiver's reaction and consequently minimizes misunderstanding.

High-performance interpersonal communicators are

- aware that body movements (kinesics)—facial expressions and hand motions—give clues as to how the message is being received;
- aware that how people place themselves (proxemics) indicates how well the message is being received;

- aware that pauses (chronemics) reflect the sender's confidence—short pauses reflect certainty, while long pauses reflect uncertainty;
- aware that eye movements (oculesis) influence the message;
- aware that physical appearance influences the receiver.

In addition, they

- consider the experience of the receiver;
- avoid technical terms whenever possible;
- select the appropriate medium to send the message;
- minimize the cause of interference or noise in the environment;
- avoid abstract words.[3]

ORGANIZATIONAL COMMUNICATION

High-performance organizational structures are designed to facilitate the flow of information. Organizational communication, like interpersonal communication, involves getting a message from one person to another person or a group. Drucker defines organizational communication as a perception, an expectation, and a demand. He explains that we perceive what we expect to perceive, we see what we expect to see, and we hear what we expect to hear. Thus, he concludes that before there can be effective communication, the sender must know what the receiver expects to perceive. Effective organizational communication, Drucker notes, involves motivation and, consequently, always makes demands. It demands that the receiver change, do something, or believe something. Organizational communication can be effective only when the message keys into the receiver's aspirations, values, and beliefs.

Drucker also sees a bond between experience, perception, and concept formation. It is impossible to communicate a concept unless the receiver can perceive it. Therefore, culture and emotion are two very important constraints on communication. Conflict is usually the result of different perceptions. He observes that what one person sees so clearly, another does not see at all. Accordingly, what the first person argues has no relevance to the other person's concerns, and vice versa. Both probably see reality, but each sees a different part of it. Hence, Drucker concludes that communication is impossible unless the sender knows what the receiver can understand. Good communicators share common experiences and values.[4]

Four factors influence organizational communication:

- formal channels;
- organizational authority structure;
- job specialization;
- information ownership.[5]

Formal channels within organizations help determine who will interact with whom. Studies show that hierarchical arrangements and centralized organizations obstruct good communication. Likewise, organizations with specialized work groups and ownership of information also obstruct the dissemination of information.

Communication networks have unique information exchange and membership characteristics. Researchers have studied the characteristics of the five typical communication networks: star, "Y," chain, circle, and completely connected. The information exchange characteristics are speed, accuracy, and saturation. Speed and accuracy are obvious, and saturation is defined as the amount of information the network can pass along. The membership characteristics are overall satisfaction, leadership emergence, and centralization. Figure 5.2, identifies the pattern of each network, classifies their information exchange characteristics, and rates their membership characteristics.

Figure 5.2
Organizational Communication Networks and Their Characteristics

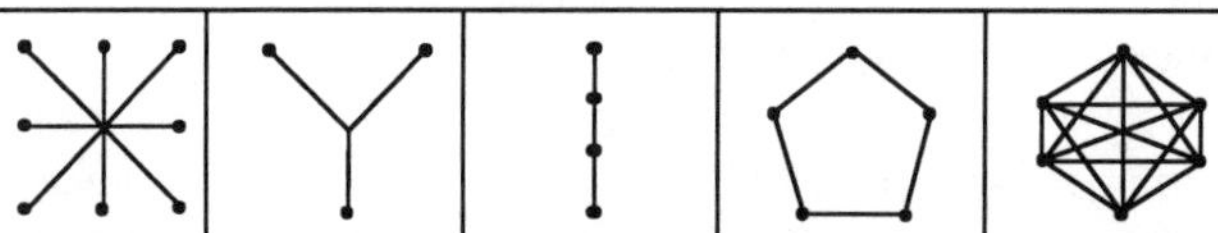

Network Patterns	Star	Y	Chain	Circle	Completely Connected
Characteristics of information exchange					
1. Speed	Fast	Slow	Slow	Slow	Fast / Slow
2. Accuracy	Good	Fair	Fair	Poor	Good
3. Saturation	Low	Low	Moderate	High	High
Characteristics of membership					
1. Overall satisfaction	Low	Low	Low	High	High
2. Leadership emergence	Yes	Yes	Yes	No	No
3. Centralization	Yes	Yes	Moderate	No	No

Source: Based on A. Bavelas, "Communication Patterns in Task-Oriented Groups," *Journal of Acoustical Society of America 22,* (1950): 725–730.

Network centrality is the critical feature that determines whether a network is effective or satisfying to the participants when performing a particular task. Centrality involves the flow of information within the network. Centralized networks, such as the star, reflect the dependence of the members on one person for information. Unfortunately, the star is probably the most common communication network in the union environment, since too many Labor leaders tend to hoard information and trickle it out on a need-to-know basis. On the other hand, decentralized networks, such as the completely connected, reflect the free flow of information among the members. In Figure 5.2 the degree of centralization decreases from the star network to the completely connected network.

Centralized networks communicated faster and more accurately when performing comparatively simple tasks, while decentralized networks worked better when the tasks were more complex. Network centrality influences the selection of a leader and degree of member satisfaction. Members were least satisfied with the star network and most satisfied with the circle and completely connected networks.

Organizational communication, classified by its flow, can be one-way or two-way. One-way communication flows in only one direction—either upward, downward, or horizontal. However, downward is the most prevalent. Two-way communication flows in the same three ways, but it involves an exchange of messages. A study of the distinction between one-way and two-way communication found that one-way communication is quicker when accuracy is easily achieved and appears to be more orderly than two-way communication. On the other hand, it found that two-way communication is essential when accuracy is important. Receivers are more sure of their judgments, but the sender can easily feel attacked in two-way communication.[6]

In addition, communication can be vertical or horizontal. Vertical communication can be from the top down or from the bottom up but usually flows from the top down. Horizontal communication takes place informally between peers and colleagues and crosses the various organizational levels. Informal, horizontal communication involves political risks, which is probably the reason it is constrained in the union environment. In an information-based environment, horizontal communication is more important than top-down, vertical information.

The primary purpose of downward communication is to direct, instruct, evaluate employees and provide information about the organization's mission and core objectives. It flows from manager, to front line supervisor, to worker. Downward communication is frequently filtered, modified, and halted as managers decide what is to be passed to whom. When subordinates lack trust in their managers, information is concealed and distorted. Conversely, insecure managers deliberately withhold information to keep the subordinates dependent on them.

Downward communication cannot work regardless of Management's commitment. Frequently, there is no provision for feedback. In an organization, feedback takes many forms from a simple verbal response to a detailed, comprehensive memorandum. By encouraging employee and member feedback, Management demonstrates concern for them beyond their roles as workers. All that can be communicated downward are commands—not understanding and motivation. Understanding and motivation require upward communication from those who perceive, to the managers who want to understand their perception. Downward communication can be effective only after upward communication has been successfully established.

Upward communication is when front line workers send messages to their superiors. In many organizations upward communication is ineffective because workers simply do not trust their superiors. As a remedy to this problem, managers need to create an environment that encourages worker participation in the decision-making process, rewards openness, and limits inflexible and arbitrary policies and programs. Effective upward communication is always focused on something common and real to both the sender and receiver. It also is firmly focused on the aspirations, values, beliefs, and motivation of the receiver. Communication based on "I" versus "you" does not work. Organizational communication can be effective only if it is based on "us" and "we."[7] Always keep in mind:

- Tell me, and I'll forget.
- Show me, and I'll remember.
- Involve me, and I'll understand.

Horizontal communication is where workers use informal, lateral channels to share information with their peers and colleagues. It usually occurs between members of the same group, between one group and another, between members of different departments and occupations, or between line and staff. Horizontal communication provides a direct channel for organizational problem solving. It is a faster process than downward communication because it eliminates the level-to-level organizational handoffs. It also establishes constructive employee relationships, which are an important part of employee satisfaction. Even though horizontal communication is outside the downward communication process, it should be encouraged by Management because of its many benefits.

The grapevine, a form of horizontal communication, is the normal result of the employee's endless pursuit of information. It is usually alive with rumors and active in all types of organizations. The grapevine is an informal communication network, outside the officially sanctioned communication process, that can either supplement or replace the formal communication network. It can have both positive and negative effects on an organization. It is usually made up of several informal networks that overlap each other at several points. Informal leaders act as message centers for receiving, interpreting, and distributing grapevine information to others. Some well-informed employees belong to more than one grapevine network. Unfortunately, many uninformed managers, believing that grapevines primarily circulate negative rumors, waste resources squelching them.

The facts are that grapevines are frequently faster and more effective than the formal organizational communication network. In addition, studies reveal that grapevines are right about 80 percent of the time and, thus, are a useful means of transmitting messages. Regrettably, they also are very hard to control. Consequently, high-performance managers work with the grapevine rather than fight with it. Some intentionally use the grapevine by "leaking" information. The quality of an organization's communications is

significantly affected by Management's success in listening to, and understanding, the grapevine. Even though the grapevine cannot be suppressed or
controlled, it can be influenced by the way Management relates to it. Given
the intensity of internal union politics and the significance of such issues as
employment security, wages, overtime, promotion, training, and representation, the union grapevine is extremely active and frequently under attack by
incumbent officers.

The four types of grapevines are single-strand, gossip, probability, and
cluster. Figure 5.3 shows the configuration of each type.

Figure 5.3
Types of Grapevines

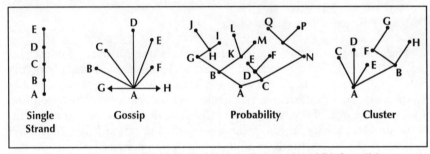

In the single-strand grapevine one person passes the information to a second person, who passes it to a third person, and so on. This is the least accurate grapevine. In the gossip grapevine, one person is the source of what
information is revealed to all the employees he or she contacts. In the probability grapevine, employees are indifferent about whom they pass the information to. In the cluster grapevine, a person shares information with a
few selected employees whom he or she trusts or favors and who share the
information with people they trust or favor. The cluster grapevine is the
most dominant pattern.[8]

Communication systems can also be classified as open or closed. Open
communication systems provide opportunities for both employees and
members to complain freely about the difficulties of the workplace or the
quality of the products and services. Closed systems stifle communication by
restricting upward and horizontal communication, and there is no provision
for feedback.

Even though complaints, grievances in a union environment, are much
more frequent in open systems, this is not necessarily undesirable. In fact, if
managed properly, complaints are valuable because they provide warning,
guidance, and reorientation.[9] Most complaints are the result of the lack of

information or misinformation. An abundance of accurate information is the best way to eliminate rumors and improve employee or member morale. Figure 5.4 presents the various activities involved in a complaint-processing situation.

Figure 5.4
A Typical Complaint-Processing Model

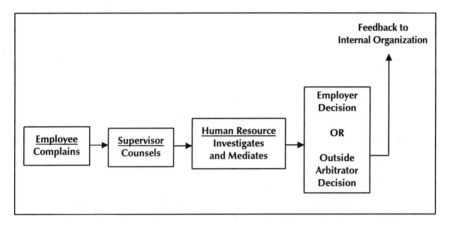

Note that the complaint-processing model is very similar to the grievance system in a union environment. The major difference is that in a nonunion environment, no matter how elaborate the complaint process, Management holds unlimited power and unrestricted authority. Complaint-processing models that include an ombudsman or some form of outside mediation and/or arbitration are rare exceptions to the unlimited power and unrestricted authority of Management. In contrast, in a union environment, the formal grievance system provides a much more equitable balance of power and authority between the grievant (complainant) and Management.

High-quality organizational communication requires

- informal communication systems;
- an extraordinary organizational commitment to high-quality communication;
- physical support and forcing devices.

COMMUNICATION AND INFORMATION

Communication is perception, while information is logic. Communication is an interdependent process that exchanges information, whereas information warns, guides, and reorients—the reasons for Management communications systems. Quality information is entirely different from quality communication. Information is specific, while communication involves the perception of a message. Historically, the problem was how to isolate the information from perception. Now, as a result of the information explosion, we have the problem of handling meaningless communication. Information overload is anything that is beyond what is actually needed. Usually, the less data, the better the information.

Information requires communication, even though communication may not be dependent on information. The more levels of meaning of a communication, the less it lends itself to quantification. Information is always encoded, and this code must be understood by the receiver. The effectiveness of an information system depends on the preestablishment of a communication process.

High-quality information systems thoroughly analyze what information is needed, by whom, and for what purposes and agree on the meaning of each specific input and output. They produce periodic, exception, demand, and predictive reports. Periodic reports show routine organizational information in detailed or summarized form. Exception reports spotlight unique situations that require Management's attention. Demand reports respond to various Management queries. Predictive reports look into the organization's future and are especially important to strategic management.

Kanter sees information as a primary organizational resource since it is critical in the circulation of power and the development of innovators. Her three primary organizational tools are information, resources, and support. She explains that an organization's structure and policies shape three kinds of markets in which an individual must compete for these tools:

- a knowledge market for information—data, technical knowledge, intelligence, expertise;
- an economic market for resources—equipment, facilities, funding, supplies, and so on;
- a political market for support—approval, endorsement, authority.

Kanter notes that "markets" cannot exist in organizations where formal hierarchies determine the allocation of these commodities. Markets can exist only when there is a give-and-take process among the participants.

Kanter teaches that empowerment—the circulation of, and access, to power—encourages innovation. Innovative organizations employ three aids to create an empowering, integrative environment. She identifies these aids to empowerment as

- an open communication system;
- a network-forming arrangement;
- the decentralization of resources.

Kanter believes that the environment, more than the person, makes the biggest difference in the level of innovative managerial activity. In an innovative environment, managers employ power tools and power tactics to implement change. They make new internal and external connections, both organizational and intellectual, and they reach beyond the limits of their jobs. As a common bond, they share the need to exercise their skills in obtaining and using power to accomplish innovation. In short, managers become change masters.

The first empowerment aid is an open communication system. Innovators agree that the most common obstacle to change is poor communications with other departments on which they depend for information. To overcome this obstacle, innovative organizations create open communication systems that

- use immediate, face-to-face information sharing;
- establish open door policies;
- create "openness" in physical arrangements.

The second empowerment aid is network-forming devices. The four major types of approaches to network formation are

- frequent mobility;
- employment security;
- extensive use of formal team mechanisms;
- complex ties that permit frequent inter-unit contact among managers.

The decentralization of resources is the third empowerment aid. Here, the existence of multiple sources of loosely committed funds and the availability of resources at local levels are essential for successful innovation.

However, Kanter warns that unlimited circulation of power without focus can be an organizational disaster. Thus, an organization has to constantly seek to balance the circulation of power with the concentration of power. In the search to balance power, it is important to know that innovation is aided by low formalization at the initiation stage and by high formalization at the implementation stage. Consequently, the employment of the various empowerment aids is most effective within organizational units that deal with the initiation of a project.[10]

COMMUNICATION AND MANAGEMENT

Communication is the foundation of the four basic management functions: planning, organizing, directing, and controlling. Managers spend 70–90 percent of their time communicating, because employees cannot do any constructive work without communicating. They spend about 45 percent of their time communicating with their peers, 45 percent with people outside their work unit, and only 10 percent with their superiors.[11] The higher a manager is in the organization, the greater the time consumed in communicating.

Managers are completely dependent on communication, because it

- is the basis for social interaction within organizations;
- is the vehicle an executive uses to conduct planning, organizing, directing, and controlling activities;
- is the primary means by which people obtain and exchange information;
- represents power in organizations.[12]

Communication is also a vital factor in three managerial roles:

- the interpersonal role, because managers are constantly interacting with people both inside and outside their work unit;
- the informational role, because managers seek and disseminate information on everything that may affect their jobs and responsibilities;
- the decision-making role, because managers collect information necessary to make decisions and send messages regarding their decisions to all people affected by them.[13]

High-performance union managers communicate through their work activities; relations with co-workers; pay, placement, and promotion practices; and constant communication with subordinates, peers, and superiors.[14] Even though high-quality organizational communication has always been extremely difficult to achieve, today's information explosion has made communication problems much more urgent and even more difficult to manage.

CONTEMPORARY COMMUNICATION PRACTICE THEORY

Contemporary communication practice (CCP) theory is based on the premise that the most important communication takes place immediately after a meeting or conference between participants on a horizontal level. In most cases, it is at this time that a peer-opinion leader, a person whose perceptions can strongly influence his or her peers, emerges. Since managers, the message senders, want a positive perception, CCP attempts to make this critical exchange of information more consistent with the intent of the sender. CCP

- makes communication more believable;
- increases the trust between Management and non-Management employees and members;
- provides managers with more opportunities to say yes rather than no;
- develops positive momentum uninterrupted by periods of inertia.

Therefore, CCP applies to almost any behavior that maximizes a positive perception. In the new American workplace, union leaders will assume a much greater responsibility for maximizing positive perceptions of shared-fate, participatory-Management decisions.

Unfortunately, wider use of CCP is often constrained because of Management's traditional assumption that the people who work for them will understand, accept, and act correctly on their communication. However, employee satisfaction surveys in hundreds of organizations prove this assumption wrong. Consequently, tools such as CCP are necessary to improve organizational communication.[15]

CCP is a three-step, behavior-change process that attempts to enlist the help of peer-opinion leaders. First, it identifies the peer-opinion leader. This is frequently difficult because the evaluation of leadership varies. Next, it outlines a strategy for using the peer-opinion leaders effectively. The CCP review process and the endorsement process are two critical opportunities for their participation. Finally, the peer-opinion leaders help augment the manager's message with statements and print communication such as newsletters, brochures, electronic bulletin board messages, and so on.

Many of today's organizations use employee surveys and focus groups more for downward communication than for diagnostic purposes. Involving peer-opinion leaders in the communication process helps create a consistency of support among employees. Therefore, subgroups of peer-opinion leaders are involved in the communication planning and evaluation process at every organizational level.

In a nonunion environment, peer-opinion leaders are usually Management-selected and -controlled, while in a union environment, the union's leaders serves as peer-opinion leaders. Union leadership includes elected officers, representatives, and stewards. For union leaders, peer-opinion roles are extremely risky, because no matter how well it is packaged, it is still Management's message, and everyone knows it. Carrying Management's message is the ultimate political dilemma of union politics. If Management's message is unpopular, no matter how reasonable and essential it is, the union officers will be challenged and possibly defeated in the next election.

Mutual trust is the critical ingredient of any plausible solution to this dilemma. Management and the union leaders must trust each other, and the union members must trust their union leaders. Only politically secure union officers, with the trust of the union members, can be effective peer-opinion leaders. Keys to building this trust are the unrestricted access to all relevant information and effective communication systems that share this information with all affected parties.

COMMUNICATION BARRIERS

Communication is an extremely challenging process involving many barriers. Since eliminating all communication barriers is impossible, the best way to improve communication is to identify the major interpersonal and organizational barriers and develop a strategic communication management plan to reduce them.

The five most common interpersonal communication barriers are

- lack of writing, oral, and listening skills;
- perception and frame of reference;
- personality, interests, emotions, and attitude;
- defensiveness and self-interest;
- assumptions about relationships with others.[16]

The first interpersonal barrier is inadequate writing, oral, and listening skills. To accurately convey meaning is a major challenge. The words or language used to encode the message influences the quality of communication. Misunderstanding and distortion are the result of using words that are too abstract or have too many meanings attached to them. In addition, the message may be overgeneralized or fail to include important subtleties. Unfortunately, this extremely complicated process is further complicated when the sender uses language to intentionally confuse the receiver. Many times superiors intentionally create misunderstandings by withholding necessary information or omitting the emotional content of the message. Likewise, subordinates distort upward communication by failing to include negative information. Solutions for this problem area include study and practice, establishing communication guidelines and standards, using the right emphasis, and requiring feedback.[17]

The second interpersonal barrier is perception and frame of reference. People see the world in different ways because of their knowledge and experience, which are their frame of reference. Language has meaning only if it relates to the receiver's frame of reference. If the sender uses terminology, knowledge, or ideas that are not within the receiver's frame of reference, very little communication takes place. To correct these problems the sender must be sensitive to the world of the receiver, provide adequate information, avoid jargon and acronyms, and actively pursue feedback. Furthermore, knowledge of the values and traditions of the receiver's culture facilitates communication. Thus, to convey the intended meaning, senders also need to try to see the situation from the perspective of the receiver's culture. This interpersonal communication barrier is becoming much more important to union officers because of the increasing diversity of the workforce.[18]

Personality, interests, emotions, and attitude constitute the third interpersonal barrier. The attitudes and emotions of each employee or group regarding collaboration and competition have an immense impact on the quality of communication. "We versus they" and/or "win versus lose" attitudes can quickly polarize positions and obstruct communication. Intense emotions always override reason and logic and, thus, distort communication. Furthermore, information is not likely to be persuasive if the receiver's mind is already made up. Problems in this area can be minimized by avoiding situations that involve bias, prejudice, and emotions. Deferring emotional issues until they can be discussed in a calmer, less emotional manner is another tactic to minimize conflict. Deliberately refraining from expressing personal judgments until the end of the session is still another means to defuse emotions.[19]

The fourth interpersonal barrier is defensiveness and self-interest. Defensive receivers protect their egos, avoid damaging issues, and make excuses for failures. Self-interest screens out negative information from the communication process. Solutions for problems of this type include refraining from verbally attacking receivers; promoting trust, acceptance, and openness; establishing objective standards that are agreed upon; conducting periodic audits; and constantly measuring customer satisfaction.[20]

The fifth interpersonal barrier is concerned with assumptions about, and relationships with, others. Information is always evaluated in terms of its source and discarded if the source is distrusted, unreliable, or uninformed. Everyone agrees that arguments should always be evaluated on their merits, but it is a fact that relations with others are a major influence on the acceptance of information. People are more likely to accept information from people they like and trust. Trust is probably the most important virtue in industrial relations and within the union organization. This barrier can be reduced by promoting trust, integrity, and openness between communicators.[21]

Communication is naturally difficult because messages are not very precise, and receivers filter the message according to their individual backgrounds, needs, ambitions, values, and experiences. An international study involving Japan, Great Britain, and the United States found that 74 percent of the executives surveyed identified communication breakdown as the greatest single barrier to corporate excellence. Poor communication is also a frequent cause of inter-group conflict.[22]

The first step to improve interpersonal communication is to understand that barriers are natural. The next step is to improve the manager's ability to communicate. Interpersonal communication can be improved by expanding the complete knowledge of both senders and receivers. The Johari grid, Figure 5.5, is a very effective tool for analyzing communication barriers and identifying individual interpersonal communication styles. The Johari grid, developed by Joseph Luft and Harry Ingham, includes the four basic kinds of information available in every human communication:

- public information, which is information known to all parties;
- blind information, which is information known to others but unknown to self;
- hidden information, which is information known to self but unknown to others;
- unknown information which is information unknown to all parties.[23]

In part A of Figure 5.5, the four kinds of information are equally balanced. In part B, the public information is expanded, while the hidden and blind information is reduced 50 percent, and the unknown is reduced 25 percent. In part C, the hidden information is expanded as the result of a 50 percent reduction in the public and unknown information, plus 25 percent reduction of the blind information.

Figure 5.5
The Johari Grid

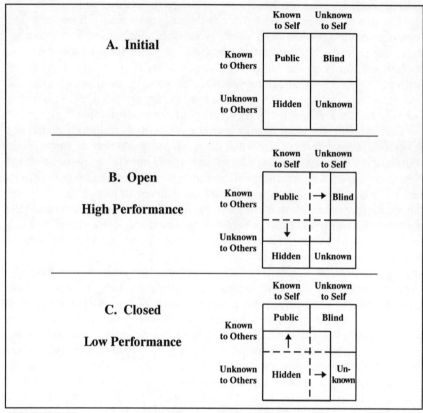

Source: First appeared in *Success Magazine*, August 1987. Reprinted with the permission of *Success Magazine*. Copyright © 1987 by Hal Holdings Corp.

Generally, the size of the public square is a good measure of the quality of the communication. The larger the public square, the greater the information and the better the communication. The more team members know about how the manager makes decisions, the more effective the manager will be. Thus, in regard to disclosure, high-performance managers always provide all relevant information and explain their motives and strategies. Further, they always solicit objective feedback. High-performance managers always share their knowledge and conceal information only when absolutely necessary. Consequently, high-performance managers always seek to increase the size of the public square. Since the Johari grid applies to all team members, every participant should always be working to expand the public square. Members of the best teams know each other so well that they need not spell out their thinking in detail. Large public squares are the key to high performance in participative Management relations.

The six most common barriers to effective *organizational* communication are

- a large, cumbersome, closed organization structure;
- ineffective use of media and internal information systems;
- communication overload for executives;
- too great a status distance between top Management and the front line worker;
- inter-group and intra-group hostility;
- a threatening organization environment.

The first organizational barrier is a large, cumbersome, closed organization structure with confusing and unclear lines of authority, functions that overlap, inadequate or inappropriate policies and programs, and unclear objectives. When lines of authority are unclear or uncertain, communication is very difficult. A large organization, spread out over many locations, makes communication even more difficult. Multi-level hierarchies also contribute to communication problems, because each level introduces some distortion into downward messages. In addition, unclear or uncertain vertical lines of authority become cluttered when too much unnecessary information is confined to very narrow channels. Thus, downsizing advocates argue that elimination of several middle Management levels will dramatically improve organizational communication.

The primary solution to cumbersome organizational size is to break down large units into semiautonomous small work units. As previously explained, this strategy is referred to as "chunking" and "hiving." Large organizations can downsize by eliminating a number of levels within the hierarchy. Delegating more authority is still another way to improve the performance of large organizations. Managers can also use various linking mechanisms such as meetings, committees, task forces, and the exchange of staff to improve communication. These subjects are covered in more detail in Chapter 7.

Ineffective in-house media are the second organizational barrier. Many organizational publications such as newsletters, newspapers, and magazines have low readership, and their credibility is even lower. They are often considered mind-manipulating "propaganda" sheets. Consequently, high-performance organizations constantly evaluate the effectiveness of their in-house media. Organizational publications should never become the propaganda tool of Management. All organizations need a comprehensive, strategic plan for their internal media. This plan should include all appropriate state-of-the-art enabling electronic technologies.

The third organizational barrier is executive overload. Many executives defer or do not pass on important information because they are too busy. Overworked executives need to delegate more responsibility to subordinates, hire more staff assistants, and manage their time more effectively. Time management is covered in the "Managing Time" section of Chapter 3.

Status distance between top Management and the front-line workers is the fourth organizational barrier to quality communication. In this situation, communication is restricted when subordinates are uncomfortable or sometimes even intimidated by the power or prestige of managers and experts. If subordinates are to provide open and objective information, the symbols of Management's power must be de-emphasized.

High-performance managers visit their employees at their workplace and participate in various organizational social events such as picnics, parties, achievement awards, and so on. Top managers stress the shared-fate environment concept when meeting with subordinates. The basis of the shared-fate environment concept is, "We're all in this together," as opposed to focusing on the subordinate's shortcomings. When a manager's prestige is so high that it is impossible to establish open, objective relationships with subordinates, he or she must rely on trusted, top staff assistants to acquire the necessary information.

The fifth organizational barrier is inter-group and intra-group hostility. Hostility between and within groups inevitably results in communication breakdown and tears an organization apart. Interpersonal communication cannot be improved until personal relationships improve. Here the problem is not improving writing and speaking skills but eliminating distrust, fear, or prejudice. The remedies to this problem start with recognizing the existence of the problem and then implementing such practices as establishing bonding objectives, issue negotiations, third-party mediation, and smoothing over the differences.

A threatening organizational environment is the sixth communication barrier. In a threatening environment employees fear reprisals for constructive criticism and, thus, suggestions are driven underground. However, even in a threatening environment, communication is inevitable. In such an environment the formal communication process is replaced by the informal "grapevine" communication as the main source of information. Frequently, this information is inaccurate and biased. To minimize this problem, managers should intensely cultivate trust, rather than force. They also should actively encourage feedback and always follow up on it. Employees should be empowered to perform, and their performance should be evaluated. Managers should implement strategies to improve employee communication.[24]

High-performance organizations promote better communication by

- establishing a supportive environment;
- encouraging assertive communication;
- encouraging active listening.

First, a supportive environment

- gives and asks for information, rather than praising and blaming;
- collaborates in defining problems and finding solutions, rather than imposing them;
- deals with others honestly, rather than manipulating them;

- identifies with others' positions and problems, rather than ignoring them;
- respects others, rather than dominating them;
- postpones taking sides and is open to new information and interpretations, rather than competing.

A supportive communication environment requires a comfortable fit among thoughts, emotions, and communication. It also recognizes the uniqueness and importance of the individual.

Second, assertive communication is self-expressive, honest, and direct. It projects personal rights without violating the other person's rights. It also expresses personal needs, opinions, and feelings openly and honestly. Nonassertive communicators do not stand up for their rights and are usually hesitant, apologetic, or fearful. It is very important to be aware that assertive communication is entirely different from aggressive communication. An aggressive communication is when an individual stands up for his or her rights without regard for the rights of the other person.

Third, listening, only about 25–50 percent efficient, is by far the weakest communication skill. This is because people can speak about 100 to 200 words per minute, while they can think at a rate of between 400 to 500 words per minute. This enormous difference between speaking and thinking permits an undisciplined mind to wander off to other subjects.

High-performance managers are active listeners. In active listening, the receiver tries to understand the sender's facts and feelings from the sender's perspective. Active listening attempts to understand the total meaning the sender is trying to convey. This involves receiving both the content and context of the message, which requires noting all the sender's cues, both verbal and nonverbal. The willingness to listen also depends on whether the sender has something significant and relevant to say. The following techniques can facilitate active listening:

- paraphrase—restate in the receiver's own words the sender's message;
- perception checking—the receiver describes what he or she perceives to be the sender's intention;
- behavior description—considering specific, observable actions of the sender to better understand his or her motives, personality, or characteristics;
- allow sufficient time to hear the entire issue;
- no talking![25]

Like most things in this world, high-quality communication does not just happen. High-performance unions develop and implement strategic communication management programs that are connected to the organization's mission. Their strategies focus on the following three factors, which are critical for high-performance organizations:

- full and open communication;
- active membership participation;
- mutual trust.

Communications management starts with situation analysis, which includes culture, history, mission, services, standards, and competition. The communication management team must recognize the need to determine the audience's values, priorities, and interests. Consequently, high-quality communication management programs analyze economic, social, legal, political, and technical systems. They also take full advantage of all advanced enabling technologies to facilitate communication. High-performance unions develop a comprehensive communications management program, have contingency plans in case of a communication breakdown, and continuously evaluate their communication programs.

SUMMARY

High-quality communication, the clearly understood exchange of information between two or more people, is a defining attribute of all excellent organizations. Communication motivates and encourages innovation, transmits knowledge and information, and permits the exchange of ideas and opinions. Communication can be classified as interpersonal or organizational.

Interpersonal Communication

Interpersonal communication includes the perception, attribution, motivation, personality, and personal development of the message sender and receiver. The most common methods of communication are speaking and writing by the sender and listening and reading by the receiver. Nonlanguage communication also plays an important role in the communication process.

High-performance union communicators

- are highly skilled at sending and receiving messages;
- recognize that how a person perceives a message depends on his or her experiences;
- use the appropriate medium for sending messages.

Organizational Communication

Organizational structures facilitate the flow of information. Organizational networks and various classifications of communication are explained in this section. Organization communication can be classified as one-way or two-way communication. One-way communication is criticized as ineffective, and the grapevine is recognized as an important form of informal, horizontal communication.

High-performance union communicators

- recognize that high-quality communication keys into the receiver's aspirations, values, and beliefs;
- provide an extraordinary organizational commitment to high-quality communication;
- establish decentralized communication networks;
- encourage informal communication systems and skillfully manage the grapevine;
- design structures to facilitate the flow of information;
- take advantage of recent advances in multi-discipline surveying techniques to better understand the attitudes, aspirations, and objectives of union members and employees of the union;
- use advanced enabling technologies to promote communication;
- provide strong physical support and forcing devices for achieving it.

Communication and Information

Information is different from communication. Information warns, guides, and reorients—three reasons for managing communication systems. Information, a primary organizational resource, is critical in the circulation of power and the development of innovators. Organizational structure and policy shape the markets in which individuals compete for information. It is important to note that markets cannot exist in hierarchical structures. Empowerment, the circulation of, and access to, information, encourages innovation.

High-performance union communicators

- provide the right information to the right people for the right purpose;
- develop an empowering environment where people compete for information;
- form open communication systems;
- form completely connected networks;
- decentralize resources.

Communication and Management

Communication is the foundation of the four basic management functions and is a vital factor in Management's interpersonal, information, and decision-making roles.

High-performance union communicators

- constantly interact with people;
- recognize that the information explosion has made communications problems even more difficult to manage.

Contemporary Communication Practice Theory

Contemporary communication practice (CCP) theory attempts to make the critical exchange of information more consistent with the intent of the sender by enlisting the help of peer-opinion leaders. In the new American workplace, union leaders and negotiators will be called upon more often to serve as peer-opinion leaders.

High-performance union communicators

- require that Management provide access to all relevant information and that high-quality communication systems are in place to share this information with all affected parties;
- use member and employee feedback techniques for upward communication and diagnostic purposes;
- recognize that mutual trust and credibility are the keys to success in the new American workplace.

Communication Barriers

This section identifies the most common interpersonal and organizational barriers and provides solutions to minimize them. Since elimination of all communication barriers is impossible, communication management is essential.

High-performance union managers

- identify interpersonal and organizational communication barriers and develop Management strategies to reduce them;
- recognize that interpersonal communication can be improved by expanding the knowledge of both senders and receivers;
- promote organizational communication by establishing a supportive environment and encouraging assertive communication and active listening.

NOTES

1. Howard M. Carlisle, *Management: Concepts, Methods, and Applications* (Chicago: Science Research Associates, 1982), 421–422.

2. Judith R. Gordon, *Organizational Behavior* (Boston: Allyn and Bacon, 1991), 296.

3. "Interpersonal Communication," *The Leader, Manager, and Supervisor* 2, no. 4, April 1993, 1.

4. Peter F. Drucker, *Management Tasks, Responsibilities, Practices* (New York: Harper & Row, 1985), 483–487.

5. James A. F. Stoner, *Management* (Englewood Cliffs, NJ: Prentice-Hall, 1978), 480.

6. Ibid., 471.

7. Drucker, *Management*, 491–493.

8. Stoner, *Management*, 485–486.

9. James T. Ziegenfuss, Jr., *Organizational Troubleshooters* (San Francisco: Jossey-Bass, 1988), 99.

10. Rosabeth Moss Kanter, *The Change Masters* (New York: Simon & Schuster, 1983), 156–177.

11. Stoner, *Management*, 466.

12. Carlisle, *Management*, 420.

13. Stoner, *Management*, 465.

14. Drucker, *Management*, 400.

15. David B. Freeland, "Turning Communication into Influence," *HRMagazine*, Sept. 1993, 93.

16. Carlisle, *Management*, 426.

17. Ibid.

18. Ibid., 428.

19. Ibid., 430.

20. Ibid.

21. Ibid., 431.

22. Ibid., 421.

23. Ibid., 433.

24. Ibid., 434–440.

25. Gordon, *Organizational*, 306.

6

High-Performance Union Decision Makers

When it comes to creating the best decisions, what will matter henceforth is collective brilliance—not individual brilliance.

Anonymous

Weigh matters carefully, and think the hardest about those that matter most.
Baltasar Gracian, *The Art of Worldly Wisdom: A Pocket Oracle*

Everyone makes dozens of decisions a day. A few are important; most are somewhere between important and trivial. Decisions can be made by individuals or made collectively. They can be personal decisions or organizational decisions. Some will be high-quality, rational decisions, and others will be faulty, irrational decisions; most will be somewhere in between. The objective of this chapter is to improve the quality of decisions and to increase the awareness of the roles of risk and ethics in the decision-making process.

DECISION THEORY

Decision making is an extremely complex process that involves managing risks. Since the management of risks affects the lives of others, decisions are always subject to ethical evaluation. Figure 6.1, shows theory, risk, and ethics as three separate, inextricably interlocked concepts. Every decision involves these three concepts in varying degrees and combinations.

Union decisions, like business decisions, have four basic characteristics. First, all decisions are concerned, to some degree, with the future. Second, all decisions will have an impact on other functions, other areas, and the union as a whole. Third, all decisions include a number of qualitative factors such as

Figure 6.1
Decision Theory-Risk-Ethics
Relationship

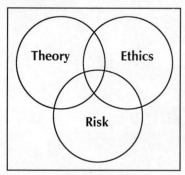

Theory   Ethics

Risk

Source: Risk, 2d ed., Spring 1989, Center for Instructional Development and Evaluation, University College, University of Maryland.

risks, ethics, and social and political beliefs. Fourth, all decisions can be classified according to their frequency of occurrence.[1]

Decision making is about evaluating alternatives and their consequences. Several criteria for evaluating the effectiveness of a nonprofit organization's decisions are public interest, political efficiency, and cost-benefit analysis.[2] The problem is to predict the results of taking an action before harm occurs. Thus, quality decision making requires information and good communication before, during, and after the decision-making process.

Since important decisions, the make-or-break points for an organization, require a lot of resources, time, thought, and hard work, high-performance decision makers make very few important decisions. Important decisions, which always involve major risk, should never be rushed, especially when the decision maker is under stress. High-performance decision makers take time to thoroughly think the problem through. Unfortunately, too many important decisions are based on habit, intuition, advice of "experts," snap judgments, impulse, and just plain chance.

Decision theory includes both the descriptive and the prescriptive decision-making models. The descriptive model is the real, rather than the ideal, decision process. It includes all the shortcuts, omissions, and decision mistakes inherent in the real world of decision making. It describes how people, given alternatives and their consequences, make decisions individually or in groups. It is concerned with group interactions, the mental processes groups go through, and the rules groups apply in arriving at preferred choices.

In contrast, the prescriptive model is concerned with how a decision should be made. It includes systematic and logically sound procedures that improve the decision-making process. The rationality of the prescriptive model is resource-related. This means that the rationality of decisions is limited by the availability of time and resources and the willingness to commit them to the decision-making process. A completely rational condition is a condition in which all the information is available for all the alternatives involved in the decision. Important decisions are usually very complex and include too many variables, too many alternatives, and too much information to consider in the available time. Therefore, even the most critical decisions are made under conditions of limited rationality.

Personality traits also limit the rationality of the decision. An individual's orientation toward risk, tolerance for ambiguity, and patience affect a decision's rationality. Ambiguity describes how well a person can tolerate unsettled conditions and disruption. Patience measures how long a person is willing to wait for the optimal decision.

There are four-, five-, and six-step prescriptive decision-making models. This book uses the four-step prescriptive model, as seen in Figure 6.2.[3]

Figure 6.2
The Four-Step Decision-Making Process

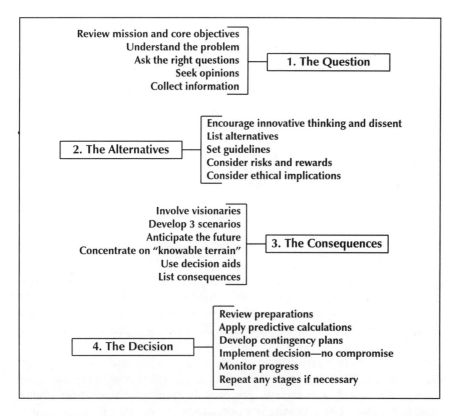

Quality decisions convert vague mental visions to more explicit pictures that can be described verbally. To make good decisions, missions and core objectives, also referred to as strategic objectives, must have real meaning to the decision maker. Consequently, clear missions, core objectives, and strategies are essential for good decisions.

Missions and strategic objectives are concerned with the future welfare of the union organization and define an ideal or perfect situation. Tactical objectives, policies, and programs are the means of achieving the strategic objectives. Operating objectives, policies, and programs include the daily operations of the union and are a means of achieving the tactical objectives.

A primary objective of high-performance union decision making is to maximize the efficiency of the union's resource-conversion process for attaining strategic objectives. A resource-conversion process refers to the various combinations of resources that are consumed to produce a product or to provide a service.

Typical union decision areas are

- resource allocation;
- scheduling of operations;
- supervision of operations;
- control of operations.[4]

The basic types of union resources included in a typical resource-conversion process are

- membership;
- equipment;
- facilities;
- technology;
- workforce;
- volunteers;
- supplies;
- information.

The Decision Process

As previously noted, there are several different decision-making models. For readers who may already be using another version there is no need to change. The critical point is that high-performance union decision makers use a formal process for all important decisions, and the decision maker ultimately determines the importance of each decision. The decision maker also determines how much time and effort he or she is going to expend on each decision. While a formal decision-making process does not guarantee a correct decision, it does increase the probability of a satisfactory or even a quality decision. The following is an expansion of each step in our four-step decision model.

The Question. To make high-quality decisions it is necessary to review the understand the problem in terms of mission and core objectives. Therefore, asking the right question in terms of mission and core objectives is the most critical step in making a high-quality decision. A high-performance union leader's first decision-making responsibility is to make sure that his or her organization is asking and answering the right questions.[5] The quality of the questions and information provided should be directly related to the complexity of the issue. Major decisions obviously take more time and consume more resources than less important ones.

The following is an often-told example of the importance of asking the right question. The Sharpe Drill Co. was unable to provide special, high-quality drills at an acceptable price to a major, longtime customer and was about to lose its business. Maxwell Sharpe, president of the Sharpe Drill Co., organized a decision-making team and called a brainstorming session. Most of the discussion revolved around changes in the present production process until the question, "What business are we in?" was asked. The unanimous answer was, "Making drill bits." However, after much discussion it became clear that the company was in the broader business of making holes. Given this entirely new perspective, a decision was made to develop a laser beam technology that could burn the holes. Thus, the Sharpe Drill Co. entered an exciting and very profitable new line of business and retained a very satisfied longtime customer. High-performance unions are in the business of representing workers' interests, providing community, and changing workers' lives for the better. The concept of providing community opens exciting, new opportunities for innovative union leaders.

To adequately define the question, it is first necessary to collect information. In general, the amount of time spent on collecting information should be balanced with the other three steps. Typical information-collecting activities include consultation with stakeholders, literature search, review of written reports, examination of case histories, field trips, and expert opinion. It is also extremely important to remember that including the right people is just as important as collecting the right information. Expertise and experience can be just as valuable as information from written reports. Further, information is useless unless communicated, in advance, to the people who need it.

The Alternatives. In the alternative stage, innovative thinking must be enthusiastically encouraged. We have already seen that innovation is synonymous with excellent organizations. New ideas must be respected and taken seriously, even if some are badly articulated, half-formed, or far-fetched. Real dissent between people is not only unavoidable but absolutely essential. The most common failure of managers is that they are not patient or stimulating enough in this creative stage. Impatience, discourtesy, and intolerance are the most serious common failings in the second stage. Ideas are ultimately rejected only with care and courtesy. Hence, waste is an indispensable element of quality decision making. High-performance union managers persuade people to suggest alternatives and learn to tolerate waste. Today, any organization in which the people believe that innovative thinking is thankless or dangerous is in serious trouble.

Personal survival is a common concern for most people, and the safest assumption is that survival is best guaranteed by gaining a reputation for soundness and orthodoxy. Thus, too many people believe that it is not worth the risk to be considered creative or imaginative. High-performance union managers recognize this problem and, thus, encourage and reward people for being innovative.[6]

All alternatives should be written down, no matter how far-fetched or foolish they may seem. Next, there must be guidelines to limit the list of alternatives. Several typical guidelines in this culling process are long- and short-range plans, objectives, structure, functions, programs, policies, costs, facilities, and capabilities.[7] Then the risks and rewards and ethical implications associated with each alternative are considered.

The Consequences. The consequences stage is concerned with the future of each alternative. This stage is the most difficult stage because it is imprecise, uncertain, unrewarding, and mentally exhausting. It is impossible to foresee everything that will happen, but it is possible to develop scenarios about what might happen. A scenario is a narrative description of a possible state of affairs or developments over time. More formal, it is a hypothetical sequence of events constructed for the purpose of focusing on the causal process and the decision points.[8] More simply, scenarios are word pictures that make excellent forecasting tools. Poetically, scenarios are freedom from bondage to the past. Scenarios are generally classified as economic, social, legal, technical, and political systems. The format of a scenario can be long or short essays, outlines, tables, graphs, or charts.

It is obvious that while the future is unpredictable, it must be anticipated. Thus, an effective plan should recognize the possibility of at least three scenarios. In large organizations, forecasters develop and distribute a manageable number of scenarios to provide managers with sufficient insight into the different major dimensions of the future. In most union organizations, the manager is also the forecaster.

Ben Wattenberg, futurist and author of *The First Universal Nation*, recommends that futurists concentrate on the "knowable terrain." His knowable terrain, the immediate to near future, not more than ten years—is composed of three parts. First are the things we have been told happened but never did. Second are the trends, conditions, and developments that have already happened and are likely to stay in place. Third are the things that are not yet in place but are likely to happen. This near-term analysis of "not happened," "already happened" and "likely to happen" is the safest and most practical approach to future studies. To Wattenberg's knowable terrain, I add a "not likely to happen" category.

In the union environment, there is a wide range of subjects for which scenarios can be developed. Economic subjects are internal trends in products, services, workforce, industry, and competition and external trends, which include gross domestic product (GDP), inflation, employment, interest rates, energy, foreign imports, and so on. Noneconomic subjects are technology, changing social values, government regulations, potential legislation, Labor union activities, future elections, political and social changes, demographic trends, and so on. Subject selection is obviously a complex issue and should be thoroughly analyzed to assure that it satisfies the needs of the union.

Next, it is necessary to determine the number of scenarios. While there is a wide range of opinions on this issue, three is ideal. Typically, to minimize risk, high-performance decision makers develop a best-case scenario, a worst-case scenario, and a most-likely scenario. Useful future scenarios. require

- the patience to systematically work through a whole range of consequences associated with each alternative;
- the experience to provide insight into the problem and how others are likely to react to the decision;
- the wisdom to apply the experience.[9]

Scenarios are used to evaluate the alternatives, identify possible dangers, and develop contingency plans. A quality scenario never depends on luck or opponents' mistakes, because the consequences of each alternative are carefully thought through. Quality scenarios are based on

- a clear appraisal of the present situation;
- a fully imagined picture of the future;
- recognition that trends are not infallible guides to the future.

Visionaries are essential in the consequence stage, so high-performance union officers surround themselves with people who are visionaries. In this stage, negative thinking is just as valuable as positive thinking, so conscientious critics and worriers are equally valuable to the team. It is important to be aware that people who are good at stage 2, the alternatives, are not necessarily good at stage 3, the consequences, because different skills are involved. The person who sees new and imaginative alternatives is not necessarily the person who can think through the consequences and imagine all the implications associated with an alternative. Each step requires special skills and talents. Forecasters, visionaries, and worriers are dependent on decisive people, and vice versa.[10]

Decision aids are techniques or tools that can help the decision maker reach the best available decision. The more common aids include decision matrices, decision trees, model forecasting, linear programming, game theory, and linear regression.[11] High-performance union decision makers use the simple- and weighted-decision matrices. Union decision makers who become part of a participative-Management decision team could be exposed to the other, more sophisticated decision aids. If you are ever in this situation, the bibliography will provide useful information.

The decision matrix is helpful when important personal or collective union decisions involve two or more alternatives with two or more common criteria. The decision matrix is especially helpful with such important personal decisions as buying a house, car, major appliance, insurance, and so on. For a union decision maker, the decision matrix can help with such decisions as purchases of supplies and equipment; personnel selection and promotion; selecting an arbitrator or consultant, an organizing target, the type of insurance coverage or investment, and so on.

It is important to remember that even though a decision matrix is intended to bring order to complex decisions, it is highly subjective. The decision matrix relates a limited number of subjectively chosen alternatives through a subjective ranking by subjectively chosen criteria. It, like most decision aids, requires self-imposed discipline to structure thinking. There are two types of decision matrices: the simple-decision matrix and the weighted-decision matrix.

The simple-decision matrix, Figure 6.3, is a decision aid that employs the concept of utility value to force a detailed analysis of each alternative according to selected criteria. Utility value is defined as the subjective value a person places on things or outcomes. It is the degree of satisfaction derived from a service, product, activity, outcome, and so on. The criteria are usually ranked on a scale of 1 to 5 or 1 to 10. The highest total is considered the best decision. As noted earlier, union decision makers who are uncomfortable with mathematics can still benefit from the simple-decision matrix by relying on their personal judgment and experience to rank alternatives.

Figure 6.3
The Simple Decision Matrix

The Alternatives	Major Decisions	Minor Decisions	Experience	Education	Primary Occupation	TOTAL
Arbitrator A	3	4	2	2	2	11
Arbitrator B	3	3	3	3	3	15
Arbitrator C	4	3	5	4	4	20
Arbitrator D	3	2	5	4	4	18

Consequences / Criteria

Selection of Arbitrators

5 = best
1 = worst

The weighted-decision matrix, Figure 6.4, adds a weighting factor that reflects the degree of importance of the criteria to the simple-decision matrix. Weighting can also be thought of as a rating. Based on the decision makers utility value, or opinion, a value, less than 1, is assigned to each criterion so the total for all criteria equals 1. The weighted-decision matrix process consists of the following five steps:

- identify all alternatives (inputs);
- establish the selection criteria (outputs);
- construct the matrix chart;
- assign the weighting factors;
- calculate the results.

Figure 6.4
The Weighted Decision Matrix

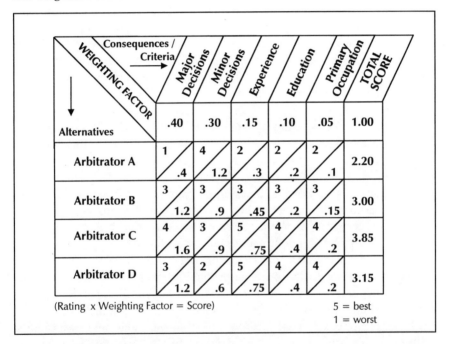

Consequences / Criteria → WEIGHTING FACTOR ↓ Alternatives	Major Decisions	Minor Decisions	Experience	Education	Primary Occupation	TOTAL SCORE
	.40	.30	.15	.10	.05	1.00
Arbitrator A	1 / .4	4 / 1.2	2 / .3	2 / .2	2 / .1	2.20
Arbitrator B	3 / 1.2	3 / .9	3 / .45	3 / .2	3 / .15	3.00
Arbitrator C	4 / 1.6	3 / .9	5 / .75	4 / .4	4 / .2	3.85
Arbitrator D	3 / 1.2	2 / .6	5 / .75	4 / .4	4 / .2	3.15

(Rating x Weighting Factor = Score)

5 = best
1 = worst

The weighted-decision matrix concept also assumes that the highest score is the best choice. However, this process is extremely sensitive to the assignment of weighting factors. Thus, the quality of the outcome is determined by the degree of honesty and objectivity of the decision maker.[12]

Decision-tree analysis, model forecasting, game theory, linear programming, and regression analysis are mathematical decision aids beyond the scope of this book. However, it should be noted that a wide variety of computerized, decision-support system applications is available to simplify the process. These applications search an organization's database for information, analyze this information in various ways, and predict the impact of alternatives before they become a decision.

It must be reemphasized that it is not the purpose of this book to teach the various theories and concepts but to merely expose the reader to them because of their relationship to management theories and concepts. The actual teaching is left to Labor education schools and junior colleges, colleges, universities, and union education departments.

The Decision. The fourth stage, the decision, requires judgment and courage because decisions trigger action—judgment because the distinction between alternatives can be very fine, and courage because most decisions involve risk.

Basically, decisions are made four ways. The first way is incremental decision making, which refers to making a series of small decisions rather than taking a comprehensive approach. The second way is the remedial decision which involves devising the rationale after the decision has already been made. The third way is the serial approach, which involves a chain of decisions, each entirely separate, with no set objective. The fourth way, by far the best way, is the rational, prescriptive approach to decision making described in the preceding material.

The quality of the decision is determined by the quality of the preparations. The time for decision making can be minutes, hours, days, or even years. The manager is responsible for setting the pace of the decision-making process and for determining the right moment to make the decision. Paralysis from fear to make a decision can be fatal. Regardless of the preparations, the following decision-making checklist helps to assure quality decisions: Were the right questions asked? Were at least three alternatives considered? Were the consequences of each alternative considered? Were plans for contingency plans developed?

Most decisions fail because managers neglect to subject their decisions to two predictive calculations—the probability of success and the balance between benefits and costs. These two fundamental calculations, both judgmental and intuitive, should precede every important decision.

Uncertainty is a critical factor in all decisions. The only way to cope with uncertainty is to subject the decision to the discipline of numbers. Assessing the probability of success and balancing the benefits of success against the risks of failure are two different calculations. Each alternative has a unique blend of probability calculations and risk/reward balance that can be compared only indirectly to other alternatives. Probability is explained in the "Risk and Probability" section of this chapter. There are no magic numbers. The probability of success can be classified as simply high, medium, or low. However, it is better to assign numbers such as 90 percent, 75 percent, 50 percent. The following questions should be asked for each alternative. What are the benefits? What are the risks? What type of risks? How expensive are these risks? Whenever possible, dollar values are the most useful for comparing options.

It is important to realize that even top-quality probability analysis and contingency planning cannot eliminate risk. Still, the greatest danger to an organization is acting without thinking through the consequences of the decision. In decision making there are no certainties, only risks. It is unforgivable to pretend that risks do not exist. The consequences of each decision must be continually monitored so contingency plans can be implemented if the consequences are not what the decision maker expected. The availability of contingency plans lessens the chances of becoming irrationally overcommitted to a faulty course of action. Unfortunately, too many union officers ignore risks and do not develop planning contingencies to minimize them.

Once the decision is made, and contingency plans are complete, the rules change. The open-mindedness associated with decision making should be replaced with the single-mindedness necessary for effective implementation. Tragically, for too many unions, the decision triggers the start of a new round of internal strife. In such unions, some people covertly attempt to rescind, delay, undermine, and sabotage the decision. In addition, many unions are unable to effectively implement their decisions because of lack of resources or because their managers, supervisors, or employees lack the necessary skills.

Decisions facing such obstacles have very little chance of achieving their expected success. Further, decisions that are seen as the arbitrary views of one person or a small faction of the organization have much less chance of success than decisions that are seen as a product of an open, participatory, decision-making process. On the other hand, properly managed decision making not only helps to create the best decision but secures the support needed for implementation.

There are three instances where decisions can be harmful or inadequate:

- when the decision-making process is poor—the implementation is irrelevant;
- when decision-making process is sound, but the decision wrong—whatever happens in the implementation stage will be harmful;
- when the decision-making process is sound, but the implementation is mishandled because of incompetent people or inadequate resources—even the right decision will be wasted.[13]

The decision-making process is ongoing and iterative, since at any point it may be necessary to repeat one or more of the stages. From the context of the union, high-performance decision making must be seen as a collective endeavor that uses the minds of all the people affected by the decision.[14]

Ben Heirs, author of *The Professional Decision Thinker: America's New Management and Education Priority*, points out that consequences, complexity, and change, three "C" factors, have emerged in the past decade to render informal decision making obsolete. Today's important decisions involve many complex economic, environmental, social, political, and legal consequences. In addition, Heirs continues, dynamic change requires more frequent and important decisions that require complex information and assumptions. Heirs concludes that today's managers cannot make decisions in isolation. They must create an organizational environment that encourages quality and collective decision making. High-performance decision makers understand and apply a prescriptive, decision-making process and communicate these rules and practices to the people who work for them.[15]

Heirs warns that organizational disasters can result from thoughtless or shortsighted decisions. In contrast, tangible benefits can accrue to an organization with a well-managed approach to decision making. An organization will thrive tomorrow only if today's managers make the right decisions. Heirs notes that a manager is both a decision maker and a manager of the efforts of other decision makers in the organization. In addition, he continues, managers have two other related tasks. First, they manage a decision-making team, and second, they manage a decision-implementing team. Heirs points out that the makeup of these teams may or may not be the same since some people are strong decision makers but weak decision implementers, and vice versa.

Heirs is convinced that quality decisions can be made only if a formal process is followed. High-performance decision making is a discipline that must be applied by both the individual managers and the collective mind of the organization. There is an overriding need for clarity and objectivity at each stage of the decision-making process. However, it is important to realize that high-performance decision makers do not submit all their decisions to a rigorous, formal decision-making process, just the ones they feel are important. The degree of effort varies for each decision according to the time and resources available. As union decision makers become more familiar with the four-step decision model, it becomes an inherent mental process—automatically proceeding from the question, to alternatives, to consequences, to decision.[16]

Quality Decisions

A quality decision is one that maximizes results with a minimum consumption of resources. In his search for this elusive combination, Peter F. Drucker found that the Japanese approach to decision making was very different from America's. He determined that the essentials of Japanese decision making were their focus on defining the question, encouraging dissenting opinions, and selecting alternatives, rather than finding the right solution.

Drucker's findings do not in any manner conflict or replace our four-step decision-making model. Rather, they significantly supplement, enrich, and enhance it—a combination that produces a more effective, rational decision maker. In regard to decision making, Drucker sees it not as a mechanical task but as a risk-taking challenge to judgment. Judgment involves a choice between alternatives, which is rarely a clear choice between right and wrong but a choice between "almost right" and "probably wrong." He contends that understanding the problem is more important than finding the right answer. He sees decision making not as an intellectual exercise but as a process that mobilizes the vision, energies, and resources of the entire organization.

In the question stage, Drucker emphasizes that decisions start with opinions, not facts. He believes that only by starting with opinions can a decision maker find out what the decision is all about. Testing the feasibility follows the gathering of opinions. High-performance decision makers ask, "What do we have to do to test the validity of this opinion?" and "What facts are necessary to support this opinion?" They insist that the persons who voice an opinion must also take responsibility for defining the tests and providing the facts. Conversely, intuitive decision makers start out with certainty that their position is the only way. As a result they never understand what the decision is really all about.

In the alternative stage, Drucker's first rule is that a decision is not made unless there is disagreement, because disagreement is the most effective stimulus. He lists three reasons why dissent is needed. First, it safeguards the decision maker from becoming a prisoner of the organization. Since everyone always wants something from the decision maker, there is a general reluctance to disagree with him or her. Also, everyone is a special pleader, trying to obtain a decision he or she favors. The only to way escape from the special pleader is to assure there is argued, documented, and reasoned disagreement. Second, disagreement generates alternatives, and a decision without alternatives is extremely risky. Even the best decisions can prove wrong because either they were wrong to begin with or a change of circumstances makes them wrong. If the alternatives are thoroughly analyzed in the decision process, there will automatically be a fallback position. Third, disagreement, above all, is necessary to stimulate imagination, and imagination provides new ways of perceiving and understanding the threat or opportunity. Imagination is critically important in all matters of true uncertainty, because creative solutions are necessary. Imagination needs to be challenged, stimulated, and reasoned.

Drucker stresses that quality decision making starts with a commitment to find out why people disagree. While high-performance decision makers are aware that there are always fools and mischief makers around, they assume that dissenters have reached their clearly wrong conclusion because they see a different reality and are concerned with a different problem. Consequently, high-performance decision makers ask, "What does this person see that I don't see?" They are primarily concerned with understanding the problem. Only then are they concerned with who is right and who is wrong.

Drucker believes that high-performance decision makers force themselves to see the opposition as a means to think through the alternatives, no matter how high emotions run, and no matter how convinced they are that the other side is totally wrong. They use conflict of opinion as a tool to make sure all aspects of an important decision are carefully considered.

Drucker points out that high-performance decision makers are always aware that one alternative is to do nothing since many situations can be expected to take care of themselves. He teaches that a decision is necessary only if a situation is likely to degenerate if nothing is done or if an opportunity is likely to vanish. Most frequently the situation is not going to take care of itself but is unlikely to threaten survival. The opportunity is for improvement rather than real change and innovation. If there is no action taken, the situation will not degenerate, but if action is taken, there will be considerable improvement.

In the consequence stage, Drucker points out that decisions always involve risk and, thus, justify a lot of effort, time, and thought. He classifies risks as

- the kind we can afford to take—those that are easily reversible with minor damage;
- the kind we cannot afford to take—those that are irreversible, involving serious harm;
- the kind that must be taken regardless of the outcome—those for which there are no alternatives.

In the decision stage Drucker views a decision as a commitment to action. He believes decisions are only good intentions until someone is made responsible for implementation. Thus, his first rule for quality decision making is to make sure everyone who will have to do something to make the decision effective—or who could sabotage it—has been included in the decision-making process.

Guiding questions in the decision phase are, Who has to know of this decision? What action has to be taken? Who is to take it? What has to be done so that the people who have to do it can do it? Are the people who must do it capable of doing it? In short, every high-performance decision maker must think through the action commitments a specific decision requires, what work assignments follow from it, and what people are available to implement it.

Drucker believes most decisions are lost after the decision has been thought through, the risks and gains have been evaluated, the assignments are made and understood, and the course of action is clear. At this critical point, decisions require courage as much as judgment since most decisions require change and therefore trigger conflict. Furthermore, since there are no perfect decisions, there is always a price to pay. Consequently, there is always pressure to compromise to gain acceptance or to hedge risks. Drucker argues that quality decisions start with a firm commitment to *what* is right rather than *who* is right.[17]

Drucker recognizes that even the best decisions run into snags, obstacles, and all kinds of surprises and eventually become obsolete. His four causes of failure are

- not including people affected by the decision in the decision-making process;
- not testing or using a prototype;
- not designating someone to implement it;
- not thinking through who is to do what.

In real life, most decisions have to be bailed out so it is essential to develop contingency plans ahead of time and assign bailout responsibilities. Moreover, unless there is feedback regarding performance, the decision is unlikely to produce desired results. Effective feedback requires that expectations be clearly understood and an organized follow-up effort implemented. Drucker recognizes the importance of reports but is convinced that direct exposure produces the most effective feedback. High-performance decision makers go out and see for themselves what is happening. If they cannot go, they send their top aide. They never rely solely on the reports of the subordinate responsible for implementing the decision. This is not a matter of lack of trust in their subordinates but a matter of a different perspective. The implementer has a narrower view, while the top manager has a much broader one. In short, high-quality decisions, Drucker believes, start with opinions and require dissenting opinions, imaginative alternatives, and a commitment to action.[18]

Faulty Decisions

Faulty decisions are decisions that do not achieve desired results or do so inefficiently. Since only people can make decisions, it is important to recognize and avoid people whose thinking is dominated by personal characteristics that preclude the objectivity and the open-mindedness that are essential for quality decisions. There are three types of decision-destructive minds that destroy the teamwork necessary for quality collective decisions:

- the rigid mind stifles originality, ignores change, and encourages complacency;
- the ego mind destroys objectivity and makes collaboration impossible;
- the Machiavellian mind turns all thinkers into bureaucratic connivers and all thinking into political thinking.

Almost all the decision problems are either "limits to the rationality" of the prescriptive, decision-making model or faulty-decision strategies that interfere with the rational decision-making process. Typical faulty-decision strategies are

- procrastination—delaying or deferring necessary actions;
- unconflicted adherence—making a decision too soon and sticking to it despite harmful consequences;
- remedial decision making—devising the rationale after the decision has been made: a form of damage control;

- satisfying—making suboptimal decisions that merely satisfy or suffice;
- disjointed incrementalism—making a series of small decisions rather than taking a comprehensive approach;
- favoring the status quo (loss aversion)—the tendency to hang on to what you have got rather than risk a gain;
- "sunk-cost" effect, or entrapment—the reluctance to write off the poor or obsolete investment;
- shortsightedness—the overemphasis on the present;
- neglect of probability—the assumption that improbable events will not happen;
- "my-side" bias—the defense of personal beliefs;
- single-mindedness—the concentration on one goal at the expense of other goals;
- "group-think"—a situation where a group of decision makers closes off communication and rejects information that does not match preconceived understandings;
- "bounded rationality"—a situation where decision makers are unable to formulate problems so as to permit optimal solutions. They formulate decisions within self-imposed constraints.

Most decision makers have worked with destructive people and have been guilty of using these faulty decision strategies at some time in their lives.

Problem Solving

Problem solving is decision making from a different perspective. The principal difference is that the decision-making process is broader and, in effect, includes problem solving. Problem solving starts by identifying the right problem instead of by asking the right questions. A problem is any question or smatter involving doubt, uncertainty, or difficulty. Aids in problem solving usually come from within the organization. A solution to a problem usually has several options (the alternatives), and each option has consequences. The problem solver selects the best option and decides whether or not to implement it (the decision).

The overall problem of any organization is to plan and direct the resource-conversion process so as to optimize the attainment of core objectives.[19] More specifically, this involves three subclasses of problems:

- There are strategic problems that are primarily concerned with the external environment and with the service/product mix the union will provide.
- There are administrative problems that are concerned with structuring an organization's resources to maximize performance potential. Administrative decisions include structuring of authority and responsibility relationships, work and information flows, distribution of resources and location of facilities, and do on. They are also concerned with the acquisition and development of resources such as development of raw material sources, personnel training and development, financing, and acquisition of facilities and equipment.
- There are operating problems involved that attempt to maximize the efficiency of the organization's resource-conversion process. The major operating-problem areas are resource allocation, scheduling, and controlling.[20]

When confronted with a problem, organizations typically look backward and forward. They look backward to establish responsibility, find the source of the problem, and analyze it. They look forward to find a solution to the problem. The backward look is an essential part of the organization's reward system but a potential source of serious problems. Punishing mistakes is a major cause of concealment and conflict. The best solution to these problems is a reputation for fairness and objectivity.

The forward look, the more important, rewards the search for problem situations and effectiveness in finding solutions. Top Management is the greatest influence on effective problem solving. As role models they practice the following principles:

- the solution takes precedence over finding the cause;
- the manager is responsible for finding and proposing solutions instead of shifting the blame;
- the manager is responsible for implementing solutions;
- the primary focus is not to fix blame but to learn so similar problems can be prevented.[21]

Typically, a traditional troubleshooter resorts to what is referred to in decision theory as "local rationality." This approach is based on the assumption that problems are best divided into subproblems, with each assigned to different subunits. Each subunit has only one objective and, thus, is one piece of the problem. "Local rationality" works best with segmented structures.

Another approach in today's integrated structures is the "integrative mode," where problem solvers do exactly the opposite of the "local rationality" approach. Here, they aggregate subproblems into larger problems so as to re-create a unity that provides more insight into required action. The problem is redefined so new solutions emerge. Instead of isolating the problem into fragments, integrative bodies are created. These new supraunits, multi-unit teams, task forces, or project centers consider the whole before taking action.[22]

The following are four innovative ways to solve problems:

- brainstorming—where several people propose and discuss a wide range of ideas;
- brain-writing—the same as brainstorming except this approach eliminates the problem of one person's or several people's dominating the discussion;
- confronting—involves ideas that challenge established policies and programs;
- guided fantasies—involves creating ideal situations.[23]

High-performance problem solvers are innovative people. They see the problem from many different perspectives. They twist and turn it. They look for other uses. They adapt it, modify it, maximize it, and minimize it. They find substitutes, rearrange it, and combine it. They turn it backward, upside down, and inside out.

The following questions can help you analyze problems, analyze other people's problem-solving processes, and prepare responses for your own decision:

WHO?
- Who are the stakeholders? What motivates them? What are their incentives? What are their perceptions of the problems and solutions?
- Who will be hurt by allowing the situation to continue?
- Who will be helped by allowing the situation to continue?

WHAT?
- What are the major issues?
- What are the possible losses or gains if the problem is not solved?
- What are the factors that are inhibiting favorable results?
- What is missing from the environment that should be added?
- What is in the environment that should be eliminated?

WHEN?
- When does the problem need to be solved? Today? Tomorrow? Next week? Next month? Next year?
- When will the problem cease to exist? Today? Tomorrow? Next week? Next Month? Next year?
- When will the problem set long-term precedents that could be damaging to the stakeholders or the decision maker confronted by them? Today? Tomorrow? Next week? Next month? Next year?

WHY?
- Why has the desired outcome not occurred?
- Why is the problem worth solving?
- Why is the investment of time and money likely to be worthwhile?

HOW?
- How likely is success?
- How important is solving the problem in terms of solving other problems?
- How important is solving the problem in terms of its effect on day-to-day operations?
- How important are the people involved to the decision maker?
- How important is solving the problem to the people involved?
- How powerful are the people involved?
- How can they affect the problem solver in the future?[24]

With minimum rephrasing these questions can also be used as decision-making guides.

Creative Thinking

Creative thinking involves relating things or ideas that were previously unrelated with the objective of creating something new. Creative thinking is a critical component of both decision making and problem solving. There are five stages of creative thinking:

- preparation—getting the facts, applying convergent thinking—a central focus, and defining the question or problem in different ways;
- effort—applying divergent thinking—no central focus—that either resolves the issue or leads to frustration. Frustration is an important by-product of the effort stage and usually leads to good ideas;
- incubation—in this stage the issue resides in the thinker's subconscious mind for an extended period. Incubation provides time for inhibitions to weaken and new ideas to enter. Time is vitally important in this mysterious process. Creative ideas take time to brew. Thus, after thorough preparation and a concentrated effort, proceed with your daily activities. Intentionally avoid thinking about the issue for at least overnight. How incubation works is nature's secret—but it works!
- insight—the eureka moment, the flash of illumination that leads to the right response to the issue;
- evaluation—the analysis of all the ideas from the effort, incubation, and insight stages.

The preparation and evaluation stages require analytical thinking—the process of breaking a whole into its basic elements. The effort, incubation, and insight stages require suspended judgment and open-mindedness. Wild ideas are encouraged, and many ideas are considered. The key to creative thinking is the conscious and deliberate separation of idea production from idea evaluation.

Creative thinking techniques include

- brainstorming—several people propose and discuss many ideas;
- synectics—a group of people interact with a "client" in suggesting and evaluating various ideas;
- attribute listing—list the main attributes of each idea and examine each one to see how it can be changed;
- forced relationships—take ideas and combine them to form a new idea;
- morphological—set all the variables in a matrix and try to combine them in new ways;
- lateral thinking—examine all options including those that appear to be outside the area of the issue;
- checklists—use lists as idea generators. For example, a list of topics is put to other uses, adapted, modified, minimized, magnified, substituted, rearranged, and combined as questions to generate new ideas. Checklists should be used with care because they tend to inhibit creativity.

No matter what technique is used, the following four guidelines always apply:

- suspend judgment—rule out premature judgments;
- freewheel—the wilder the ideas, the better the results;
- quantity—the more ideas, the better;
- cross-fertilize—combine and improve on the ideas of others.

High-performance managers continually struggle against barriers to creative thinking. Most people are trained to think analytically, but only a few are trained to think creatively. Creative thinking is restricted by

- self-imposed barriers;
- the belief that there is only one right answer;
- conformity;
- lack of effort to challenge the obvious;
- evaluating too quickly;
- fear of looking foolish;
- respect for authority;
- excessive individualism.[25]

Creative thinkers are innovators, and innovation is a defining characteristic of all excellent organizations.

RISK AND PROBABILITY

As we have seen, life requires us to make numerous decisions, and decisions usually involve risks. Risk is the exposure to hazard or danger and, therefore, has an enormous influence on everyone's life. More specifically, risk is the probability of the occurrence of the significance of the consequence of the occurrence. Risk is a complex concept subject to individual perception. Consequently, it is very important to be aware that the real fear of perceived danger is more important than actual danger. Individuals may be classified on a spectrum that ranges from "risk-seeking" or "risk-adverse." An individual's attitude toward risk is influenced by his or her:

- need for stimulation and excitement;
- comfort level;
- ability to accept losses.

Hence, it is difficult to develop a universal set of rules for dealing with risk. While the principles and theories presented in this section hold true in nearly all situations, under certain circumstances the rules by which risk is evaluated change dramatically. For example, in times of extreme threat ordinary people do extraordinary things. They take risks they would normally consider "unacceptable." However, high-risk undertakings are not always bad and do not always have to be avoided. Rather, they should be rigorously monitored and controlled.[26]

Risk seekers are drawn to highly stimulating and exciting activities that tend to be short-term and involve danger to the body. Risk-adverse people tend to avoid hazards, seek security, and pursue long-range goals. Movies, television programs, and books idolize the James Bond-type of "risk seeking," automatic-weapon-blazing, karate-chopping hero. However, in the union world, where all important decisions involve increasing, decreasing, or transferring risk among workers, the deliberate, thoughtful, and ethical decision makers are the true heroes. Most risk seekers are too dangerous, and risk avoiders are paralyzed with caution and fear. High-performance union decision makers are found in the middle of the "risk seekers-risk-adverse" spectrum.

The level of risk present in any situation is the result of the probability of the loss's occurring—likelihood, and value of possible loss—impact. Figure 6.5 groups risks as low, moderate, and high on the basis of these two variables.[27] The probability of loss (y axis) ranges from zero to one, with zero being no chance of loss and one being certain loss. The probabilities in between are expressed as decimals such as .2 for a 20 percent chance of occurring or .75 for a 75 percent chance of occurring. The value of loss or impact (x axis) ranges from zero to infinity, with zero being no loss and infinity being total loss. The act of assigning values for both probability of loss and value of loss is, as previously explained, extremely subjective since most of life's events are very difficult to predict mathematically.

Figure 6.5
Levels of Risk

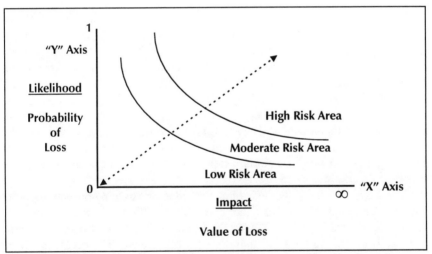

Source: "Risk Management Concepts and Guidance," Defense Systems Management College, Fort Belvoir, VA 22060.

Although risk and uncertainty are often used interchangeably, they are not the same. Therefore, it is important to distinguish risk from uncertainty. First, uncertainty is broader than risk. If there were no uncertainty, there would be no risk, but if there were no risk, there still could be uncertainty. Uncertainty refers to a state of ignorance, while risk involves known alternatives and probabilities. With uncertainty the alternatives are also all known, but their probabilities are not.[28] Second, risk is concerned with value, while uncertainty is not. Consequently, the key point is that risk involves taking a chance with something of value.

Probability is a concept used every day by most people. Probability is the likelihood that an event will occur. It can also be thought of as the personal belief that an event will occur. For example, weather forecasters typically predict weather as a 30 percent (.3 or 3/10) chance of snow. Gamblers are risk seekers with strong personal beliefs about the outcome of events such as Big Shot, at 15 to 1, will win the fifth race, or a 9 is "coming out" on the next roll of the dice, or one more "hit" is blackjack. Thus, the actual source of a probability is ultimately the individual decision maker.

This broad definition of probability opens a wide range of possibilities and applications to be explored. It also minimizes dependence on mathematical calculations. High-performance decision makers are always aware that probability is a major consideration in decision making and that the probability of a desired outcome's occurring is always less than 1. It is the judgment of the decision maker that determines how much less than 1. For example, the chance of a local union's reaching an organizing goal of 100 new members in the next year is only 50 percent (.5 or 1/2), but the chance of reaching a goal of only 30 new members in a year is 75 percent (.75 or 3/4).

Mathematically, probability is a number expressing the likelihood of the occurrence of a specific event and is used to draw inferences about unknown population characteristics. Consequently, probability is a key quantitative measurement associated with many risk-assessment techniques. Any group of numbers may be described with the following basic statistical terms: mean; median; mode; range; and variance or standard deviation.

To nonstatisticians these terms are used to represent a typical group or body. To statisticians, mean is the average number, median is the middle number, mode is the most common number, range is the lowest and highest numbers, and variance or standard deviation describes the scattering of the numbers around the mean.

There are four basic methods of determining or assigning probability. The first method, enumeration, or equal probability, is the best known. It utilizes the mathematical formula $1/n$, where n equals the number of possible occurrences, to determine the probability of each occurrence. The events involved must be mutually exclusive and collectively exhaustive. For example, a die has six sides or six possible outcomes. Therefore, the probability of any one side's occurring is 1/6, or .166, or 16.6 percent. In order to use this approach, all possible outcomes (collectively exhaustive) must be known, and each outcome must be independent of the other outcomes (mutually exclusive). This method is limited to controlled situations and ignores actual experience.

The second method, the relative frequency approach, determines probability on the basis of historical information. It is the basis for statistical sampling and extrapolation. This approach relies on repeated trials or sampling to establish the probability of a future event. The major shortcoming with this model is that it assumes the situations will be nearly equal, when in reality there are certain differences that reduce its accuracy and reliability.

The third method, mixed collectives, relies also on historical information but categorizes the elements of a situation in order to create homogeneous classes of events. For example, life insurance categorizes by age, gender, health history, family illnesses, lifestyle, and so on. Even though this method is the basis of actuarial projections, it is also weakened by the unrealistic assumption that history will repeat itself.

The final method, subjective assignment, is more general than the previous objective methods. This approach uses subjective means to determine the probability of an event. This is a more realistic method and, therefore, a very useful approach, since many problems are too complex for simple calculation.

Subjective assignment can be improved through the use of the Delphi technique, which uses a group of knowledgeable individuals to elicit feedback through a structured exchange of opinions to determine the probability of an outcome. The Delphi technique physically separates the group's members from each other in order to reduce irrelevant interpersonal influences. Each group member provides opinions and reasons to support these opinions. To preserve anonymity, a facilitator reduces the opinions to standard statements and circulates them to each member for reevaluation and substantiation. This feedback process continues until there is no further substantial change.

For those readers with a math background, the following formulas are several of the most frequently used ways to calculate probabilities:

- "Mutually exclusive" refers to events that are not causally related. The probability of event A (1/n) or B (1/n) happening equals the probability of A plus the probability of B:

    $P(A \text{ or } B) = P(A) + P(B)$

    Example: Find the probability of rolling a 3 on one of two dice.

    $P(1/6 \text{ or } 1/6) = P(1/6) + P(1/6)$

    $P = 2/6 = 1/3 = 33.3\%$

- "Not mutually exclusive" means both events can occur. The probability of event A or B happening equals the probability of A plus the probability of B minus the probability of A and B:

    $P(A \text{ or } B) = P(A) + P(B) - P(A \& B)$

    Example: Find the probability of drawing either an ace or a diamond from a deck of cards.

    $4/52 + 13/52 - 1/52 = 16/52 = 4/13 = 30.7\%$

- "Joint probability" means two or more independent events occurring together or in succession. The probability of events A and B happening equals the probability of A times the probability B:

    $P(AB) = P(A) \times P(B)$

    Example: Find the probability of tossing heads on two consecutive throws of a coin.

    $0.5 \times .5 = 0.25 = 25\%$

- "Conditional probability" means the probability a second event (B) will occur only after the first event (A) has already occurred. The probability of B happening equals the probability of event B happening divided by the probability of A happening:

    $P(B) = P(B/A)$

    Example: Find the probability of tossing two consecutive heads if one head has already happened.

    $0.5 = 0.5/1.0 = 50\%$

There are other ways to calculate probabilities, but they are beyond the scope of this book. However, it is extremely important to know that the lack of a math background does not prevent union leaders from becoming high-performance decision makers. Common sense and experience can establish very realistic and useful probabilities, and probability plays an important role in the risk management process.

Risk Management

High-performance union managers recognize the importance of the element of risk in all their decisions and try to manage it. They realize risk

- is usually at least partially unknown;
- changes with time;
- is manageable in the sense that human action changes its form and degree.

The risk management process (Figure 6.6) involves four steps—planning, assessment, analysis, and handling.[29] Like decision making, risk management formalizes a natural process. Also like decision making, it consumes resources and requires personal discipline. The arrows in Figure 6.6 show the process flow. Risk management starts with risk planning that is organized, purposeful planning about eliminating and minimizing or containing undesirable occurrences. Its purpose is to

- eliminate risk whenever possible;
- isolate and minimize risk;
- develop alternative plans;
- establish time and money reserves to cover risks that cannot be avoided.

Risk planning, the first step, should be an integral part of a typical planning process and is concerned with the mission, core objectives, strategies, programs, policies, necessary resources, techniques, responsibilities, and requirements. The planning process is explained in more detail in Chapter 7.

Risk assessment, the second step, is concerned with risk identification, which is a systematic effort to seek out the risks associated with a project. The work product of risk identification is a straightforward statement that describes the project risks. Several techniques that are very useful for risk identification are expert interviews, analogy comparisons, evaluation of program plans, past experiences, technology assessments, and alternative creation and evaluation.

Figure 6.6
The Risk Management Process

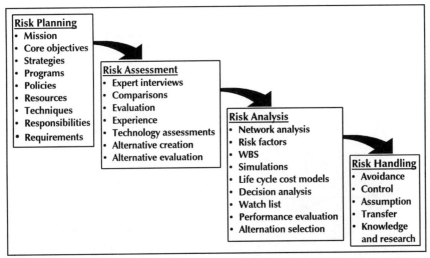

Source: "Risk Management Concepts and Guidance," Defense Systems Management College, Fort Belvoir, VA 22060.

Risk analysis, the third step, is a study of the changes in the consequences caused by changes in the project inputs. The switch from risk assessment to risk analysis is not always clear, since some analysis usually occurs in the assessment step. However, at some point, risk assessment becomes an independent step. Generally, risk assessment provides an in-depth understanding of the sources and degree of the risk. The various risk analysis techniques include network analysis, risk factors, work breakdown schedules (WBS), simulations, life cycle cost models, cost/risk evaluation, decision analysis, watch lists, performance tracking, and alternative selection.

Risk handling, the final step, is the action or inaction taken to address the risk issues identified and evaluated in the risk assessment and risk analysis efforts. Risk handling falls into the following categories: avoidance, control, assumption, transfer, and research and knowledge. Risk avoidance rejects the risks associated with one decision by choosing an alternative. Risk control involves the development of a risk control plan, tracking the plan, and taking necessary corrective actions. Risk assumption is a conscious decision to accept the consequences of an event should the event occur. Risk transfer reduces the risk exposure by sharing the risk. Contracts, performance incentives, warranties, and insurance are various ways to share risk.

Research and knowledge supply valuable information to the other methods of handling risk. It consists of gathering additional information to further assess risk and develop contingency plans.[30]

As seen in Figure 6.7, the five sources of management risk are technical, strategic, support, cost, and schedule.[31] Technical risks are risks associated with a new design to provide an improved level of performance. The nature and cause of technical risks are as varied as the system design. Each added design requirement can be another source of risk. However, what is technically risky at first usually becomes routine within a few years.

Figure 6.7
The Five Sources
of Management Risk

Source: "Risk Management Concepts and Guidance," Defense Systems Management College, Fort Belvoir, VA 22060.

Strategic risks are risks that include obtaining applicable resources and support that may be outside the Management's control but can affect the program's direction. Strategic risks are grouped into categories based on the nature of the factors that have the potential to disrupt the program implementation plan. Typical disruption categories are high-level decisions, external events, production-related problems, inadequate capabilities, and unforeseen problems.

Support risks are risks associated with developing, implementing, and maintaining, operating systems. Support risk includes both technical and strategic risks. Typical support risk categories are maintenance planning, workforce, equipment, facilities, logistics, technical support, and training.

Cost risks are risks associated with unreasonably low cost estimates, and schedule risks are risks resulting from unrealistically tight schedules. Cost and schedules are primarily dependent on the skill of the program manager to accommodate unanticipated problems related to technical, strategic, and support risks. Generally, true cost and schedule risks are minimal when the source of the risk is thoroughly analyzed.

RISK AND ETHICS

While all decisions involve some risk, risk management conveys the idea of at least limited control of risk. In terms of risk, if decision makers cannot control the outcome of alternatives, they can at least choose the alternatives that should lead to certain outcomes. Also, managers can control conduct even when the choice of alternatives is severely limited. In most situations, even though Management has less than total control, it can do more than just cope. The degree of control can be enhanced through increased information and knowledge. Progress, the gradual improvement in conditions of human life, depends on the quality of decisions. Thus, decision making is inherently and inescapably an ethical issue.

This section explores the moral dimension of the decision-making process. As human beings we are continually making moral judgments. We make moral judgments on the "goodness" of abortion, the death penalty, homosexuality, euthanasia, fetal tissue research, genetic engineering, environmental protection, affirmative action programs, and so on. The study of moral judgments, known as ethics, can be extremely complicated. Philosophers dedicate entire careers to deliberating the morality of various controversial acts or actions. While it is not necessary for union decision makers to become philosophers, it is important that we start to think more formally about how to make moral judgments.

Ethics is the study of what actions a person should or should not take and the reasons for or against these actions. Ethics are the moral guidelines that are supposed to guide the behavior of people. Ethical behavior generally stresses virtues that promote community such as charity, justice, kindness, courage, civility, honesty, wisdom, decency, honor, temperance, truthfulness, trustworthiness, and so on. It condemns vices that destroy community, such as greed, hypocrisy, dishonesty, foolishness, indecency, deceit, deception, cruelty, selfishness, and so on. Even though the list of virtues and vices can be very long, some philosophers argue that there are only two core virtues: charity and justice—two ideal virtues for building a community of workers—the new American union.

More formally, ethics is defined as a reflective philosophical endeavor that classifies actions into three basic categories: the morally permissible, the morally impermissible, and the morally obligatory.[32] An ethical decision, as distinct from other decisions, is based solely on some ethical rule, moral principle, standard, or norm. In other words, the decision maker would have made another decision if he or she had not relied on that ethical rule, moral principle, standard, or norm. Nonethical decision guides include self-interest, national interest, organizational interests, and so on.

A rule, principle, standard, or norm is ethical if, and only if, it takes into account the interests and situation of other persons affected by the decision maker's conduct and treats them impartially.[33] Ethical decision makers can be seen as finding the right answer to questions of conduct. A classic example of a moral rule is the physicians' Hippocratic oath which advises, "Above all, not knowingly to do harm." Clearly, this ancient wisdom applies to all decision makers, especially union decision makers, whose decisions can be very harmful for workers since they could expose some of them to a wide range of risks.

Ethical decision making acknowledges three factors that determine how we judge human conduct. First, ethics occur in a society of other persons, each with his or her own interests, goals, and projects. Second, ethics apply in the center portion of the spectrum between scarcity and abundance. Third, ethics seek to build equal opportunity into the decision-making process. Ethical decision making is distinct from other kinds of decision making because it assumes the presence of a moral agent—a person who is morally responsible for his or her actions.[34]

Robert Solomon and Kristine Hanson, authors of *It's Good Business*, teach that the essence of ethics is compliance, contributions, and consequences. Organizational compliance is concerned with the rules, such as laws, principles of morality, culture, traditions, expectations of the community, and a general concern for fairness. Organizations contribute to society through the value and quality of their products or services, the jobs they provide, and the usefulness of their activities to the community. Organizational consequences include internal and external consequences, intended and unintended consequences, and consequences to the organization's reputation.[35] In regard to ethics, what is good business is also good unionism.

An understanding of ethics helps the union decision makers better understand who and what really matters. It helps balance moral principles with the need for short-term economic and politically expedient results. Ethical considerations improve the quality of decisions by uncovering relevant facts, accommodating different factions, and making legitimate trade-offs. There are two main approaches to help union decision makers judge the morality of their decisions. The first is the ethics of consequences, and the second is the ethics of duty.[36] In regard to the ethics of consequences, the word "good" measures the degree of happiness brought about by a decision. For the ethics of duties, "good" is measured by the conformity of an action to certain principles of morality.

Ethics of Consequences

An ethic of consequences justifies an action in terms of the risks associated with its intended results. Generally, a "good" act will be one that produces the desired result with the least chance of producing undesirable consequences. Goodness is based primarily on the principle of utility. The principle of utility, the cornerstone of economic theory, holds that rational persons strive to maximize their happiness within the constraints of their resources. According to this principle, a decision is good or morally right, if, and only if, it brings about the greatest happiness for the greatest number of people. The difficulty with consequential ethics is in measuring the goodness of the greatest happiness for the greatest number of people.

Risk-benefit analysis, used to measure the goodness of a decision, includes both the possible and probable costs, as well as the actual costs that are associated with a risky decision. Risk-benefit analysis attempts to determine

- the probability that some harmful event will occur;
- who and how many people will be harmed by it;
- how the harm can be avoided or minimized.

Risk-benefit analysis utilizes both objective and subjective measurements to achieve a middle ground called acceptable risk. Decisions that involve the imposition of greater risk on others always require justification. Issues like consent, compensation, and cultural values are critical in the justification of acceptable risk.

Risk, from this prospective, is seen as a combination of knowledge about the future and consent about the most desired outcome. The less knowledge about the future and the greater the dissent, the less ethical the decision. Figure 6.8 identifies the appropriate responses to four situations involving knowledge and requiring consent.

Figure 6.8
The Knowledge and Consent, and Situation and Response Matrix

		KNOWLEDGE	
		Certain	**Uncertain**
C O N S E N T	**Complete**	**I** <u>Situation</u> • Certain knowledge • Complete consent <u>Response</u> • Calculate outcome	**III** <u>Situation</u> • Uncertain knowledge • Complete consent <u>Response</u> • More research
	Contested	**II** <u>Situation</u> • Certain knowledge • Contested consent <u>Response</u> • Discussion or • Coercion	**IV** <u>Situation</u> • Uncertain knowledge • Contested consent <u>Response</u> • Calculate outcome • Discussion • More research • Coercion

Source: Based on Mary Douglas and Aaron Wildavsky, "Risk and Culture: An Essay on the Selection of Technological and Environmental Dangers." Copyright © 1982. The Regents of the University of California.

In quadrant I, the situation is certain knowledge and complete consent. Typically, the response is to reach agreement by calculating the outcome. In quadrant II, the situation is certain knowledge but contested consent. The response is to reach agreement through discussion or, if that fails, through coercion. In quadrant III, the situation is uncertain knowledge but complete consent. The response is to reach agreement through more research. In quadrant IV, the situation is uncertain knowledge and contested consent. This is the most difficult situation, and agreement is reached by some combination of the solutions in the three previous quadrants.[37]

A decision maker applying the ethics of consequences is faced with two problems: first, how to measure and evaluate the possible consequences and second, how to devise a procedure for determining consent. Consequential ethics holds that the only way to think about morality is to think about consequences. Thinking about consequences involves thinking about and discussing, the consequences of decisions. A union's culture is a major source of social values, rules, and norms that are used to measure the possible consequences. Many ethical judgments are not simply "good" or "bad" but sometimes mixed, partly good and partly bad. Therefore, ethics, for even an apparently simple issue, can be a very complex subject.

The second problem is determining consent. There are three reasons that consent plays a crucial role in ethical justification. First, consent is always required to support a decision when only a few people are involved. Second, for union decision makers, consent is especially significant since their ultimate duty is to represent their members' interests. Third, other decision-guiding concepts such as equity, justice, rights, or efficiency all have serious shortcomings in particular situations.

Four types of consent make a continuum that ranges from actual informed consent to nonconsent. The first type, actual informed consent, is where the individual actually consents to the decision after receiving all necessary information. Actual informed consent is always fully ethical.

The second type, implicit consent, is where individual preference for risk is revealed through a properly functioning market. For example, there is the labor market, where workers accept extra pay or benefits for accepting greater physical risks. When market indicators are unavailable, the general preference for risks is determined and projected for the particular situation. The assumption is that rational persons would have consented had they been able to make a free and informed choice. Basically, implicit consent attempts to determine an individual's preferences and then generalizes from them.

The third type, hypothetical consent, is determined by assuming what an individual would agree to under certain favorable conditions. This requires the idealization of the conditions and never involves actual consent. This type holds that any reasonable person would consent to the alternative that imposes these losses and that it is "good" that these losses be suffered because of hypothetical consent.

The fourth type, nonconsent model, recognizes that justification of some decisions, because of the harm involved, requires direct appeals to the basic value system. This approach involves identifying and ranking social values of the union. This model requires a political mechanism for making decisions, assuring that decisions represent the interests of the workers and that they are not authoritarian.[38]

In situations that involve losses and the lack of consent, the concept of compensation becomes critically important. Unions have traditionally sought compensation whenever a decision necessarily harms some workers for the common good. For example, a union agrees to allow a new technology that will result in a 25 percent reduction in the workforce but requires retraining and extra severance pay based on the years employed to compensate those workers who will lose their jobs. An example of lack of consent and failure to compensate is where a local union is forced to end its seniority provision to facilitate organizing and fails to compensate senior workers for their increased risk of unemployment.

Ethics of Duty

An ethics of duty is another approach to measure the goodness of a decision. This principle claims that a decision is right or good only when made from duty or complying with certain principles. To measure the goodness within the ethics of duty, a moral decision must satisfy the three following conditions:

- the action must be broadly acceptable in the sense that a rational human would want anyone to use the rule to determine his or her action;
- the action must treat all involved persons as naturally valuable individuals;
- the action is consistent with one's own rational will.

There are two major differences between an ethics of consequences and an ethics of duty. First, in an ethics of consequences, the individual is subordinated to overall community happiness, while an ethics of duties is based on respect for the individual. An ethics of duty holds that people have rights by virtue of their status as moral agents. Thus, the duty of the decision maker is to bring about the most valued state of affairs and yet protect the rights of the individual. Second, an ethics of consequences holds that what makes an action right or wrong is its consequences, whereas the ethics of duty maintains that whether an action is right or wrong depends on one's reasons for doing it. For ethics based on duty, risk assessment is irrelevant to determining the morality or immorality of a decision.

Conflict between these two theories of ethics is common when decisions advancing general interest diminish the rights of individuals. The ethics of consequences, knowingly or unknowingly, is used to justify most union decisions. In most cases, union decision makers favor an ethics of consequences because it is almost always politically expedient, and it is a legitimate approach to determining morality. Decisions that provide the greatest happiness for the greatest number of people usually assure the greatest number of votes for the decision maker. However, high-performance union decision makers also recognize their duty to workers and retirees as individuals. They are aware that the ethics of duty will become increasingly important as the result of the trend toward individualism and increased workforce diversity.

A surprising implication of the ethics of duty is that decision makers are duty-bound to certain actions even if the risk of harm to innocent people is high. Seniority is an example of harm to many to protect the rights of a few longtime employees. Seniority, an example of the transfer of risk, is justified because its negative consequences are irrelevant as long as a moral principle is upheld. Seniority reduces the risks of unemployment for workers employed the longest time but exposes newer workers to a greater risk of unemployment. The ethics of consequences would judge seniority as good only if there were more senior workers than junior workers. However, in most cases junior workers outnumber senior workers; thus, according to the ethics of consequences, seniority would be "bad." In contrast, according to the ethics of duties, seniority is good because union tradition recognizes the inherent value of the senior worker's greater investment in the job.

Union decision makers affect the risks other people must take in two ways. First, they make decisions that are intended to reduce the risks of workers. For example, they negotiate wage increases and health and welfare benefits that limit the workers' economic and physical risks. Second, they make decisions that expose the workers to greater risk. For example, calling a strike exposes workers to financial risk, especially in an era of replacement workers. Also, union decision makers frequently agree to changes in work rules or permit the installation of a new technology, and these decisions subject some workers to greater economic risk.

Since collective bargaining transfers a variety of risks from the worker, to the employer, and ultimately to the consumer, it has major implications concerning the ethics of duty. For example, the chief union negotiator, for personal political gain, demands a 6 percent across-the-board increase, without fully considering the consequences to company and the union members, and without obtaining the members' informed consent. If the settlement is too high, the company Management will relocate the plant or invest in new laborsaving technologies. Both alternatives result in the loss of jobs. On the other hand, if the settlement is too low, the workers would be denied an equitable settlement, thus increasing their economic risk. According to the ethics of duty, the chief union negotiator is obligated to obtain sufficient information to recommend a good settlement that maximizes the wage and fringe benefit increases, while protecting jobs and permitting the employer to remain competitive. Then he or she must inform the workers and obtain their consent. Fortunately, most union negotiators do this every day without even realizing the ethical aspects of their actions.

Unfortunately, for many reasons, some union leaders are unaware of, or simply ignore, the issue of ethics, while others apply ethical considerations only when convenient. A major problem is that in the union environment an ethical code must be more sensitive to the union's need for unity than the members' need for protection against leadership abuses. This very complicated problem is a major source of internal conflict. It flows from the old analogy of the top union officer as a military general in constant battle with the employer, and the argument goes that the only way to win a war against an employer is a unified strategy that has very little tolerance for dissent. Therefore, the primary objective of many unions is to maintain unity at all costs.

The suppression of dissent, in the name of solidarity, not only discourages present members but also is a major impediment to organizing new members. To the extent that national union leaders are insulated from democratic pressures, they are free to arbitrarily reject new ideas and ignore membership concerns. Realistically, today's high-performance union leaders are very much unlike military generals. Consequently, a new, flexible, much less legalistic code of ethics is necessary to guide union decision makers.

Organizations implement codes of ethics because they

- set guidelines for appropriate behavior;
- make individuals totally and unavoidably responsible for their own actions;
- recognize the concept of individual dignity as the central force that drives all human interaction;
- provide a consistent, value-driven basis for determining what is right or wrong in a given situation;
- define the uniqueness of the organization.[39]

The following is a proposed model code of ethics for union officers and representatives.

As a union leader, I am dedicated to providing excellence in the service to the members, union, employers, and community in compliance with the highest ethical standards.

I recognize my responsibility to:

- pursue excellence as a leader, manager, and workers' representative;
- maintain the highest standards of professional and personal conduct;
- promote the general welfare of union workers;
- support the objectives of organized Labor;
- support and advance the principles of representative democracy;
- uphold the local union bylaws, the national union's constitution, and all local, state, and federal laws and regulations;
- acquire and maintain the necessary expertise to perform as a top-level professional;
- strive for personal growth;

- recognize that all union funds are held in trust for the benefit of union members and retirees;
- comply with generally applicable accounting, financial, and other fiduciary standards;
- manage union funds in a manner that effectively and efficiently achieves the union's objectives;
- manage union funds in a manner that does not result in personal profit or the profit of any officer, representative, or employee of the union;
- avoid all conflict of interest situations;
- recognize members as individuals deserving respect and fair and equal treatment;
- protect the members' right to full and equal participation in the affairs of the union;
- improve the public understanding of trade unionism.

In the absence of a code of ethics, union decision makers should ask the following questions to determine the morality of a decision:

- Are there any obligations involved?
- What ideals are involved?
- Who is affected?
- How are they affected?

Further, they can also apply the following practical guide for doing the right thing:

- when two or more obligations conflict, choose the most important one;
- when two or more ideals conflict, choose the action that honors the highest ideal;
- when the action is necessary, choose the action that produces the greatest good or least harm.[40]

Ethics has always been a very sensitive issue for the AFL-CIO, and its record is mixed. Historically, the AFL-CIO has focused on corruption instead of promoting ethics. The dictionary definition of corruption uses such words as "perversion," "disbasement," "depravity," "putrefaction," and "rotten" to describe corruption. Thus, the AFL-CIO has been concentrating on eliminating the lowest levels of human conduct, which leaves a lot of room for very marginal conduct. Further, the elimination of corruption is not inspirational, whereas promoting ethics is concerned with the highest community-building moral principles—the highest levels of human conduct.

In 1957, under pressure from the U.S. Congress, the AFL-CIO Ethical Practices Committee recommended, and the AFL-CIO convention affirmed, three constitutional amendments, four resolutions, and six codes on ethical practices. Unfortunately, this elaborate codification approach left enforcement to the individual national unions. While a few national unions implemented meaningful reform, most unions simply ignored the problem. For example, the United Auto Workers, very sensitive to the importance of ethics to unions, established a public review board made up of prominent citizens, which has been very successful.

In 1991, the AFL-CIO's nineteenth constitutional convention adopted a resolution on ethics that noted that American society is riddled with corruption that has infected public institutions but declared trade unions to be remarkably free from this pervasive corruption. However, it also noted that since unions were trying to enhance the image of organized Labor a resolution on ethics was necessary. Thus, the AFL-CIO resolved to "do all that is possible to maintain the highest standards of personal and professional integrity and commitment to the ethical values that will attract working people to our movement. We affirm our determination as expressed in our Constitution to keep the Federation free from any taint of corruption." Predictably, the AFL-CIO further resolved that in dealing with this serious question it would not encourage the expulsion of any affiliate as a remedy.

The AFL-CIO appears to be much more concerned with perception than substance. While it is aware that it has an image problem, it is unwilling to admit that ethical shortcomings contribute to its negative image. Tragically, this defensive attitude immunizes corrupt union officials and precludes the open-mindedness necessary for a positive approach to improve the quality of union ethics.

Even though trade unions are among society's most democratic institutions, and "the overwhelming majority of union officials have a proud record of ethical integrity and dedicated service to their members and society at large," the fact is that even a small minority defiles Labor's image and totally undermines the efforts of tens of thousands of dedicated, hardworking, law-abiding union leaders. It is unlikely the AFL-CIO will ever improve its image until it is willing to implement a comprehensive top-down ethical program that includes training, ethical standards, and discipline for affiliates that do not comply with them.

This endless pursuit of ethical excellence should be a defining characteristic of the new, high-performance American union. High-performance union officers see ethics as a positive force to be enthusiastically encouraged, not a negative force that is merely tolerated. They soar through the skies in pursuit of ethical excellence, while uninspired union officials are mucking around in the mud in search of corruption.

As the twentieth century nears its end, the rules and values by which unions play are rapidly changing. The transnational corporation, cooperative and collaborative industrial relations, an increasingly diverse workforce, and a trend toward individualism are today's dominant forces in the union environment. Like the environment, unions must change. For survival, an increased ethical sensitivity and awareness are needed at all levels of organized Labor.

Clearly, since ethics is a factor in almost every important union decision, high-performance union decision makers always seek to do the right thing, consider the consequences of their decisions, and recognize their duties to their members as individuals. They achieve impartiality by avoiding conflicts of interest and the appearance of impropriety. High-performance union decision makers make informed, ethical decisions, keep their members informed, and recognize the importance of obtaining their consent.

Top union officers, at very little cost and in a very short time, can transform their unions from ordinary unions to high-performance unions simply by implementing a top-to-bottom quality, decision-making training program. All successful decision-making programs require the total support of the top union officers because they are ultimately responsible for the efforts of other decision makers. In effect, once union leaders begin using the four-step decision-making model for all their important decisions, recognize that every decision involves risk to others, and always apply ethical considerations, unions will be fundamentally changed forever. Quality decisions will attract new members, increase the loyalty and support of present members, and earn the respect and admiration of the public.

SUMMARY

The objective of this chapter is to help union leaders become better decision makers. Consequences, complexity, and change have rendered the informal decision-making process obsolete. This chapter consists of three parts: "Decision Theory," "Risk and Probability," and "Risk and Ethics." The decision theory section explains how decisions are made. The risk and probability section explains risk as a combination of value of loss or impact and the probability or likelihood of loss. The risk and ethics section explains that because of risk, decision making is an inherently and inescapably ethical issue.

Decision Theory

Systematic and logically sound procedures can improve the decision-making process. Quality decisions, the make-or-break points of an organization, require time and resources. They start with clear missions and core objectives and require information and good communication before, during, and after the decision-making process.

The Decision Process

A logical thought process increases the probability of a satisfactory or even a quality decision. Our prescriptive model includes the following four steps:

- the question;
- the alternatives;
- the consequences;
- the decision.

High-performance union officers create an organizational environment that encourages high-quality and collective decision making.
High-performance union decision makers

- use a formal decision model for all important decisions;
- make sure everyone who has something to do with making the decision work has been included in the decision-making process;
- use decision-making aids.

Quality Decisions

A quality decision is one that maximizes results with a minimum consumption of resources.
High-performance union decision makers

- start with opinions, encourage dissent, identify innovative alternatives, understand why people disagree, and then commit to action;
- are aware that there is always the alternative to do nothing;
- realize that even the best decisions may have to be bailed out, so they always have contingency plans.

Faulty Decisions

Faulty decisions are decisions that do not achieve desired results or do so inefficiently.
High-performance union decision makers

- avoid people with decision-destructive minds;
- avoid faulty-decision strategies.

Problem Solving

Problem solving is a similar, but narrower, process than decision making.
High-performance union problem solvers

- reward the search for problems and effectiveness in solving them;
- use a formal problem-solving process for all important problems;
- use innovative ways to solve problems.

Creative Thinking

Creative thinking, a critical component of decision making and problem solving, involves relating things or ideas that were previously unrelated with the objective of creating something new. The five stages of creative thinking are preparation, effort, incubation, insight, and evaluation.
High-performance union creative thinkers

- apply the four guidelines for creative thinking;
- use creative thinking techniques;
- avoid the barriers to creative thinking.

Risk and Probability

Risk is defined as the exposure to hazard or danger, and decisions usually involve risks. Risk involves loss of something of value and the probability of that loss's occurring. Probability is a mathematical concept, but in its simplest form, it is a personal belief regarding the likelihood that an event will occur. High-performance union decision makers realize the probability of a desired event's occurring is always less than 1, and thus most decisions involve some degree of risk.

Risk Management

Risk management is a formalized process intended to minimize risk. High-performance union decision makers

- recognize the importance of the element of risk in their decisions;
- use the formal, four-step risk management process to determine the amount of risk involved and its impact on their decision.

Risk and Ethics

Decision making, since it involves managing risk, is an inherently ethical issue. Ethics is the study of what actions a person should or should not take and the reasons for or against these actions. An understanding of ethics helps the decision maker better understand who and what really matters. The ethics of consequences and the ethics of duty are two principal approaches to judge the morality of decisions. Ethical considerations improve the quality of decisions by uncovering relevant facts, accommodating different factions, and making legitimate trade-offs. In a dynamically changing society, where ethics are constantly evolving, it is important that union decision makers think more formally about how to make moral judgments. Union decision makers, as leaders, need to know what actions they should or should not take and the reasons for or against these actions.

High-performance union officers implement comprehensive education and training programs to improve ethical decision making at all levels of the union structure.

Ethics of Consequences

An ethic of consequences justifies an action in terms of the risks associated with its intended results. Generally, a "good" act will be one that produces the desired result with the least chance of producing undesirable consequences.

High-performance union decision makers

- use risk-benefit analysis to measure the impact of the decision;
- are sensitive about the consequences of their decisions on individuals and realize consent is a critical ethical consideration;

- use public opinion surveys to determine their members' consent on all important issues;
- realize the concept of compensation becomes extremely important in nonconsent situations that involve a loss.

Ethics of Duty

An ethics of duty recognizes that a decision is right or "good" only when made from duty or complying with certain principles. High-performance unions adopt codes of ethics for union officers and representatives.

High-performance union decision makers recognize that

- their duty is to protect the rights of the individual member;
- that the ethics of duty will become increasingly important as the result of the trend toward individualism and increased workplace diversity.

This chapter is basically concerned with a fundamental change in Management style for many union leaders. The new style is prescriptive as opposed to descriptive and participative versus autocratic. It is based on doing the right thing and the duty to represent their members, which requires obtaining their consent or compensating them. This is the most important chapter in the book! A quality decision-making program can produce immediate and tangible results with a minimum investment of money and resources. A very big bang for a very few bucks!

NOTES

1. Peter F. Drucker, *Management Tasks, Responsibilities, Practices* (New York: Harper & Row, 1985), 545.

2. George A. Steiner, *Strategic Planning* (New York: Free Press, 1979), 322.

3. Ben Heirs with Peter Farrell, *The Professional Decision Thinker* (New York: Dodd, Mead, 1987), 32–32.

4. Igor Ansoff, *The New Corporate Strategy* (New York: John Wiley & Sons, 1988), 5.

5. Heirs, *The Professional*, 56.

6. Ibid., 67–68.

7. Percy H. Hill et al., *Decision Making* (New York: University of America Press, 1986), 23.

8. Joseph Coates, *Issues Management* (Mt. Airy, MD: Lomond, 1986), 87.

9. Heirs, *The Professional*, 88.

10. Ibid., 90-93.

11. Hill et al., *Decision*, 24.

12. Ibid., 120–127.

13. Heirs, *The Professional*, 94–108.

14. Hill et al., *Decision*, 25.

15. Heirs, *The Professional*, 25–26.

16. Ibid., 9–15.

17. Drucker, *Management Tasks*, 465–480.

18. Peter F. Drucker, *Managing the Nonprofit Organization* (New York: Harper-Collins, 1990), 127.

19. Ansoff, *The New Corporate*, 5.

20. Ibid., 3–6.

21. Judith R. Gordon, *Organizational Behavior* (Needham Heights, MA: Allyn and Bacon, 1983), 266.

22. Rosabeth Moss Kantor, *The Change Masters* (New York: Simon & Schuster, 1983), 29.

23. *Across the Board*, June 1991.

24. *Pryor Report* 3, no. 9, "Formula for Case Injury Method," Paul G. Friedman, ed. (Clemson, SC: Fred Pryor, May 1987), 8.

25. Milan Kubr, *Management Consulting: A Guide to the Profession* (Geneva, Switzerland: International Labor Office, 1988), 171.

26. *Risk Management Concepts and Guidance*, developed by the Analytic Sciences Corporation under contract to the Defense Systems Management College, fw-3.

27. *Risk*, 2d ed. (Center for Instructional Development and Evaluation, University College, University of Maryland, spring 1989), 7.

28. *Risk*, 145.

29. *Risk Management Concepts and Guidance*, 5:2.

30. Ibid., 4:1–13.

31. Ibid., fw-3.

32. William James Earle, *Introduction to Philosophy* (New York: McGraw-Hill, 1992), 177.

33. Hill et al., *Decision*, 37.

34. Ibid., 27–34.

35. *Pryor Report* 3, no. 10, June 1987, "The Three Cs of Ethics," 8.

36. More commonly known as deontological ethics from the Greek word *deon*, which means "duty."

37. Mary Douglas and Aaron Wildavsky, *Risk and Culture* (Berkeley: University of California Press, 1983), 5.

38. *Risk*, 154–160.

39. Karp, Dr., "Why Have a Code of Ethics?" *The Fact Finder* (Jamestown, NY: The Jamestown Area Labor Management Committee), 1.

40. *Pryor Report* 4, no. 2, Oct. 1987, "Guidelines for Making Moral Decisions," 10.

7

High-Performance Union Planners and Organizers

An achievement today is but a challenge for tomorrow.
Eric Hoffer, *The Ordeal of Change*

A clear structure which enables people to work within clear boundaries in an autonomous and creative way.
Rosabeth Moss Kanter, *The Change Masters*

The four basic roles of a manager are planner, organizer, director, and controller. This chapter covers the planner and organizer roles. Planning is the beginning of the management process. It underlies even the simplest activities, and, thus, it is important to understand its development as a science, art, and profession. Before managers can organize, direct, and control, they must make plans that give purpose and direction to these activities. Planning is the key to success because it is the stage at which managers set objectives and determine near and long-term strategies. Organizing is a process that establishes a system of relationships, arranges work in subunits, and establishes authority relationships. An organization is a deliberately established social unit composed of people who coordinate their activities to achieve common aims.

HIGH-PERFORMANCE UNION PLANNERS

Planning is part of our daily lives. There many types of plans—from simple to complex, from long- to short-term. There are personal plans for daily activities, vacations, careers, retirement, and so on. Planning is also a pervasive part of every organization. It is the basic process by which organizations identify their visions, missions, objectives, and goals and decide how to achieve them. While planning is a process, a plan is a specific commitment to present and future actions.

Planning is a continuous process, because an organization's internal and external circumstances are continually changing. Managers must constantly monitor these circumstances to determine if changes are required in the organizational aims or the programs for achieving them. Consequently, flexibility, crucial to the ultimate success of the organization, is an essential part of the planning process.

In today's dynamic environment, union officers can no longer rely on their intuition to manage their organizations. Planning minimizes risk and uncertainty by providing a more formal, rational, fact-based procedure for making decisions. It also helps prepare the organization for change. Further, it promotes the efficient and effective allocation of resources by focusing on the organizational aims. Planning provides benchmarks, or reference points, to measure accomplishments. It is important to note that union planners are extremely dependent on the plans of the employer and the conditions affecting the occupation, industry, and economy.

While planning exists at all levels of an organization, the need increases at the higher levels, since top Management sets the organization's core objectives and strategies. Planning is important to all managers, but in the sense of time spent on planning and the potential impact of planning on the organization's success, it is much more critical at the higher levels of the organization.

The basic planning process is pretty much the same for every manager, but planning takes many forms, because

- the planning approach that works well in one organization does not always work in another organization;
- even within the same organization, there will be a need for different types of planning at different times;
- different managers have different planning styles.

The five key elements of union planning are seen in Figure 7.1. The subject of a plan determines how a manager will approach the planning process. There will be a different approach for developing a strategic plan for organizing than for collective bargaining. A plan's elements, part of the organization's larger planning process, help guide the execution of daily activities and provide starting points for other types of plans. The time horizon of a plan should cover a time period that is long enough for the desired target to be attained. A plan's characteristics describe the policies of the organization and the styles of the manager. The organizational level of a plan refers to the organizational structure of the planning unit. Obviously, the larger the unit, the more complex the plan.

Figure 7.1
Five Key Elements of Union Planning

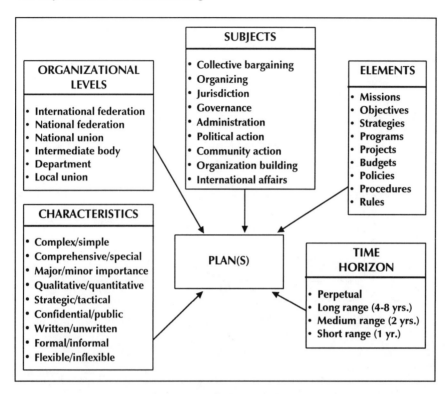

Organizational plans are also classified as strategic, tactical, and operational. Strategic planning involves decisions regarding the major aims of the entire organization and what strategies will be implemented to achieve these aims. Tactical planning involves allocating resources to achieve the organization's strategic objectives. Operational plans are short-range plans that are implemented at the operational levels to guide and control everyday activities.

Strategic planning is concerned with a longer period of time and, thus, is more uncertain than tactical planning. Strategic planning is also generally concerned with the external environment, while operational planning and tactical planning are concerned with the internal environment. Tactical planning is concerned with the delivery of the product or service. Operational planning involves having the people, supplies, and equipment available on a specific schedule to perform certain activities. Operational and tactical planning can rely on past performance for allocating resources.

The relationship of planning levels to the environment and the participants involved is seen in Figure 7.2. Part A of this figure is a two-dimension graphic with the environment on the y axis and the planning level on the x axis. The planning-level continuum ranges from the highest strategic plan to the lowest operational plan. The diagonal line between the upper left-hand corner and the lower right-hand corner divides the environment according to the relative importance of external and internal factors to the range of planning levels. For example, external environmental forces are extremely important at the strategic level but unimportant at the operational level. As the planning process moves from left to right, the relative importance of the external environment decreases.

Figure 7.2
Strategic, Tactical, and Operational Planning Level Relationship and Participants

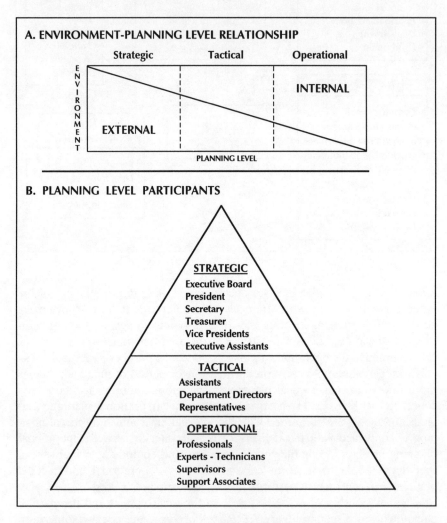

Different people participate in each of the three planning levels, as seen part B in Figure 7.2 It is important to be aware that the distinction between strategic planning, tactical planning, and operational planning is usually not as clear-cut as pictured. In part B, the triangle represents a typical union organization structure with many people at the operational level or bottom, fewer people at the tactical level or middle level, and very few at the strategic level or top.

A strategic plan by top-level Management triggers a series of increasingly detailed plans at each lower level of the organization, each contributing to the success of the strategic plan. This hierarchy of plans can be divided into three broad groups: aims, plans, and guides. Figure 7.3 shows the relationship of aims (mission and objectives), strategies, and standing plans (policies, procedures, and rules) and single-use plans (programs, projects, and budgets). Single-use plans are those that achieve a specific end, and standing plans are intended for situations that occur often enough to justify a standardized approach. It also shows the ranges of their scope, change, deviation, and hierarchy.

Figure 7.3
The Planning Sequence Model

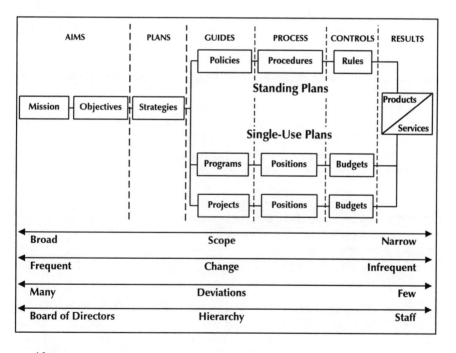

Aims

Aims are an organization's broad targets toward which the strategies and more detailed single-use plans and standing plans are directed. Aims provide a sense of direction for an organization's activities and consist of vision, mission, objectives, and goals. The reader should be aware that many authors and managers rank goals above objectives in the hierarchy of aims. However, in this book objectives are always higher than goals.

Vision is shared understanding of the organization's nature and purpose, and it sets broad limits within which the organization must operate. It specifies what the organization should be, rather than what it does.[1] High-performance organizations employ the concept of the strategic vision to better understand and operate in a dynamic and complex environment. While state and federal laws define the nature and purpose of unions, it is the vision of union leaders that provides the inspiration that brings these legalistic definitions to life. Properly written, very few organizations would have a more unifying, inspiring, and enduring strategic vision than Labor unions.

Mission identifies the underlying purpose of an organization. It is the broad aim that sets the organization apart from other organizations of its type.[2] The way in which an organization defines its mission is crucial to its success. The mission provides general guides for strategic planning, a specific reference for the formulation of program and policy strategies, and serves as the organization's driving force. Missions are highly dependent on the values of the top officer, tend to be stated in both product and market terms, and are expressed at high levels of abstraction that should be clearly written. Useful missions require a common thread such as products, technology, or user needs. While a mission cannot be proved either right or wrong, it can be approved or disapproved, both of which are exercises of value judgments.

Drafting mission statements is challenging and a potential source of constructive conflict. It has been said that a mission statement that cannot be reasonably disagreed with is probably of limited value. So conflict is an expected by-product of the mission-developing process.

In brief, a mission statement should

- identify the union's purpose and thrust;
- differentiate the union from other organizations;
- be relevant to all the union's stakeholders;
- be feasible and measurable;
- be exciting and inspirational;
- be challenging.

Every union organization, no matter how small, should have a specific mission statement that is relevant to today's environment, and each performance unit of that union organization should also have a mission statement that reflects the primary purpose of the unit. Performance units range from international federations to local union committees. The mission, while in many cases not glamorous or of momentous significance, should always be viewed as a service to others.

While the vision sets the broad limits for all similar types of union organizations, each organization chooses its own mission—a narrower, more specific version of its vision. As human-change agents, successful nonprofit executives begin by defining the fundamental change their organization wants to make in society and in human beings. Then they project that aim onto the concerns of each of the organization's constituencies. Labor organizations usually have written mission statements, or something similar to them, in their constitutions, charters, or bylaws.

A problem for the AFL-CIO is its multiplicity of possible mission statements. For example, the AFL-CIO constitution's preamble pledges:

- "more effective organization of working men and women;
- securing for them full recognition, and enjoyment of the rights to which they are justly entitled;
- achievement of ever higher standards of living and working conditions;
- attainment of security for all the people sufficient to enable workers and their families to live in dignity;
- enjoyment of the leisure, which their skills made possible;
- strengthening of our way of life, and the fundamental freedoms, which are the basis of our democratic society."

Another example of a potential AFL-CIO mission is also found in its preamble, which states: "We shall combat resolutely the forces which seek to undermine the democratic institutions of our nation, and to enslave the human soul. We shall strive always to win full respect for the dignity of the human individual whom our unions serve." However, in this case the language is dated and vague. There are two or three other sentences in the preamble that could be considered mission statements. Still another example is found in its constitution: "to assist working people in achieving their aspirations for decent, productive lives in a democratic society."

Consequently, every union leader and every union speechwriter has his or her version of the AFL-CIO's mission. Equally troublesome, every nonunion and antiunion writer has his or her version of Labor's mission. Thus, the AFL-CIO urgently needs a single, formal, inspirational mission statement that identifies its underlying purpose and direction. A review of other national union constitutions reveals that many also need new, formal mission statements, consistent with their culture and tradition, to guide them into the twenty-first century.

Organizational *objectives* are the results necessary to achieve an organization's mission. Objectives translate the mission into specific, concrete terms for measuring actual results. The basic purpose and mission of an organization must be translated into objectives in order to both guide and characterize the organization. The three basic elements of an objective are character, size, and goal. Objectives are a commitment, provide for participation, and link the mission to units of the organization.

Objectives should be

- mission-based;
- definable;
- measurable;
- feasible;
- acceptable;
- flexible;
- understandable;
- motivating;
- operational.

Objectives should be set for every performance unit of every Labor organization. However, setting objectives is a complex process because of the many considerations and trade-offs involved. In reality, objectives are the negotiated consensus of the influential participants, so power is the major factor in the formation of objectives.

Objectives are defined as a

- result to be achieved by a specific time;
- value sought by an individual or a group;
- specific category of a mission that the objective defines more concretely;
- desired future state of the organization.

Organizational objectives can be derived from the organization's external environment, internal structure, functions, and history, and require a schedule or time period to optimize their resource-conversion process. The following are several methods used in establishing objectives:

- past performance;
- past performance adjusted for trends;
- industry trends;
- resource utilization;
- negotiation;
- top Management directed;
- iteration with strategy;
- organizational analysis;
- strategies;
- analytical tools.

An objective-threshold range is the measure for evaluating future opportunities. A range of values is associated with each objective so that the value at the high end represents a highly desirable objective, and the value at the low end represents the threshold below which opportunities are not acceptable. This value is determined by the

- past, present, and future characteristics;
- number of opportunities and threats;
- urgency of strategic action;
- amount of resources to be committed.

It is extremely important to be aware that the opportunity to participate in objective setting reduces resistance, since people like to shape the system to fit their needs. Participation also minimizes misunderstandings related to objective setting by improving communications.[3]

In brief, objective setting enables unions to

- organize and explain a whole range of union activities in a few general statements;
- test these statements in actual experience;
- predict behavior;
- appraise the soundness of the decisions while they are still being made;
- let managers on all levels evaluate their own performance.[4]

Union leaders should always set objectives in specific terms of service to their members and judge themselves by their performance in creating objectives, standards, values, and commitment to enriching the lives and competence of their members. They should review their constitutions, charters, bylaws, and other governing documents to determine if their union's mission and objectives can lead them into the twenty-first century. Necessary revisions should incorporate today's language and yet be consistent with tradition and culture of the union. Also, gaps in the hierarchy of aims should be filled in. Broad-based participation is essential for developing a hierarchy of aims to meet the challenges of the future. Every stakeholder should be fully informed and have the opportunity to participate in establishing the union's hierarchy of aims. Those who would oppose changing major documents should consider that even the Bible, God's words, over 3,000 years old, has been revised several times to improve communications between eras.

Goals are targets that are shorter in time range and narrower in scope than objectives. They also set a particular value on the scale that the organization seeks to attain. Meaningful goals should

- focus on significant organizational needs;
- be expressed in clear and understandable terms;
- be reasonable;
- be tied to performance.

For all practical purposes, most union planners will not need to use a four-level hierarchy of aims, since there is little need to distinguish between *vision* and *mission* or between *objectives* and *goals*. With few exceptions, union planners should be able to develop top-quality plans using just a mission and objectives. However, the four-level hierarchy of aims may be useful if major national unions use planning consultants. A four-level hierarchy could be useful for union representatives involved in shared-fate, participative-Management activities.

Strategies

Strategies are broad policies, programs, and projects that provide direction for a union in terms of its many objectives. They also guide the allocation of resources that are necessary to achieve these objectives. Strategies are carried out by two groups of plans—single-use and standing.

Single-use plans are for activities that will probably not be repeated in the future. The major types of single-use plans are programs and projects.

Programs involve a relatively large set of activities and are schedules used to guide and coordinate operations. Typical programs include the

- major steps required to reach an objective;
- individual or organization responsible for each step;
- order and timing of each step;
- budgets.

Projects consist of the same components as programs but do not involve as many activities. Projects may be independent plans or part of programs.

Positions are concerned with the duties, tasks, and responsibilities of a particular task and the knowledge, skills, and abilities required to perform the task.

Budgets are commitments of financial resources to achieve specific ends. Budgets are primarily used to control organizational activities and usually accompany programs and projects.

Standing plans enable a single decision or set of decisions to guide repeated actions in frequently recurring situations. Standing plans save decision-making time and permit managers to handle similar situations in a consistent manner. The major types of standing plans are policies, procedures, and rules.

Policies are guidelines for decisions that include those that can and cannot be made. Policies are usually established by top-level Management and are used to

- improve the effectiveness of the organization;
- reflect some aspect of a top manager's personal values;
- clear up confusion or conflict.

Polices are adopted by an organization to influence and determine decisions in repetitive situations. They are an efficient response when a contingent event is recognized, and the outcome of such contingencies is well known, but the occurrence cannot be predicted in advance. Policies are vehicles for delegation downward within an organization. It should be noted that policies can also emerge at the lower levels of the organization through a series of consistent decisions on the same subject over a period of time.

Procedures are detailed sets of instructions for performing a sequence of tasks that occur on a regular basis, even if only once a year. Procedures are used to implement policies and ensure that high levels of consistency exist throughout the organization.

Rules are statements regarding specific requirements that usually relate to employee or member conduct. Rules can be seen as substitutes for decision making since the only alternative rules left to the individual are whether or not to apply them in a given situation.[5]

The High-Performance Union Planning Process

High-performance union planners involve all stakeholders in the planning process and are guided by the ten attributes and seven dominant values of excellent unions. First, they draft mission statements for every performance unit. These mission statements, written in terms of service to others, focus on representing members' interests in the workplace, providing common purpose and community, and changing members' lives for the better.

Second, they establish core objectives. The primary core objectives of high-performance unions are to

- be more effective representatives of member interests in the workplace;
- be more effective advocates of workers' interests in society;
- be more effective union organizers;
- restructure based on the nine basic union functions;
- maximize the efficiency of Labor's resource conversion process for attaining core objectives.

Third, they evaluate the union's capabilities relative to achieving the core objectives. Determining the union's strengths and weaknesses—organizational analysis—is a critically important phase in the planning process. Peters and Waterman decided that the traditional business problem-solving tools, which stressed strategy and structure, were inadequate. They reasoned that effective management was much more complicated than just the design of the structure of an organization. They concluded that any intelligent approach to building organizational capability has to include, and treat as interdependent, seven variables. To make their new business diagnostic tool kit easier to remember, they called it the McKinsey 7-S framework. They further classified these variables as hardware and software. Hardware referred to the formal organizational variables of structure and strategy. Software, or the informal organizational variables, includes style, systems, staff (people), skills, and shared values. The following is the McKinsey 7-S framework:

Hardware	Software
• strategy	• staff
• structure	• style
	• systems
	• shared values
	• skills

Strategy, probably today's most misused, bruised, abused, and overused word, deals with the future and is a top-Management responsibility. Strategy is the process of allocating scarce resources to achieve core objectives. Structure is how the boxes are arranged and is characterized by the chart, organizational. Staff refers to the demographics of the people who work for the organization and the various occupations within the organization such as office workers, technicians, representatives, economists, accountants, system analysts, programmers, and so on. Style describes the patterns of behavior top Management uses to achieve the organization's objectives. Systems are concerned with how information moves within the organization. Shared values refer to the mission, core objectives, and guiding values. Skills include the knowledge, skills, and abilities of the staff. High-performance union planners use the 7-S framework to help them develop plans that take advantage of their union's strengths and avoid its weaknesses.[6]

Fourth, they identify strategies. The key high-performance union strategies for attaining the core objectives are to

- adapt and apply management concepts, principles, and techniques;
- build strong, autonomous, democratic, value-based, mission-driven local unions;
- empower executive councils as executive boards;
- enrich union democracy at all levels of the union structure;
- build trust and credibility;
- improve and individualize the collective bargaining process;
- prepare workers' representatives to be equal partners in shared-fate, participative-Management environments;
- increase member participation and recognize members as individuals;
- "customerize" union operations;
- encourage innovation;
- develop high-quality communication and information systems;
- develop a global Labor communications network;
- promote the intense use of enabling technologies;
- encourage the widespread use of formal decision making;
- establish the AFL-CIO Institute for Managing Labor Organizations;
- recruit and develop union members for key union management and specialist positions;
- promote lifetime union member categories;
- decentralize to empower members, and form ASCs to minimize the need for mergers;
- stress excellence in quality, service, and performance;
- increase global union solidarity.

Fifth, they develop standing and single-use plans for implementing strategies. Sixth, they identify risks, determine the probability of their occurrence, and consider the ethical issues before approving plans. Seventh, they develop contingency plans, and eighth, implement the plans.

HIGH-PERFORMANCE UNION ORGANIZERS

The purpose of an organization structure is to help achieve the organization's aims. There is a clear distinction between organizing and organization. The formal structure, intentionally designed by Management, is relatively durable and consists of relationships that determine how the organization is "supposed to function." It dictates who has what responsibilities and who has what decision-making and directing authority. The formal organization defines relationships among positions, while the informal organization involves relationships among people. It is extremely important to be aware that formal structure is a fiction, since people never perform precisely as planned.

At this point, it is important to develop a better "feel" for structure. An organization is not rigid but constantly changing. There are daily changes in the organization in response to an ever-changing flow of people reacting to a dynamic combination of threats and opportunities. This concept is referred to as an organic or living structure and is entirely different from the traditional, rigid, bureaucratic structure. While the intent of structure is to organize work to flow in a systematic way, reality recognizes the need for flexibility. It must be stressed that there is no ideal organizational design and, thus, each organization is unique and requires its own structure.

The classical school of organization preached "one best way" to organize. Its primary concern was to eliminate loose ends. The classical organizing process defined the function of each work unit, specified the duties of each position, established procedures and rules for every activity, and delegated authority through a chain of command. The weaknesses with the classical principles are that they

- are too general;
- consider only one factor among the many that determine the structure and functioning of organizations;
- result in structures that are too rigid and static;
- relate only to internal factors;
- are not responsive to motivational or organizational change.

Even though the classical approach to organizing ignores reality, it is still useful as a starting point and, thus, remains an everyday Management working "tool."

Since the 1960s, management experts have recognized that there is no "one best way" to organize, and different structures are appropriate for different situations. The design must be appropriate for the organization's activities, technology, strategy, people, and external environment. This is referred to as the contingency approach to organizing and means that design is dependent on many variable forces. Another approach, the comprehensive-situational model of organizational design, recognizes that both the internal and external forces influence organizational design. In this model, the internal forces are aims, tasks, technologies, and people, and the external forces are economic, social, legal, technical, and political systems.

Organizational mission and its related objectives and strategies are important organizational design determinants because structure follows strategy.
People and groups make up organizations, so their behavior and relationships
not only make up the informal structure but frequently dominate the formal
structure as well. The type of technology employed also influences the structure. Mechanistic structures are related to stable environments, while organic
structures are characterized by dynamic environments.

The newer methods of organizational design are based on behaviorist
theory. Behaviorists argue that organizations can benefit by encouraging the
participation of subordinates in the organizing process. This trend is encouraged by the success of Japanese companies. Like previous organizational design concepts, the behaviorists approach is not the "one best" way
since to be effective it must fit the organization and the situation.

The structure of an organization is usually shown in an organization chart.
The organization chart, a graphic display of the organization structure, is a
convenient tool for understanding the functions, departments, and levels of
Management in an organization and the relationships between them. Organization charts are useful in determining authority relationships, career paths,
salary levels, and the division of work. They also can help identify structural
weaknesses, duplication of effort, and inappropriate relationships.

Critics, however, point out that organization charts overemphasize the
vertical aspects of the organization, while the fact is that work flows horizontally. Also the charts can inaccurately reflect power and status, since managers at the same level have different capacities to influence operations. Furthermore, the charts do not show informal relationships and give the im-
pression of being static.

With this material as background, it is time to begin the organizing process. The organizing process includes two basic activities—division and integration. Division means dividing the organization into specialized units. Integration refers to tying these specialized units together. Since these two
activities work against each other, the Management challenge is to achieve a
balance between the two.

High-performance union organizers build their unions in response to the
need for efficiency around the basics—the stability pillar, the need of regular innovation—the entrepreneurial pillar, and the need to break old habits—the habit-breaking pillar. As noted in chapter 4, these are the prime
needs of high-performance organizations. The stability pillar is based on
maintaining a simple and consistent underlying form, and on developing and
maintaining broad, yet flexible, enduring values. The entrepreneurial or
innovative pillar sees smallness as a requisite for continual adaptiveness and
includes simple measuring systems and small staffs. The "habit breaking"
pillar is concerned with a willingness to reorganize regularly in response to
a rapidly changing environment.

The organizing process consists of four basic steps. The first step, breaking it up horizontally, divides the organization horizontally into divisions,

departments, and other performance units. The second step, breaking it up vertically, establishes vertical units and delegates authority. The third step, putting it together, is concerned with lateral coordination and integration of performance units. The fourth step, fitting people in, involves putting the right people in the right place at the right time.

Step 1: Breaking Unions Up Horizontally

In the first step, horizontal division, the organization is divided horizontally into common groups according to all the work that must be done to achieve the organization's mission. This step involves identifying the work necessary to achieve the organization's aims and assigning it to divisions and departments and their support units. As organizations grow, the administrative and support functions are usually set up as separate units. Administration and support units provide services to operational departments, rather than produce the product or provide the service. They are established to relieve operations managers of administrative duties and to provide operating departments with access to specialists.

The first step groups logically related work activities. Businesses typically use the following nine different groupings: functional, product, process, geographical, customer, time, equipment, support, and matrix. High-performance union organizations structure on a functional basis, as indicated in Figure 7.4, where the nine basic union functions are considered divisions.

Figure 7.4
Breaking Unions Up Horizontally

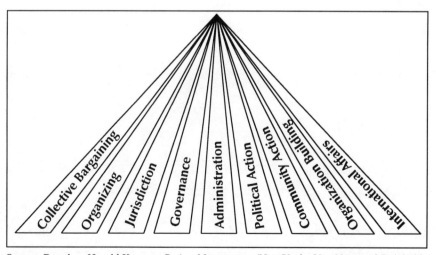

Source: Based on Harold Kerzner, *Project Management* (New York: Van Nostrand Reinhold, 1989), 5.

The following is a guide for horizontal division:

- establish organizational mission and core objectives and develop strategies for each division before beginning the organizing process;
- limit the number of performance units associated with each division;
- group related performance units together;
- consider the work flow when assigning responsibilities;
- focus the organization structure on the services or products that need emphasis;
- establish consistent departmentalization at each level of the structure;
- base departmentalization on the aims of the division, its strategy, and tasks to be performed;
- clearly identify and segregate the divisions;
- balance efficiency and integration equally when separating the divisions.[7]

Step 2: Breaking Unions Up Vertically

The second step, vertical division, establishes levels within each group and lines of authority. Figure 7.5 shows a typical union organization structure and is primarily concerned with power, authority, and influence. Vertical division:

- establishes clear lines of authority from the top to the bottom of the organization;
- keeps the number of organizational levels to a minimum;
- delegates decision making to the level where it can be most effective;
- defines authority and responsibility very carefully;
- assigns subordinates, whenever possible, to only one supervisor;
- avoids duplication and breaks in the chain of command;
- avoids overcontrol.[8]

Exceptions to these guidelines are necessary when designing matrix structures.

Figure 7.5
Breaking Unions Up Vertically

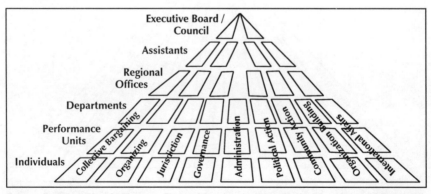

Source: Based on Harold Kerzner, *Project Management* (New York: Van Nostrand Reinhold, 1989), 5.

Power refers to the ability to produce or the capacity to mobilize people and resources to get things done. Power is always present; it permeates human relationships and, thus, is viewed as a collective act. Power and leadership are basic elements in a system of social causation. Power can be brutal or sensitive. It exists, whether or not it is quested for, and is both the glory and the burden of humanity.

The power process is always the same. Power wielders draw from their power bases resources relevant to their own motives and the motives and resources of others upon whom they exercise power. Power bases may be narrow and weak or broad and strong. Dominated by personal motives, a leader draws on supporters, funds, ideology, institutions, old friendships, political credits, status, and his or her own skills of calculation, judgment, communication, and timing to mobilize those elements that relate to the motives of the persons he or she wishes to control. Power wielders are not free agents but are subject to pressures working on them and in them. Even at the naked power extreme of the power continuum, power wielders such as Iraq's Saddam Hussein and Syria's Hafez Assad are always subject to both empowering and constraining forces. Power takes many forms: insignia, symbols, money, sex appeal, authority, administration regulation, charisma, weapons, and staff resources. However, all resources must be relevant to the motivations of the power recipients.

Power also has four dimensions: distribution, scope, domain, and arena. The first dimension, distribution, is concerned with the concentration and dispersion of power among persons of diverse influence in various political, social, and economic locations, such as geographical areas, classes, status positions, skill groups, communications centers, and so on. The second dimension, scope, distinguishes between the extent to which power is generalized versus specialized. Persons who are relatively powerful in relation to generalized power may be relatively weak in specialized relationships, and vice versa. The third dimension, domain, measures power by the number and nature of power respondents who are influenced by power wielders compared to those who are not influenced. The fourth dimension, arena, refers to the number of relationships in which power is exercised. Micropower refers to simple power wielders and respondent relationships. Macropower describes a multiplicity of power wielders and power respondents. Power relationships become vastly more complex as a greater number of power actors and power components come into play.[9] High-performance union leaders redefine power within the union environment by assuring that the legitimate power, the power derived from their elected offices, is sensitive to needs of their members.

Figure 7.6, part A, shows the sources of power that converge to constitute total power. The six sources of power are

- reward power, derived from the ability to distribute rewards for good performance and achievements and punishments for poor performance and failure;
- coercive power, based on the ability to force an action. Frequently, coercive power is used as an implied threat;

- legitimate power, sanctioned by union constitutions and bylaws; it can be enhanced with titles, office size and placement, salary, and reporting channels;
- referent power, derived from the position in the union and the personal characteristics of the immediate superior;
- expert power, based on ability, credibility, and reputation;
- personal power, derived from an individual's traits and characteristics.[10]

Figure 7.6
Power and Authority Convergence

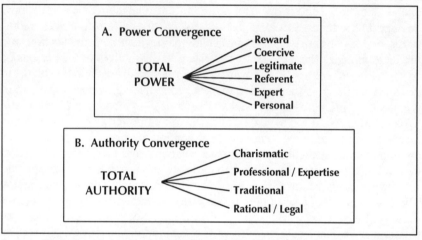

Source: Ziegenfuss, James T., Jr. *Organizational Troubleshooters: Resolving Problems with Customers and Employees,"* Figure 5 (p. 82) and Figure 6 (p. 88), adapted as submitted. Copyright © 1988 Jossey-Bass Inc., Publishers.

Authority is legitimated power, or the right of an individual to make necessary decisions required to achieve organizational objectives or fulfill his or her responsibilities. There are two types of authority—substantive and procedural. Substantive authority is legitimated by tradition, religious sanction, rights of succession, and the rights of the individual against rulers. Procedural authority is legitimated by constitutions, judges, legislative bodies, doctrines of due process, protection of property, and judicial review.

There are four basic sources of authority. The first source, charismatic authority, is derived from the leader's personal traits and attributes. Professional/expertise authority, the second source, is derived from the leader's reputation, credibility, training, or education. The third source, traditional authority, is derived from the historic role of the office or position in the organization. The final source, rational/legal authority, is derived from the organization's official constitution, bylaws, rules and regulations, policies and procedures, and the practical implications of internal and external perceptions and pressures. Part B of Figure 7.6 shows how the sources of authority converge for total power.

Authority is the legal right to command, while responsibility is the obligation to respond to an order. From another perspective, responsibility is the assignment for the completion of an event or activity. When authority is delegated, another individual becomes accountable for the duties and responsibilities assigned. Accountability involves the personal acceptance of success or failure.

It is important to remember that authority is delegated, but responsibility is shared. The delegation of authority gives the subordinate the right to make commitments, use resources, and take actions in relation to the assigned responsibilities. However, the delegation of authority never relieves the supervisor of responsibility. A supervisor always retains ultimate responsibility for the work performed by lower-level units or individuals.

In the union environment, the ultimate source of authority, as seen in Figure 7.7, is the membership.

Figure 7.7
The Flow of Authority in a Union Environment

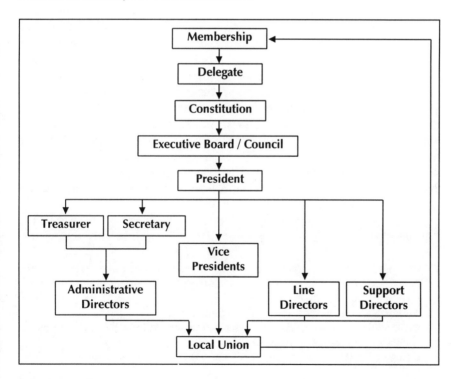

This authority, in most cases, is entrusted to elected delegates who, in convention, are responsible for amending the constitution—the ultimate source of rational/legal authority in the union environment. Next, authority flows to the executive board or council, then to the president, and down through various levels of the organization. This chain of command traces authority and responsibility to every individual in the union. It creates a continuous link from the rank and file to the top. It also forms a major system of communication channels and facilitates coordination by providing structure to the organization.

In most cases, a chain of command should not be violated. However, in crises or emergencies it is frequently necessary to go directly to the source and bypass intermediate subordinates. In today's world of management, the tendency is toward a flat chain of command with a high degree of informality.[11]

The primary task of Management is to achieve a high performance level for the entire organization. Since no individual can know it all or do it all, delegation is essential. The delegating process—decentralization—starts with the premise that every position in the organization has specified tasks and the responsibility for carrying them out. Delegation empowers people and involves trust in their ability to make good decisions. Without trust in their ability, important decisions would never be turned over to them. Empowerment, a currently popular management topic, adds a new dimension to delegation. Delegation is a down-through-the-organization process, while empowerment is an upward, shared, decision-making process. The empowerment process predisposes individuals to make choices, take actions, and assume responsibility about meaningful matters—it changes the entire organization.

The key to empowerment is common purpose, accountability, and the ability to measure results. These are necessary conditions for organizational alignment where all performance units use the same information and have the same motive for making decisions. An organization is aligned when all its performance units are moving roughly in the same direction. Tools for measuring performance are also essential for successful empowerment. In short, statistical tools that generate data and information empower people. While it is easy to empower people, it is also important to be aware that people can unintentionally be disempowered.

While there are no absolutes or fixed principles regarding delegating, the following are broadly accepted guides:

- Responsibility for specified tasks should be clearly defined and assigned to the lowest level of the organization at which there are sufficient ability and information to complete them effectively;
- Authority should be sufficient to fulfill responsibility;
- By accepting responsibility and authority, individuals must be willing to be accountable for their performance;
- Delegated authority should be clearly defined regarding assignments, decisions, and results;
- There should be agreed-upon deadlines for progress reports and deadlines;
- Supervisors should show trust and confidence in their subordinates' ability and commitment;
- Supervisors should establish a simple control system;

- Subordinates should have sufficient freedom to accomplish their objectives;
- Subordinates should keep their supervisors informed.

Managers do not delegate because

- of self-importance;
- they enjoy power;
- they believe they must know everything "just in case";
- they are perfectionists and lack trust in others.

The delegation process includes three basic principles:

- the scalar principle;
- the principle of unity of command;
- the span of Management principle.

The scalar principle states that there must be a clear line of authority from the highest level to the lowest level of the organization. A clear line of authority identifies for members of the organization to whom they can delegate, who can delegate to them, to whom they are accountable, and who is accountable to them. The delegating process must assure the completeness of delegation. In other words, all necessary tasks in the organization must be assigned. There should be no gaps, which are unassigned tasks; or overlaps, where responsibility for the same task is assigned to more than one person; or splits, where responsibility for the same task is assigned to more than one organizational unit.

The principle of unity of command holds that a subordinate should report to only one supervisor. The unity of command principle minimizes confusion and identifies responsibilities for performance appraisal, promotions, and pay increases. As organizations become more information-driven as opposed to hierarchy-driven, the unity of command tends to break down.[12]

The span of Management principle is concerned with the number of subordinates whom one manager can effectively supervise. The span of Management has many implications for the organization structure. Experts have long argued whether the ideal span of Management is 5 to 1, 8 to 1, or 12 to 1. Yet Japanese managers frequently use 30 to 1 or even 50 to 1 ratios! The higher the ratio, the flatter the organization; the lower the ratio, the taller the organization.

The span of Management is strongly influenced by the

- similarity of the tasks;
- geographical proximity of the tasks;
- complexity of the tasks;
- degree of supervision required by the subordinates;
- degree of coordination required of the supervisor;
- amount of planning required of the supervisor;
- amount of organization assistance provided to the supervisor.[13]

The span of Management is important for two reasons. First, the span of Management affects the utilization of Management personnel and the performance of subordinates. Overcontrol is the result if the span is too narrow, and too much freedom is the result if the span is too broad. Second, a narrow span of Management results in a "tall" organization, while a broad span of Management results in a "flat" organization. Tall organizations have many levels of supervision between top Management and the lowest organizational level. "Flat" organizations, with the same number of employees, have fewer levels of Management between the top and the bottom.[14]

"Tall" organizations are more costly, and communication is more difficult. They are more costly because they have more managers, with salaries and fringe benefits, who require offices, equipment, and support personnel. Communication is more difficult because the more levels that communication must pass through, the more likely it is to become diluted, distorted, or inaccurate. These are the major reasons behind today's tidal wave of corporate "downsizing."[15] However, my guess is that "downsizing," like most trends, has been excessive and inefficient. If people are the main asset of an organization, then, for many organizations today's enormous "downsizing" is a serious problem. The pendulum has, in many cases, swung much too far, and more middle Management is necessary to operate organizations effectively and efficiently.

The results of corporate downsizing are already becoming evident. A recent Wyatt Co. survey of 531 companies that employ more than 2,000 employees revealed the following:

- more than half refilled some of the jobs;
- only 21 percent were able to reduce waste or inefficiencies;
- fewer than half increased their profitability;
- only one-fourth saw improved customer satisfaction;
- only about one-half were able to improve cash flows;
- sixty percent saw their employees' commitment to the company decline.[16]

In the union environment, for the midlevel union manager, a span of Management ratio between 5 to 1 and 10 to 1 is probably best for most cases.

Virtually every function in excellent organizations is decentralized. Whether an organization is centralized or decentralized is determined by how much authority top Management delegates to the lower levels. Centralization or decentralization is a condition, not a process. The organizing concepts that determine this condition involve the span of Management and the delegation of authority. In a centralized organization most of the authority is held at the top, whereas in a decentralized organization a considerable amount of authority is delegated to the lower levels.

Decentralization is dependent on the following situational variables:

- knowledge, skill, and abilities of the people;
- size of the organization;

- geographical dispersion;
- complexity of the technology;
- time frame for decisions;
- importance of the decisions;
- status of the planning and control systems;
- conformity and coordination required for the work flow;
- stability of the environment.[17]

Frequently, the final decision regarding centralization or decentralization is not clear-cut because these variables often point in different directions. Regardless, no organization is either completely centralized or decentralized and, thus, organizations should be placed somewhere on a continuum. Since modern management theory clearly leans strongly toward decentralization, its emphasis is toward setting up autonomous plants and divisions and delegating authority downward in the organization to the level where the most capable person makes the decisions. The extent of decentralization depends on the need for flexibility, the aims of the organization, and an awareness of trade-offs associated with decentralization. The question for top union managers is not whether or not the union should be decentralized, but how best to do it. Their challenge is how to provide coordination, maintain control, and still achieve sufficient flexibility and sensitivity to thrive in the twenty-first century.

The organizing process traditionally distinguishes between line and staff authority. Line authority is the exercise of direct command over subordinates and is concerned with activities that apply to the basic purpose and goals of the organization. While staff authority is not authority in a pure sense, it is a specified relationship with clearly defined obligations concerned with providing service and advice to line units. Staff personnel advise, analyze, report, study, give reactions and opinions, recommend, provide services, and generally assist the line personnel—they do not direct them.

There are two types of staff groups. The first type, personal staff, personally assist the top union officers and have such titles as "executive assistant," "assistant to the president," or "assistant to the secretary." The personal staff tend to be an extension of the person they work under. The second type is the specialized staff, who possess special expertise and serve as advisers to the line personnel but have line authority over employees in their own units. For example, the research director has line authority over economists and research associates, and staff authority when advising line directors.

In many situations, line and staff are not distinguishable in absolute terms since all units contribute to achieving the aims of the organization. While some units contribute more than others, the differences are relative. Unfortunately, the basic assumptions underlying line and staff organizing theory ignore the concepts of power and influence. Figure 7.8 shows an example of a union line and staff structure.

Figure 7.8
Typical Union Line-Staff Structure

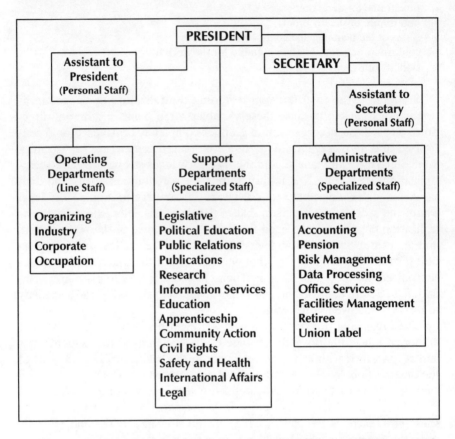

The advisory designation tends to relegate staff personnel to second-class citizenship; thus, the line and staff distinction is frequently the source of organizational conflict. The staff units hold knowledge-based authority, while the line units hold position-based authority. However, in modern, information-based organizations this advantage is rapidly changing. The staff units, with their greater access to specialized knowledge, are frequently more capable of solving today's complex problems. Consequently, the line units are becoming more dependent on the staff specialization. Thus, the growth of expertise-based authority erodes the line authority.

Staff personnel have two types of authority—functional and concurring. Functional authority is the limited right of staff persons to give orders or instructions to those outside their functional unit on certain matters. Concurring authority, the most common of staffing activities, is the right to approve a line decision before it is valid. In general, too much staff authority will create conflict with the line personnel and undermine the basic line-staff concept.[18]

Influence is a more moderate form of power where leaders can modify or affect their followers, but leaders do not have complete control. Influence is any form of behavior that modifies the behavior of someone else. In reality, all interpersonal relationships fall on a continuum that ranges from little control to total control. Influence relationships have many implications for managing and interacting in organizations.

Step 3: Putting Unions Together

Steps 1 and 2 divided the union organization into various units and sub-units; horizontally and vertically. The third step, horizontal integration, links together all the newly divided groups and subunits to obtain lateral coordination and integration. The two critical components in linking the organization together are good communication and the effective use of groups. It is worth noting that today's management literature frequently refers to teams instead of groups. Since communication is covered in Chapter 5, this section covers only the effective use of groups.

In successful organizations, with very few exceptions, the organizational aims are achieved through team activity. A team or group is two or more people who interact and influence each other. Basically, there are six types of teams:

- command teams that are composed of managers and their subordinates;
- task forces and ad hoc committees that are disbanded when their objective is completed;
- standing permanent committees that remain in existence to advance organizational aims;
- boards that consist of individuals who are appointed or elected to manage the organization;
- councils that are made up of individuals to advise the top officer and carry out specific constitutional responsibilities;
- informal groups that emerge in an organization without the support or control of Management.

Command teams, task forces and ad hoc committees, standing committees, boards, and councils are called formal groups because managers appoint their members and establish their formal aims. Permanent formal groups include command groups, standing committees, boards, and councils, while temporary formal groups include task forces and ad hoc committees. Temporary formal groups are created to solve a particular problem or achieve a specific objective and are disbanded upon completion of their objective.

In spite of many criticisms, temporary and permanent formal teams have very important roles in advancing organizational aims. Their major functions are to

- provide members with the opportunity to exchange views and information;
- make recommendations to higher levels in the organization;
- generate ideas or solve problems;
- make policy decisions for the organization.

On the positive side, teams

- improve decision making;
- improve coordination;
- enhance the likelihood of the acceptance of decisions;
- empower participants;
- are a form of Management training.

On the negative side, teams

- can waste time and money;
- provide a potential for individual domination;
- have a tendency for premature agreement and mediocre compromises;
- lack individual responsibility.

The following guide can help teams function more effectively:

- clearly defined objectives, preferably in writing;
- clearly specified committee authority;
- carefully chosen membership;
- a chairperson selected for his or her ability to run an efficient meeting;
- a permanent secretary responsible for handling all communications;
- an agenda known to all members and staff, with time allocated for each item;
- supporting materials distributed before each meeting, and members aware what materials to bring to the meeting;
- short, focused meetings that start and end on time;
- meeting minutes circulated as soon as possible after the meeting to all participants and all others who are affected by the decisions. The minutes summarize who said what and list all decisions, action items, and assignments.[19]

The effectiveness of a committee ultimately depends on the ability of the chairperson to run the committee. The chairperson must be sure the membership is fully informed regarding the committee's objective. He or she is responsible for scheduling the meetings, setting the agenda, and providing all necessary information well in advance of scheduled meetings. In addition, the chair has the following five major responsibilities:

- getting the discussion started;
- keeping the discussion going;
- maintaining focus on the subject;
- managing conflict;
- obtaining an appropriate conclusion.

To get the meeting started, the chair can

- state the problem and explain its importance;
- identify the objectives;
- dramatize the problem with a specific example;
- encourage participation;
- ask a question that focuses on the problem.

To keep the discussion going, the chair can

- use problem-solving techniques;
- periodically summarize the progress of the meeting;
- provide transitions, when appropriate, to the next stage.

To maintain focus on the subject, the chair must be diplomatic but firm. In addition, he or she can

- acknowledge the new topic by tactfully summarizing it and deferring it to another time with specific details for future action;
- reinforce the commitment to following the agenda and completing the meeting on time by restating the meeting's objectives and noting the schedule;
- move the meeting back on course by directing an appropriate question or request to another person or the entire group;
- take an opposing position to make sure all positions are given full consideration;
- set time limits on the amount of time allowed each participant.

To manage conflict, the chair must remain calm and unemotional. Further he or she can

- interrupt the argument, summarize the conflicting positions, and announce it is time to move on;
- summarize the conflicting positions and ask the disputants if the summary is fair and accurate. If there is general agreement, make a judgment as to which is better. If this approach is unsatisfactory, table the subject for future deliberations;
- solicit opinions of the nonconflicting parties;
- take a break to allow cooling off.

To conclude the meeting, the chair can

- summarize the issues;
- review the main points of discussion;
- summarize the conclusions;
- provide a tactful, but honest, evaluation of the group's progress;
- assign responsibility for action.

The chairperson is part contributor and part facilitator but always the diplomat in pursuit of maintaining a climate of focused collaboration. The chair always has the opportunity to improvise, but the preceding guides and techniques will provide the best chance of having a successful meeting.[20]

The secretary is also important to the success of meetings. He or she should always write the minutes at the meeting because this technique can help prevent the group from wandering off the subject and can help clarify the status of decisions. It also gets accurate information out more quickly. Minutes should report all required actions and assignments. This can be facilitated by identifying who said what, actions recommended, decisions approved, and responsibilities assigned. These notations can be modified to accommodate the makeup of the committee and the writer's own particular style. The important point is to focus in a systematic manner on the necessary actions before the next meeting.

The basic objective of committee decision making is to resolve conflicts by reaching a consensus. A consensus is a condition in which each member accepts the group's decisions because they seem the most logical and feasible. To facilitate the consensus process

- state your position clearly and logically, then listen to, and consider, other members' reactions before arguing for your position;
- when a discussion gets bogged down on a specific point, suggest the next most acceptable position;
- accept solutions only when based on sound logic, never just for the sake of harmony or to compromise.[21]

Since meetings can be a waste of time and money, it is important to know when and when not to call them. Meetings should be called to

- get participation—meetings can provide a forum to exchange ideas;
- bring about uniformity of direction—meetings can promote a common understanding;
- acclimate your people—meetings can encourage flexibility and willingness to compromise;
- pack more weight—team decisions can carry more weight than individual decisions;
- neutralize political infighting—meetings can permit dissenters the opportunity to participate.

Meetings should never be called to

- make fast decisions—committees can stall action on almost anything;
- come up with innovative ideas—formal brainstorming aside, creative thinking rarely benefits from group thinking;
- resolve a crisis—a crisis calls for clear direction and inspirational leadership, not group decision making.[22]

The seventh group, the informal group, emerges whenever people interact regularly. Informal groups emerge within the formal organization structure and sometimes have objectives that are counter to the organization's aims. Members of the informal group tend to subordinate their personal goals to the goals of the group.

On the positive side, informal groups

- reinforce the social and cultural values that members of the group hold in common;
- provide status and social satisfaction;
- help members communicate;
- upgrade the work environment.

On the negative side, informal groups

- tend to encourage conformity and resist change;
- may be a source of conflict and rumors.

Managers must learn how to overcome the disadvantages so informal groups can perform at a high level in achieving organizational aims.

Step 4: Fitting People In

The fourth step divides the work and fits the people into the organization. This step is primarily a human resource department responsibility. Human resource management is growing in importance for unions, just as it is for business, government, and other nonprofit organizations. However, unlike other organizations, many Labor unions have been very slow to develop policies with respect to human resource management.[23]

People are an organization's most valuable resource and, thus, are essential to its future success. Even the best strategy has little hope of success if the right people are not in the right place at the right time. The corporate world, recognizing this fact, has upgraded the role of strategic human resource planning. Strategic human resource planning links organizational missions and objectives to human resource missions and objectives. Its purpose is to ensure that appropriate personnel are available to provide the necessary expertise and leadership. Obviously, there can be no strategic human resource planning until there is some form of formal strategic, organizational planning.[24]

Fitting people in can be divided into ten interrelated subfunctions:

- workforce planning;
- job analysis;
- recruiting;
- selection;
- orientation;
- training and development;
- performance appraisal;
- promotion and career planning;
- compensation;
- separation.

Union officers should view the following material as workers' representatives and as employers. From the workers' representative perspective it can provide insight into corporate human resource strategies and motivation. From the employer's perspective, strategic human resource management is necessary to become a high-performance union.

Workforce planning looks into the future of the organization, evaluates the various trends that will take place in the planning period, and projects what skills will be necessary to achieve the organization's mission. The planning information is derived from the strategic planning process and includes many variables. The external variables include demographics, government laws, cultural influences, the education system, economic conditions, technology, and international competition. The internal variables include job analysis, recruiting, selection, orientation, training and development, performance appraisal, promotion and career development, compensation, and separation systems. The workforce forecast compares the present workforce to the projected future workforce so that actions can be taken to make up the difference.

Today work is more clearly divided as production and knowledge. Since union members are moving from production work to knowledge work in greater numbers and faster than ever, local union leaders must become more involved in shared-fate, participative management activities to influence decisions that affect their union's destiny. The AFL-CIO Strategic Approaches Committee and the AFL-CIO Institute for Managing Labor Organizations should monitor industries and major corporations so that union organizations can anticipate necessary adjustments in their workforce and their employer's workforce.

Job analysis includes job description, specification, and classification. Job analysis considers all aspects of a job such as its design, responsibilities, value to the organization, physical and mental requirements, work flow, relationships with other positions, and communication linkages. The process involves collecting all information about the operations and responsibilities of a position and analyzing, describing, and classifying it. The line director or supervisor, working with the human resource department, is primarily responsible for dividing the unit's work into individual jobs.

Job analysis includes two work dimensions—depth and scope. Depth is the degree to which an individual can control his or her work. The job depth is low when there are narrow, rigid rules and high when there are broad, general rules. The scope of a job refers to the number of different operations that make up a job and the frequency with which they are repeated. The division of labor, the first classical principle of management, holds that the more that people specialize, the more efficiently they perform their work. However, as jobs became highly specialized, the workers lose their sense of identity and achievement, with a subsequent loss of productivity and quality. Consequently, over the years, management experts have struggled with this specialization versus satisfaction trade-off. Attempts to solve this problem concentrated on job enlargement and job enrichment. Job enlargement increased the scope of the job, and job enrichment increased the depth of the job.

Job descriptions, written statements of the tasks, duties, and responsibilities (TDRs) of a specific job, are developed from the job analysis. Job descriptions identify each job's physical and mental requirements and typically include the knowledge, skills, and abilities (KSAs) employees must have to perform effectively in the job. These are valuable documents for selecting, inducting, and training new employees, for performance evaluation, counseling, determining compensation, and establishing career paths. However, writing job descriptions is difficult and time-consuming, and they must be frequently reviewed and updated. Unfortunately, even though the organization and the people in it are continually changing, there is a common tendency to ignore job descriptions until they are a source of serious problems.

Accurate job descriptions are extremely important because employees need to know what is expected of them and their location on the organization chart. Each box on an organization chart should have a description that lists the title, duties, standards, and broad responsibilities for each job, who it reports to, and who reports to it. It is worth noting that job description is the term used at the operational level, while position description is the term used at the Management level.

Job classification is a process that divides jobs into different categories based on difficulty and skills required. Along with wage and salary schedules, it ties together and structures all the different jobs in the organization.[25]

Every job and position, including the top officers, in every union organization should have current job descriptions, specifications, and classifications, and they should be periodically reanalyzed and updated. Excellent organizations recognize that people are the source of all innovation and have broad, nonroutine, flexible job descriptions. They also feature intersecting territories that permit workers to look beyond their jobs to collaborate with others for higher performance levels.

Recruiting. Typically, national unions recruit middle and top managers from the ranks of local union officers who have distinguished themselves at the local union level, the convention, or the intermediate union level. In Chapter 1, this approach was referred to as the from-the-rank career ladder. Universities with industrial relations and Labor education schools are another primary source of middle managers. Professionals and experts who work under contract and others with various ties to Labor are also recruited for union Management positions. Nonprofessional support employees are recruited in traditional ways, such as employee referral, Management referral, newspaper advertising, and employment services.

If unions are to survive as an effective voice of American workers in the twenty-first century, they must develop nontraditional recruiting practices. As previously noted, a new professional union manager and specialist track urgently needs to be added to the present from-the-ranks track. Developing a professional union manager and specialist track involves finding, recruiting, and developing talented and dedicated young union members. If a professional union manager and specialist track are not developed, academics, professionals, and experts with no actual experience as union workers will inevitably take over unions or unduly influence the union decision-making process. Consequently, a sacred and extremely valuable tradition of unions' being managed by union members will be destroyed.

Over the years traditional Labor education programs have touched hundreds of thousands of union members who are still active in their union organizations. The providers of these traditional Labor education programs include college degree programs in Labor studies; short-term, noncredit courses/workshops; the AFL-CIO Education Department; the George Meany Center for Labor Studies; university Labor education centers, community colleges; Coalitions for Occupational Safety and Health (COSH) groups; nonprofit Labor research and education centers; national unions; intermediate union organizations; and local unions. In this enormous pool, there are thousands of candidates, with the ability and motivation, qualified to become professional union managers or specialists.

The new expanded membership database, with records of previous educational achievements and training experiences, could also be used to recruit qualified candidates. In addition, the national union's monthly journal or other periodic publications, could be used to explain the professional union management and specialist program and to solicit applications. This exciting, never-before opportunity has enormous political, union-organizing, and organization-building potential. Labor educators, professionals, and experts will continue to play important support roles as teachers and consultants.

Selection. The objective of this critically important process is to place the right person in the right job at the right time. The selection process is complicated because of the many laws and regulations involved. The common tools used in the selection process are application forms, reference checks, screening interviews, tests, and physicals.

Tests, the most common selection tool, is any assessment procedure used to make decisions about a job applicant's qualifications. Tests can be written or oral, such as interviews and situational hands-on simulation. Employers determine what factors are important for success on the job and then develop rules to determine the most appropriate means for assessing them. The format of the test is insignificant compared to what is being measured.[26] In order to avoid major personnel problems and related litigation, all tests must be validated against relevant criteria of job performance. Title VII of the Civil Rights Act requires that tests must be professionally validated as an effective and significant predictor of effective job performance. It also requires that all records be kept for documentation and that the employer identify, analyze, and monitor every step of the selection process to determine if any practices have an adverse impact on protected groups.

A recent survey of national unions found that only 44 percent of the responding unions had formal selection policies, and yet 75 percent required "specific qualifications." The two most common qualifications were specific degrees and training (46 percent) and union membership (37 percent). Twenty-two percent of the respondents indicated they frequently hired employees who had worked for other unions, and 61 percent hired these types of employees "on a few occasions."[27] These findings reveal major inconsistencies in union selection policies.

In regard to selecting candidates for the professional union manager and specialist track, the process should include résumés, student achievement tests, community and union achievements, and personal references. It should also include such hands-on tests as the assignment of special projects and essay competition to identify union commitment and intelligence. To assure a lasting identity with and empathy for the workers, there should be a minimum of three to five years' work experience as a union member. It is also critically important to avoid any politicizing of the selection process.

Orientation. The human resource department usually administers the orientation process. Since local union officers are responsible for orienting both new employees and new members, the material in this section has a dual purpose. The orientation process includes acquainting new employees or new members with the organization, their job requirements, and their co-workers. The supervisor and steward usually is the person primarily responsible for the new employee's or member's socialization process.

Welcoming employees and members properly is critically important to the development of a high-performance workforce and a committed membership. Unfortunately, the first day is usually an exasperating experience for most new hires and members. To minimize these unavoidable negative experiences, they need a strong message that the union cares, is interested in them as special persons, and that they are an important part of the union team. Furthermore, the union should always present a positive initial image—effective, efficient, and caring for the individual. The first day should be a positive experience.

Training and development (T&D) are intended to create or enhance individual knowledge, skills, and abilities (KSAs) that enable workers to perform their tasks, duties, and responsibilities (TDRs) at higher levels.[28] Generally, training involves improving current performance, is usually technical in nature, and is aimed at nonmanagerial personnel. On-the-job training is by far the most common and successful method. Other methods include readings, lectures, role-playing, computer games, and job rotation. Development, on the other hand, is usually broader in scope and designed to enhance the long-term growth or potential of the employee. It is usually conceptional in nature, with emphasis on human relations skills and technical competence.

Workers acquire skills through the interaction of the three major modes of training: informal, formal on-the-job, and classroom. Typically, skills first develop through a dynamic interaction of informal and formal on-the-job training. More formal training is added as skill requirements increase. Finally, classroom programs are added to satisfy the next level of skill requirements. An increasingly wide range of educational programs has been developed to prepare people for a wide range of careers. It is estimated that business spends more than $52 billion annually to upgrade the talents of nearly 50 million employees.[29]

There are three phases to training needs analysis:

- the organization must determine where it intends to go in the future;
- next, it must analyze how operations are to be changed;
- then, the competencies of the employees or applicants are assessed to determine how well their KSAs fit the proposed TDRs.[30]

Needs analysis bonds strategic organizational planning with strategic human resource planning. This is an obviously crucial bond since there must be some idea of where the organization is going in order to prepare appropriate training and development programs and materials.

Labor's T&D efforts have focused on traditional courses such as collective bargaining, organizing, union administration and leadership training, political education, Labor law, economic education, Labor history, communications, and international Labor affairs. More recent Labor education subjects are health and safety, joint Labor-Management activities, technological change, basic skills instruction, and worker culture.

A recent study, *New Directions in Labor Education* by Lois S. Gray, Cornell University, and Joyce L. Kornbluh, University of Michigan, reports on innovative union education efforts. The authors note that the union leader as a manager is a new thrust for full-time staff and officers. Harvard's Trade Union Program has adapted its curriculum to incorporate material and insights from the Harvard Business Executive Development program, and added a new course, Long-Range Strategic Planning for Unions. The University of California at Los Angeles conducted a seminar, Human Resource Management for Union Chief Executives. The Bricklayers and Allied Craftsmen National Union is training local union officers and business agents in self-assessment techniques that become learning objectives to guide the selection of subjects to be studied. The University of Wisconsin and Indiana University have taken the lead in applying the computer to a variety of union functions.

Gray and Kornbluh also note that some Labor educators question the desirability of training union leaders to "manage" their organizations. Further, even those who support the concept of Labor leaders as managers express concern about the applicability of concepts and materials and particularly the use of instructors from business schools.[31]

This book, *Managing Tomorrow's High-Performance Unions*, is in response to the AFL-CIO Committee on the Evolution of Work's *The Changing Situa-*

tion of Workers and Their Unions, which recommended that *"some* of the management, budget, and planning techniques so highly developed in American business circles can be successfully *adapted* to union needs." It is important to note that the Committee on the Evolution of Work referred to some and deliberately chose the word "adapted" as opposed to "adopted."

In regard to the use of instructors from business administration schools, again *The Changing Situation of Workers and Their Unions* recommended "Unions should devote greater resources to training officers, stewards, and rank and file members. In a vastly more complicated world, there is an increased need to provide training opportunities for local leadership and potential leaders. Training *must* encompass the skills local leaders need to function effectively and the information needed to confront the issues of the day." Here again the language is clear: "training *must* encompass the skills local leaders need to function effectively." Obviously, the most urgently needed skills are those required to manage complex union organizations in an extremely dynamic environment. Union leaders as high-performance professional managers are absolutely essential for the survival of free, democratic unions in the twenty-first century.

Therefore, it is extremely important to stress the need for exciting new forms of collaboration with nontraditional academic disciplines, not abandonment of Labor's long-trusted and loyal friends—Labor educators. The AFL-CIO Institute for Managing Labor Organizations' mission is to identify what management concepts, principles, and techniques are to be adapted for the union environment and how to implement them. It also must serve as a permanent forum to facilitate urgently needed collaboration between the various educational disciplines such as Labor and industrial relations, business administration, various enabling technologies, psychology, philosophy, sociology, and political science, economics and union leaders to develop curricula and materials for the professional union Management and specialist development program.

The union Management and specialist development program could be patterned after the U.S. Office of Personnel Management's Senior Executive Service Candidate Development Program. This comprehensive program includes seminars and university courses. It also includes a wide variety of career developmental assignments within their union and external assignments with other union organizations, corporations, government agencies, and other nonprofit organizations. In addition, it includes sabbaticals and fellowships with universities and think tanks similar to the pioneer program that the Service Employees International Union established with Harvard University.

Performance appraisal. For most managers, performance appraisal is difficult, subjective, unpopular with both parties, full of problems, and generally not well handled. For most union organizations it is generally not handled at all. However, unions can no longer afford to waste our most precious resource—people.

There are five basic reasons for performance appraisals:

- employees need to know their weak areas so they can be improved and their strong areas so they can be emphasized;
- employees need to be recognized as individuals for promotions and rewards;
- managers need to know the effectiveness of their training programs and other Management initiatives;
- appraisals provide a formal record of an individual for the term of employment;
- managers need a means to analyze the overall performance of the organization.[32]

The primary goal of performance appraisal is to improve work performance. Studies show that nothing improves until it is measured and that once job behaviors and skills are measured, they automatically begin to improve simply because people are giving attention to them and are getting feedback.[33] A typical formal appraisal system includes specific rules and procedures for assigning ratings to employees. Performance is considered a function of ability and motivation and is typically rated on a scale of 1 to 5, with 1 the worst and 5 the best.

Another approach includes on the entire work system rather than just the employee. The work system includes everything that influences the quality and the quantity of the product or service, such as availability of supplies and materials, training, compensation, style of leadership, the efficiency of the process, the culture of the organization, and so on. This approach recognizes that opportunity also influences performance and can account for up to 90 percent of the variance in work performance.

This new, system-focused approach to employee appraisal involves not only a shift in process but a change in values for both managers and workers. Greater emphasis is placed on team performance and rewards, rather than individual performance and rewards. Managers must learn to think in terms of the impact of how the system affects individual performance, while workers must learn to adjust to the lack of competition between the individuals and the lack of differentiation. Appraisal is more frequent and, thus, brings no surprises and no cause for alarm. The manager is more of a coach than an evaluator. Meetings emphasize praise, recognition, and problem solving rather than criticism.[34]

Job-relevant behaviors and work outcomes are two basic performance areas. Job-relevant behaviors lead to work outcomes—the primary focus of the organization. Both person factors and system factors influence job-relevant behaviors. Person factors are knowledge, skills, ability, motivation, and personality. System factors include economic, social, political, cultural, and stakeholder influences. Work outcomes are primarily influenced by job-relevant behaviors and system factors, not person factors.

Promotion and career planning. A critical problem in workforce planning is the development of a reservoir of managers for promotion to higher positions. Deliberate planning is essential to ensure that capable candidates receive the necessary training and experience to assume middle- and top-level Management positions. Therefore, it is important to identify them early in their careers, so that they can receive the training and job variety necessary to prepare them for these positions.[35]

In the corporate world, promotions will become a less and less viable option because of the ever-increasing trend toward flatter structures—fewer levels of Management and broader spans of Management. Consequently, in the future there will be fewer opportunities to move up the ladder. While this may be a major problem for businesses, it will not be as important for union organizations, since they are already relatively flat. In fact, because of the trend toward specialization and greater complexity, most unions will most likely need more middle-level managers and specialists. The problem for unions is to anticipate the need and develop the expertise.

A common problem facing both unions and business involves the many obstacles that prevent women, minorities, and the disabled from achieving top-level Management positions. In the case of women, this is frequently referred to as the "glass ceiling." You cannot see it, but it's there. They bump against it and cannot go any further. Glass ceilings have unfairly and unlawfully excluded too many talented people from achieving their leadership potential and deprived organizations of their many skills and abilities.

In regard to women, there are three explanations for the ceiling. First, the criteria are based on a male leadership model. Here, employers need to reassess the criteria for selecting applicants for Management positions. Second, men misinterpret women in determining whether they meet established criteria. Here, the need is for sensitivity training to understand the differences in leadership styles. Third, women are frequently criticized for acting too male. Here, employers need to assess the extent to which they subconsciously penalize women for copying the male leadership model. Typically, the male leadership model is seen as authoritarian, assertive, confident, objective, and controlled. On the other hand, the female leadership model is seen as interactive, appreciative, fair, accessible, participative, and collaborative. It is clear that where there are gender differences, not only must they be recognized but special efforts must be made to assure that the female leadership model complements the male leadership model to create a new organizationl synergy based on diversity.[36]

Labor, as the primary advocate of all workers, has a special responsibility to assure that women, minorities, and the disabled have equal access to the full range of opportunities to achieve their leadership potential in the workplace and, equally important, within the Labor movement.

Compensation is important because it attracts employees, provides incentives, affects turnover, and motivates people to improve their knowledge, skills, and abilities. The human resources department is primarily responsible for developing a graduated wage and salary scale that is primarily determined by three basic factors: external competition, internal consistency, and individual contributions. Various compensation models include

- annual bonus plans;
- small- group incentive plans;
- individual incentive plans;
- current cash profit-sharing plans;
- gainsharing plans;
- skill- or knowledge-based plans;
- spot or technical achievement plans;
- key contributors' plans.

Calculation of total compensation is complicated and difficult because it combines salary, bonuses, insurance, various benefit plans, stock options, stock ownership, profit-sharing plans, and retirement benefits.

Compensation consultants Edward J. Giblin, Frank Sanfilippo, and Linda Ulrich suggest that compensation strategies of successful companies will be based on performance. They predict that organizations will stop copying other organizations' compensation systems and design a system that aligns with their organizational priorities. They believe that variable pay will become more important as organizations reward performance and that this new, reward-for-performance system will emphasize a shared-fate environment. Shared-fate environments place less emphasis on differentiating Management pay from that of other employees. Finally, they feel companies will be more concerned with long-term performance. This means an increased willingness to accept short-term reversals for long-term advances.[37]

Compensation, like all successful human resource relations, starts with the basic concepts of fairness and trust. Fairness cannot stand alone; there must be a basic trust in people to be fair. A system can be fair, but its administrators may not be trustworthy. Trust can be earned only over a period of time. The basic concept of total mutual trust is absolutely crucial to all successful employer-employee relations. The lack of trust debilitates and destroys most employer-employee relations. To earn trust, both the employer and employee must resist all temptation to exploit the other party. A trust-building agenda is simple. Say what you mean and mean what you say. No hidden agenda, no stacked deck, and all cards face up. The ultimate objective is a true shared-fate, mutually beneficial partnership based on fairness and trust and sharing the common purpose of customer satisfaction. This is especially true when unions are the employers in the employer-employee relationship.

Recent compensation research reveals that people are more likely to think their pay is fair when they believe that the process used to distribute that pay is fair. Researchers M. J. Wallace and C. H. Fay suggest four criteria for evaluating the procedural fairness of a compensation system:

- an open system;
- two-way communication;
- employee participation;
- an appeal process.

Openness refers to the availability of information about the employer's compensation system. Two-way communication refers to the degree to which the employer actually collects and exchanges information with the employees. Employee participation refers to the degree of actual influence the employee has in the design and administration of the compensation system. The appeal process is a means by which the employee can appeal a compensation decision.[38]

These four criteria are, in varying degrees, basic to successful collective bargaining relationships. As workers' representatives, the union leader's objective is to pursue the greatest possible degree of fairness. As employers, union officers have the responsibility to earn the trust of their employees and to assure complete fairness.

Obviously, today's trend is to reward performance by aligning pay with the organization's strategic priorities. Successful organizations, unions included, need a competitive advantage, and a high-quality workforce is the greatest competitive advantage. Consequently, the union compensation system must also be aligned with the union's strategic priorities.

As noted in Chapter 4, all excellent organizations stay close to their customers. Like business, the highest strategic priority is satisfied primary customers. In a union environment the primary internal "customer" is the member, and the primary external customer is the employer. Improved quality and service go to the basic purpose of the union. Satisfied customers are the surest way to achieve other strategic priorities. Thus, a union's compensation system should be designed to reward employees based on their collaborative efforts to satisfy their "customers." Typical factors that determine an employee's pay, such as the local labor market, independent performance appraisal, seniority, and the knowledge, skills, and abilities an employee possesses, do not focus on the really important issues, such as customer satisfaction, number of new "customers," number of "customers" lost, or the "customers' " perception of product/service.

To assure satisfied customers, many businesses are adopting compensation systems based on performance models. Performance models

- determine what is needed at each level within an organization to produce high-level performance;
- measure and reward performance at each level;
- refocus individuals and units on satisfying customers, rather than pleasing those higher in the organization.

Performance models clarify roles and focus on objectives rather than the hierarchical organization chart. First, they identify each performance unit, individual or group, that has an identifiable and measurable output impacting the organization's performance. Next, they identify the level of each performance unit in the organization and establish the criteria for measuring and rewarding performance. As each unit's mission and objectives become clearer, the criteria for measuring performance become easier to define. Even though performance models may look very much like an organization chart, they bear little resemblance to it, because performance units may have entirely different boundaries.

Performance-unit charters, which focus on customer satisfaction, are written for each performance unit and attempt to identify all external and internal customers for each unit. As previously noted, excellent organizations use the internal-customer model as the primary management tool to promote customer satisfaction. The linkage of customer levels ultimately leads to the primary internal customer—the rank-and-file member. As seen in Figure 7.9, servicing is interactive with, and sensitive to, the environment, and feedback loops are necessary to enable performance units to determine what customers perceive to be happening. It is always important to keep in mind that what the customer perceives to be happening is usually more critical than what is actually happening.

Figure 7.9
The Universal Performance Management Model

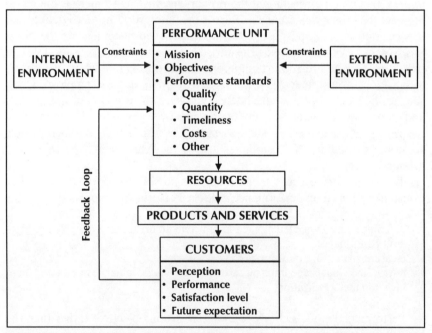

Source: Reprinted with Permission of *HR*Magazine published by the Society for Human Resource Management, Alexandria, VA. An exhibit from "A 90s Model for Performance Management" by Robert J. Green, Apr. 1991, p. 64.

Each performance-unit charter must be integrated across other units to ensure that objectives are not in conflict. In addition, each performance unit must justify its consumption of resources. When there is an effective demand for certain outcomes, the performance unit has a viable purpose. However, when its product is not worth the resource consumed to produce it, the performance unit has not performed at an acceptable level.[39]

The union environment is unique and, thus, most business compensation models will never fit and others will require major "adaptation." However, revising the union compensation system, in a manner consistent with union culture and traditions, has enormous potential for improving union performance.

Separation includes resignation, layoff, discharge, retirement, illness, and death. The loss of trained employees, for whatever reason, is always extremely costly to an organization. Typical replacement costs include recruiting, selecting, training, and developing the new employee to function at the same level of effectiveness as the separated employee. However, separation is inevitable and, when handled properly, can benefit both the departing individual and the organization.

The fact that our society values and protects the rights of citizens through fair treatment and due process is finally having an impact on the separation process. Recent legislation and litigation have forced employers to rethink their industrial justice policies. The traditional employment-at-will doctrine is becoming more rationalized and sensitized. Most Management realizes it can no longer simply fire workers, and to avoid expensive litigation, employers are beginning to apply a just-cause standard for discharge policies. There also has been a significant increase in formal complaint procedures. Since most arbitrators require that Management apply just-cause or fairness standards, discharge is not allowed after only one incident except for extremely serious and disruptive actions such as gross insubordination, theft, or violence. Further, decisions that can be justified to arbitrators or third-party reviewers are almost always upheld in courts.

Relatively recent federal legislation has further complicated the separation process. The Worker Adjustment and Retraining Act (WARN) requires employers to give 60 days' notice of a plant closing or mass layoff to all affected employees or their union representative and to state and local governments. Severance programs, whether written or unwritten, formal or informal, are generally considered "employee benefit plans" subject to the Employee Retirement Income Security Act of 1974 (ERISA). The Consolidated Omnibus Budget Reconciliation Act of 1986 (COBRA), still another federal law, establishes regulations for continuation of health coverage after separation. The Civil Rights Act protects against discriminatory separations based on race, sex, religion, or age. Clearly, separation is no longer a simple matter of paying off an employee and changing the locks. Mistakes can be very disruptive and very expensive.

Organizations, hoping to reduce unnecessary turnover, use exit interviews to determine why people leave the organization. Both the unit manager and the human resource department usually conduct exit interviews. Properly handled exit interviews can reveal a lot of useful information, even though the separating employee is probably no longer very committed and possibly even hostile. The type and quantity of separations provide insight into the quality of Management. For example, a high rate of turnover could indicate potentially serious Management problems, too many resignations could mean the pay is noncompetitive, too many layoffs might be the result of poor scheduling, too many discharges could indicate poor supervisor training, and too many retirements could indicate poor workforce planning.

Exit interviews that reveal a pattern of unfair treatment can be used to correct the situation before it affects the morale and performance of loyal, but silently suffering, employees. Loyal employees who perceive themselves to have suffered some injustice usually do not complain until just before quitting. However, once a loyal employee decides to complain formally, the relationship has been disrupted, and the possibility of quitting the organization is a realistic option. This suggests that tolerating perceived unfair treatment in silence may be a realistic interpretation of how loyalty and complaints interrelate—the more loyal employee is less likely to complain until it is too late to remedy the complaint.[40] Several other typical separation interventions are advance announcements, outplacement programs, and workshops on stress management.

In summary of Step 4, excellent organizations recognize that people are their most important asset. They build upon the fact that people need meaning, some control over decisions that affect their lives, and positive reinforcement. They are people-oriented organizations built upon trust and caring as core values. They realize that even the best strategies within the soundest structure cannot work without a skilled and motivated staff. They excel in their ability to achieve extraordinary results with ordinary people.

The union manager, as an organizer, is responsible for structuring the union organization to efficiently and effectively achieve its mission and core objectives. This four-step organizing process requires a wide range of skills involving a variety of management concepts, principles, and techniques. Given the importance of designing and implementing appropriate union structures for the twenty-first century, the AFL-CIO Institute for Managing Labor Organizations should provide comprehensive research and support programs necessary to help union managers with this critically important function.

SUMMARY

Everyone plans and organizes—two basic functions common to everyday living. Since it is clear that some people are better planners and organizers than others, the objective of this chapter is to help union leaders become better union planners and organizers.

High-Performance Union Planners

The entire management process starts with planning. Nothing can be done unless a plan is in place. There are some good plans, but unfortunately there are too many bad plans. To improve the planning process, this section shows the relationship between the environment and planning and identifies the participants at strategic, tactical, and operational planning levels. It also defines the hierarchy of organizational aims and shows the sequence of planning relationships.

Aims
Organizational aims—mission and core objectives—trigger the union planning process. Mission is the underlying purpose of the organization, and core objectives are the results necessary to achieve the organization's mission. High-performance union plans start with missions and core objectives.

Strategies
Strategies are broad programs and policies that provide direction for an organization in terms of its core objectives.

The High-Performance Union Planning Process
High-performance union planners

- draft mission statements;
- select core objectives;
- evaluate their union's capabilities relative to the core objectives;
- identify which strategies will help the organization achieve its core objectives;
- develop standing and single-use plans for implementing strategies;
- identify the risks involved, determine their probability of occurrence, and consider the ethical issues before approving plans;
- develop contingency plans;
- implement plans.

They always involve all stakeholders in the planning process and are guided by the ten attributes and nine dominant values of excellent unions. They also stress service to others, quality, reliability, and innovative problem solving.

High-Performance Union Organizers

Union organizers design and build organizational structures to achieve their union's aims. The structure takes shape in the arrangement of the blocks of an organization chart. The intent of the organization structure is to organize work to flow in a systematic way. Since organizations are made up of people, they are constantly changing. There is no "one best way" to design and build an organization, since both internal and external forces influence organizational design. However, high-performance union organizers build on the stability pillar, the entrepreneurial pillar, and the need to break old habits.

The organizing process consists of four basic steps.

Step 1: Breaking Unions Up Horizontally

In the first step, breaking it up horizontally, logically related work activities are grouped together. High-performance union organizers

- divide the work among the nine basic union functions;
- establish the organizational mission and core objectives and develop strategies for each division before beginning the organizing process;
- limit the number of performance units associated with each division;
- group related performance units;
- consider work flow when assigning responsibilities;
- focus the organization structure on the products and services that need emphasis;
- establish consistent departmentalization at each level of the structure;
- base departmentalization on the aims of the division, its strategy, and tasks to be performed;
- clearly identify and segregate the division;
- balance efficiency and integration equally when separating the divisions.

Step 2: Breaking Unions Up Vertically

The second step, breaking it up vertically, is concerned with the concepts of power, authority, and influence. Modern management literature leans strongly toward decentralization. Whether an organization is centralized or decentralized is determined by how much authority top Management delegates to the lower levels. The question for union organizers is not whether the union should be decentralized but how best to decentralize.

High-performance union organizers

- establish clear lines of authority;
- keep the number of organizational levels to a minimum;
- delegate decision making;
- delegate authority;
- assign subordinates to one supervisor;
- avoid duplication and breaks in the chain of command;
- design broad spans of Management and flat organizations;
- avoid overcontrol.
-

Step 3: Putting Unions Together

Horizontal integration, the third step, links together all the newly divided groups, units, and subunits to obtain lateral coordination and integration. Two critical linking components are good communication and the effective use of teams. A team or group is two or more people who interact and influence each other. In most excellent organizations, organizational aims are achieved through team activity. High-performance union organizers promote open communication and the effective use of teams.

Step 4: Fitting People In

The fourth step fits the people into the organization. People, an organization's most valuable resource, are essential to the future success of the organization. Fitting people in, a strategic human resource management function, is divided into ten interrelated subfunctions. High-performance union organizers

- project future workforce needs;
- have current job descriptions, specifications, and classifications for every job;
- select qualified candidates;
- make orientation of new members and employees a positive experience;
- have a wide range of training and development programs for members and employees;
- recruit and develop union members to become professional union managers and specialists;
- evaluate employee performance;
- develop an expertise in promotion and career planning;
- eliminate "glass ceilings" for women, minorities, and disabled;
- search for innovative ways to reward performance;
- have compensation systems based on procedural fairness and trust;
- use exit interviews to reduce employee turnover and identify potential internal problems.

NOTES

1. Susan Walter and Pat Choate, *Thinking Strategically* (Washington, DC: Council of State Planning Agencies, 1984), 60.

2. James A. F. Stoner, *Management* (Englewood Cliffs, NJ: Prentice-Hall, 1978), 98.

3. Igor Ansoff, *The New Corporate Strategy* (New York: John Wiley & Sons, 1988), 38.

4. Peter F. Drucker, *Management Tasks, Responsibilities, Practices* (New York: Harper & Row, 1985), 100–101.

5. Stoner, *Management*, 95–103.

6. Thomas J. Peters and Robert H. Waterman, Jr., *In Search of Excellence* (New York: Warner Books, 1982), 8–11.

7. Howard M. Carlisle, *Management: Concepts, Methods, and Applications* (Chicago: Science Research Associates, 1982), 490.

8. Ibid., 491.

9. James MacGregor Burns, *Leadership* (New York: Harper & Row, 1978), 12–18.

10. James T. Ziegenfuss, Jr., *Organiozation Troubleshooters* (San Francisco: Jossey-Bass, 1988), 87–93.

11. Ibid., 81–87.

12. Stoner, *Management*, 277–278.

13. Ibid., 260.

14. Ibid., 250.

15. Ibid., 253.

16. "Pfizer Cuts Work Force," *Chicago Tribune*, 20 Oct. 1993.

17. Carlisle, *Management*, 520.

18. Stoner, *Management*, 272–276.

19. Ibid., 306–308.

20. Charles E. Henderson, "Taking the Lead," AS&M, Feb-Mar. 1985, 24–28.

21. Stoner, *Management*, 309–310.

22. "Attacking Meetingitis," *Working Smart '87* (Stamford, CT: Learning International, 1987), 5.

23. Paul F. Clark and Lois Gray, "The Management of Human Resources in National Unions," *Proceedings of the Forty-Fourth Annual Meeting* (Madison, WI: Industrial Relations Research Association, 1993), 414.

24. Kay Stratton-Devine, "Unions and Strategic Human Resource Planning," *Proceedings of the Forty-Fourth Annual Meetings* (Madison, WI: Industrial Relations Research Association, 1993), 424–425.

25. Stoner, *Management*, 233–238.

26. Scott I. Martin and Karen B. Clora, "Employee Selection by Testing," *HRMagazine*, June 1992, 68–70.

27. Clark and Grey, "The Management," 418.

28. John A. Fossum, "Issues in the Design and Delivery of Corporate Training Programs," *Proceeding of the 1991 Spring Meeting* (Madison, WI: Industrial Relations Research Association, 1991), 575.

29. Knight-Ridder, "Making Education Their Business," *Washington Post*, 17 Nov. 1996.

30. Fossum, "Issues," 577.

31. Lois S. Gray and Joyce L. Kornbluh, "New Directions in Labor Education," *Proceedings of the 1991 Spring Meeting* (Madison, WI: Industrial Relations Research Association, 1991), 574.

32. Kenneth B. Carlson, Robert I. Cards, and Gregory H. Dobbins, "Upgrade the Employee Evaluation Process," *HRMagazine*, Nov. 1992, 88.

33. Kate Ludeman, "Customized Skills Assessment," *HRMagazine*, July 1997, 67.

34. David A. Walderman and Ron S. Kenett, "Improve Performance Appraisal, *HRMagazine*, July 1990, 66–69.

35. Carlisle, *Management*, 466.

36. Jonathan A. Segal, "Women on the Verge . . . of Equality," *HRMagazine*, June 1991, 117–123.

37. Edward J. Giblin, Frank Sanfilippo, and Linda Ulrich, "Fixed Pay Ratio Is Bad Theory at Any Odds," *HRMagazine*, Jan. 1991, 96.

38. Daniel J. Koys, "Process Equity in Compensation Administration," *Proceedings of the Spring Meeting 1990* (Madison, WI: Industrial Relations Research Association, 1990), 586–591.

39. Robert J. Green, "A 90s Model for Performance Management," *HRMagazine*, Apr. 1991, 62–65.

40. Karen E. Boroff, "Loyalty—A Correlate of Exit, Voice, or Silence," *Proceedings of the Forty-Second Annual Meeting* (Madison, WI: Industrial Relations Research Association, 1990), 307–314.

8

High-Performance Union Directors and Controllers

In a free society the leader must follow the people even when he leads them.
Eric Hoffer, *The True Believer*

There is a measure in all things.
Horace, *Satires*, 35 B.C.

HIGH-PERFORMANCE UNION DIRECTORS

Directors are leaders who are responsible for implementing the approved plans for achieving the organization's objectives. They clarify expectations, communicate objectives, motivate people to take action, and maintain high productivity. The position of director is very common in the union structure. For example, I served as the assistant director and director of the Department of Research and Education. As the administrative assistant to the International Secretary, up to eight directors reported to me. Included were Research and Education, Skill Improvement, Safety, Legislative, COPE, Computer Services, Personnel, and Office Services. The title of director is also associated with various industry and occupational departments. In today's world, a union director's most important responsibilities are leadership, motivating members and employees, and building teams. This section covers these subjects.

Leadership

First and foremost, high-performance directors are good leaders. James MacGregor Burns believes leadership is inseparable from the followers' needs and goals. The essence of his leader-follower relationship is the inter-action of persons with different levels of motivations and resources in pur-suit of a common or, at least, a joint purpose. Burns also sees leadership as an aspect of power but a separate and vital process in itself. Chapter 7 re-lated Burns' views on power to organizational structure. This chapter relates them to leadership. Power, he teaches, is a process that power wielders use to realize their objectives, even though their objectives may not be the ob-jectives of the followers. Effective leaders with motives and power bases use followers' motives to realize both their motives and their followers' motives. Consequently, leadership is always exercised in a condition of competition and conflict in which leaders must contend for potential followers. It is im-portant to note that naked power does not tolerate competition or conflict. In brief, both power and leadership are relational, collective, and purpose-ful. Leadership shares with power the central function of achieving purpose through personal values and motivation.

Leaders control other humans, not things. Since things do not have mo-tives, the control of things is not an act of power. Leaders convince followers to act for certain objectives because they represent the wants, needs, aspira-tions, and expectations of both leaders and followers. While the leader and follower may be inseparable in function, they are not the same. Leaders al-ways take the initiative in making the leader-follower connection—it is the leader who creates the links that allow communication and exchange to take place. The genius of leadership lies in the manner in which leaders see and act on their own and their followers' values and motivations. Most impor-tant by far, successful leaders address themselves to their followers' motiva-tion and, thus, they serve as an independent force in changing the makeup of the followers' motives through gratifying their own motives. Successful leaders continue to exert moral leadership and foster needed social change long after they are gone.

Burns divides this leader-follower interaction into two fundamentally dif-ferent forms—transactional leadership and transforming leadership. A transactional leader takes the initiative to contact others with the purpose of an exchange of valued things, that is, economic, political, psychological, goods, money, votes. Each party recognizes the other party as a person and is conscious of the power, resources, and attitude of the other party. Fur-ther, their purposes are related as counterweights and can be advanced by maintaining the process.

Transforming leaders build on the follower's need for meaning to create an institutional purpose. They engage with others in such a way that leaders and followers raise one another to higher levels of motivation and morality. Their purposes become fused; power bases are linked, not as counter-weights, but as mutual support for a common purpose. Transforming lead-ership ultimately becomes moral because it raises the level of human con-duct and ethical aspirations of both leader and follower.

Transforming leaders, morally purposeful and objective-oriented, set direction and are the vehicle of continuing and achieving purpose. The failure to set inspirational objectives is a sign of faltering leadership. They choose key values and create social structures that embody them. Both leaders and followers are responsible for shaping the purpose of leadership. Often, today's dilemma is not so much the absence of leadership but the paucity of values that sustain leaders. Thus, the problem is not a failure of leadership but a failure of the popular will from which leadership draws strength. Transforming leaders give voice to a higher value system, which fills followers with a sense of justice and equity and lifts them above petty differences. Thus, the transforming leaders' greatest contribution is clarifying the value system and breathing life into it. They do not shun conflict—they confront it, exploit it, and ultimately embody it.

A grand leadership theory that closely links the aspirations and expectations of both leaders and followers, requires hard and detailed information about the followers. It also involves such disciplines as history, psychology, sociology, and political science. In the past, combining these disciplines and gathering such information were impossible. However, recent advances in information-gathering and in-depth analysis of public attitudes, aspirations, and goals combined with computer-driven technologies have made possible a thorough understanding of followers' response to leadership.[1] High-performance unions expand membership records as the first step toward a grand leadership process that provides meaning and institutional purpose and strengthens the bond between union leaders and the rank-and-file members.

High-performance leaders use the following four-step formula, either consciously or unconsciously, as a blueprint for action:

- Vision—High-performance leaders have a clear vision of a desirable and realistic future state that currently does not exist and have a credible plan for achieving it.
- Communication—High-performance leaders communicate their vision to others in such a way that they are inspired to be part of it.
- Positioning—High-performance leaders are positioned so that the followers can at all times see their devotion to the vision, and every organizational objective, strategy, policy, and program is aligned with their vision.
- Self-management—High-performance leaders manage themselves in a manner that is flexible, tolerant, and encouraging.

This empowering combination provides leaders the ability to motivate and inspire and to grow and learn, while they translate the vision into a reality. Taken separately, none of these qualities are the key to high-performance leadership, but together they are greater than the sum of their parts.

Furthermore, University of Southern California graduate school professors Warren Bennis and Bert Namus observed that high-performance leaders

- have a strong, defined sense of purpose;
- are persistent and willing to invest whatever time is necessary to achieve results;
- know their strengths, weaknesses, skills, and abilities;
- stay informed, develop new skills, and strengthen old ones;
- love their work;
- attract and unite people in a unified effort;
- build human relationships based on trust, respect, and caring;
- are willing to explore and experiment with any resource that serves their ultimate purpose;
- transform even the most serious mistakes into positive experiences;
- are always guided by the people they serve.

However, today many leadership theorists are more concerned with the style of leaders than their leadership traits. One way to study the style of leaders is to observe the extent to which they demand complete obedience or encourage democratic participation in decisions. All leaders fall somewhere between these two extremes as seen in Figure 8.1. Authoritarian leaders like to have everything under their personal control, while democratic leaders encourage participation in the decision-making process.

Figure 8.1
Continuum of Leadership Style

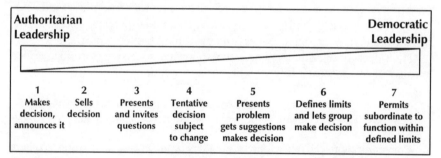

1	2	3	4	5	6	7
Makes decision, announces it	Sells decision	Presents and invites questions	Tentative decision subject to change	Presents problem gets suggestions makes decision	Defines limits and lets group make decision	Permits subordinate to function within defined limits

Source: Reprinted by permission of *Harvard Business Review*. An exhibit from "How to Choose a Leadership Pattern," by Robert T. Gorin and Warner Schmidt, May/June 1973, 164. Copyright © 1973 by the President and Fellows of Harvard College, all rights reserved.

"Concern for production" and "concern for people" are other ways of describing leadership style. "Concern for production" is oriented toward getting the work done efficiently, while "concern for people" is oriented toward encouragement of human relationships and the development of individual potential. Figure 8.2 presents the various combinations of these two variables. For example, grid 1.1 represents a low concern for both people and production; grid 1.9 represents high concern for people and low concern for production; grid 5.5 represents a moderate concern for people and production; grid 9.1 represents a low concern for people and a high concern for production; and grid 9.9 represents a high concern for both people and production.[2]

Figure 8.2
The Leadership Grid

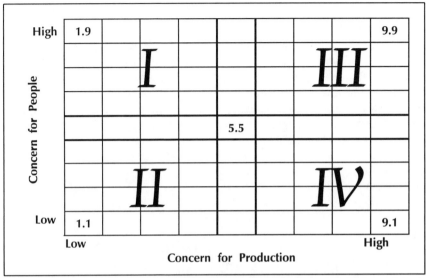

High-performance union leaders work from the right side of the range of leadership skills and the third quadrant of the Management grid. They are democratic leaders, equally concerned with production and people. They also, as noted in Chapter 4, are value-shaping, hands-on leaders. Value-shaping leaders deal with the highest level of abstraction and lowest level of detail and "hands-on" refers to the leader's role in instilling organizational values. Clarifying the value system and breathing life into it are the greatest contributions a leader can make.

Motivation

Productivity through people, an attribute of excellent organizations, is concerned with motivating employees through various techniques to achieve consistently high levels of performance. High-performance leaders recognize that people are an organization's most valuable asset and excel in their ability to achieve extraordinary results from ordinary people. Since a director's output is the output of his or her organization, he or she depends on the skills and motivation of the people who make up the organization. Consequently, the most important task of a director is to encourage increased effort from his or her subordinates. Motivation is concerned with encouraging others to higher performance levels by providing incentives. Motives are an individual's internal conditions that energize, direct, and determine the intensity of effort. Effort is the end result of being motivated. Motivation, broader than motive, includes the entire process by which effort is intensified, sustained, or diminished.[3]

Andrew S. Grove, one of Intel Corporation's founders and author of *High Output Management*, believes there are only two reasons people are not doing their job. Either they cannot do it, or they will not do it. Consequently, training and motivation are two ways to improve performance. Figure 8.3 shows that performance can be improved from point A to point B by training and a higher degree of motivation.[4] Clearly, motivation has an extraordinary impact on performance.

Figure 8.3
Individual Capability and Performance

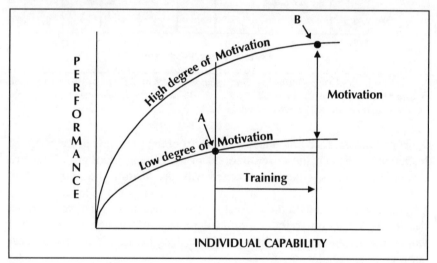

Source: From *High Output Management* by Andrew S. Grove. Copyright © 1983 by Andrew S. Grove. Reprinted by permission of Random House, Inc.

Since there are many theories regarding motivation and behavior, no one theory adequately explains them. Thus, this section summarizes four primary motivational theories: needs, environment, expectancy, and composite-contingency.

Needs motivation stresses the importance of understanding an individual's internal needs. The variety and intensity of these needs determine the effort expended to satisfy them. Needs theories are extremely complicated, because individuals

- have different needs;
- respond differently to the same needs;
- pursue different needs-satisfying actions;
- respond differently to successful and unsuccessful needs-satisfying actions.[5]

While people have many concurrent needs, one is always stronger than the others. That one special need is the one that largely determines the individual's motivation and, consequently, his or her level of performance. It also is very important to understand that once a need is satisfied, it stops being a need and, thus, is no longer an incentive. These are known as self-limiting needs. In short, fulfilled needs are not motivators.

Maslow, as noted in the second chapter, grouped human needs into a five-step hierarchy. He further grouped them into two categories: primary needs and secondary needs. Primary needs include physiological needs and safety/security needs and are considered unlearned. Secondary needs are psychological and are learned through experience. They vary significantly by culture and somewhat by individual. Maslow's theory of a hierarchy of needs is especially important to Management since it classifies human needs in a rational manner that has direct implications for managing human behavior in organizations.

Physiological needs, the lowest level, include the basic physical requirements, such as food, shelter, clothing, water, and rest. Desirable job features are a convenient job location, an adequate wage, and comfortable work conditions. These are the things that money can buy.

Safety/security needs include the need to feel safe, secure, and protected from threats and danger. Workplace features include adequate health and welfare benefits, job security provisions, and a safe work environment.

Social needs are very powerful and include love, affection, affiliation, acceptance, community, respect, and shared values and common objectives. They reflect the inherent desire of humans to belong to groups. However, people do not want to belong to just any group; they want to belong to a group whose members share something in common with them. The social need level is concerned with the worker's need to belong. At this level, the worker looks for friendly co-workers, acceptance by others, organization-sponsored activities, shared values, and common objectives. The employer and the union are in constant competition for satisfying these worker needs. The physiological, safety/security, and social needs levels get people to work, but the next two levels, the esteem and self-actualization needs, influence their performance.

Esteem needs relate to a worker's need to feel a sense of prestige, respect, status, importance, and recognition. Accordingly to Maslow, there are two types of esteem needs. The first, achievement, is the desire to excel or succeed in challenging situations and includes the need for achievement and competence. The second is the need for prestige, respect, status, importance, and recognition. At this level a worker needs recognition for performance, the admiration of others, influence over others, and high wages. The need to keep up with, or emulate, someone is a powerful source of positive esteem motivation.

Self-actualization needs, the highest level, cover the individual's need to find realization of potential, advancement, and self-fulfillment. Workers need freedom of expression and creativity to actively seek out new responsibilities, and they need the opportunity to fully develop their skills and talents. Self-actualization needs include the need to find meaning and personal growth.

Self-actualization continues to motivate even after needs are fulfilled. It drives people to ever-higher levels of performance. Self-actualization can be either competence-driven or achievement-driven. Competence-driven is concerned with a particular task or job. Here it is common for star athletes or great musicians to devote thousands of hours developing their special skills. Achievers are driven by the need to excel in all that they do. They are continually testing themselves. By challenging themselves, they gain satisfaction and a sense of achievement.

Since both competence-driven and achievement-driven people test the outer limits of their abilities, successful managers create environments that encourage self-actualization motivation. Such an environment values and emphasizes performance. Objective setting, as a specific means of increasing motivation, is extremely important to attaining high performance. At the self-actualization level, the greatest fear is the fear of failure. The fear of not satisfying oneself comes from within. Extensive studies on knowledge workers demonstrate clearly that knowledge workers want achievement and, indeed, will perform at high levels only if that achievement is built into their job.[6]

Research reveals that difficult and challenging, but realistic, objectives that clearly specify what is to be accomplished foster the highest level of performance. However, if objectives are to be accepted, workers must trust Management not to raise the goals if they are met and not to punish them if they are not met. Another study found that performance is improved only when workers participate in the setting of objectives. Task-relevant feedback mechanisms that measure performance are also very important in this mode.[7]

Environmental motivational theorists consider external factors to be the most important influence on behavior. They see the environment as an endless source of stimuli that energize the individual. The individual chooses a particular course of action from the opportunities that exist as he or she perceives them. Most theorists agree that work behavior is learned and that workers learn to perform either well or poorly. Thus, environmental theories deal with how the consequences of past action influence future actions. Environmental motivation, frequently referred to as behavior modification techniques, attempts to arrange the consequences of an individual's behavior so that his or her future behavior will be influenced. These theories have been the source of heated controversy for being manipulative.

Environmental theories are based on the worker's ability to learn the relationship between cause and effect and to adopt the behavior that causes the desired effect. This behavior modification, operant conditioning, is based on the "law of effect," which holds that behavior followed by a reward tends to be repeated, while behavior that is punished tends not to be repeated. Thus, the various kinds of organizational behaviors are contingent on the immediate consequences of those behaviors. This suggests that directors can change subordinate behavior by changing the consequences of that behavior. Punish undesirable behavior and reward desirable behavior.

Environmental motivation involves making choices as well as extending effort. The amount of effort the individual extends is based on how rewarding the outcome is expected to be. Rewards can be either intrinsic or extrinsic. Intrinsic rewards, internal rewards, relate to the psychological needs of feeling competent, challenged, autonomous, and so on. Extrinsic rewards are tangible and come from others. Included here are pay, benefits, security, promotion, safety and health, and so on.

The principal conclusion of environmental theorists is that to properly motivate subordinates, Management should be more concerned with changing the environment than with changing the individual, since the environment is much easier to change than the individual. As workers' representatives, union leaders can play an important role in changing the environment to benefit the membership by participating in job redesign. As employers, union leaders must include the employees in job redesign projects.[8]

For consequences to influence behavior they must be clearly tied to behavior. The following are six basic guides for changing behavior:

- reward individual contribution;
- no response also changes behavior;
- let individuals know what they must do to be rewarded;
- let individuals know what they are doing wrong;
- discipline in private;
- be fair.[9]

Chacko in "Member Participation in Union Activities: Perceptions of Union Practices, Performance, and Satisfaction," suggests that union members' participation in union activities is affected by their perceptions of, and attitudes toward, the union. They are more likely to participate if they perceive the union is effective in obtaining both intrinsic and extrinsic benefits for the membership. Thus, the study concluded that "to stay attuned to, and to obtain participation of their membership, it appears that unions may have to emphasize their resolve to seek non-economic, intrinsic benefits that they may have traditionally downgraded in the past." [10]

Expectancy motivation theory is based on the belief that an individual's motivation is determined by expectations about what will occur as the result of his or her behavior. It assumes that workers make conscious judgments about whether they are capable of meeting Management's requirements for a particular reward, how much they want the reward, and the probability they will get it once they have performed the requirements. Expectancy theories respond to differences between individuals and between situations.

Expectancy is based on four assumptions:

- behavior is determined by a combination of forces in the individual and the environment;
- individuals make conscious decisions about their behavior in organizations;
- individuals have different needs, objectives, and desires;
- individuals behave according to their expectation that this behavior will lead to a desired outcome.

These assumptions are the basis of the expectancy model, which has three major components:

- performance-to-outcome expectancy;
- value expectancy;
- effort-to-performance expectancy.

The performance-to-outcome component states that whenever an individual engages in a certain behavior, he or she expects certain consequences from that behavior. The value component holds that the outcome of any particular behavior has a specific value for the individual, and this value is always determined by the individual, not an objective quality of the outcome itself. The effort-to-performance component states that an individual's expectation of how difficult it will be to perform successfully affects the individual's decision on whether or not to perform.

The expectancy model provides the director with six clear guides on how to motivate subordinates:

- determine the rewards valued by each subordinate;
- establish performance standards;
- establish attainable performance objectives;
- link rewards to performance;
- analyze the factors that might undermine the effectiveness of the rewards;
- make sure the reward is adequate to motivate higher performance.

The expectancy model also has implications for the organization:

- organizations usually get what they reward;
- the job itself can be intrinsically rewarding;
- the director has an important role in motivating workers.
-

Expectancy theories are concerned with satisfaction as a dimension of behavior. Individuals compare their actual experiences with their expectations, and satisfaction or dissatisfaction is the result of this comparison. Satisfaction is a personal condition at a particular time. The opposite of satisfaction is not dissatisfaction, but no satisfaction. Conversely, the opposite of dissatisfaction is not satisfaction, but no dissatisfaction. In other words, satisfaction and dissatisfaction are separate and not on a continuum. Thus, workers can be both satisfied and dissatisfied at the same time. Their job can be challenging (satisfying), but their pay poor (dissatisfying). It is also important to be aware that a satisfied worker is not necessarily a productive worker. Research reveals there is no strong relationship between satisfaction and productivity. However, studies also show that satisfaction reduces turnover and absenteeism, which, in turn, reduces costs and increases output.

In the late 1950s, Frederick Herzberg identified two sets of factors that determined job satisfaction and dissatisfaction. His two-factor theory, while subject to some criticism, is still recognized as an important contribution to understanding the effects of job characteristics. The factors that motivate, or satisfiers, are related to the content of the job, while factors that do not motivate, or dissatisfiers, are related to the context of the job. Job content determined satisfaction, and job context determined dissatisfaction. Included in job content are achievement, recognition, advancement, responsibility, opportunities, and challenging work. Included in job context are policy and administration, salary and fringe benefits, job security and working conditions, supervision, and relationships with peers, supervisors, and subordinates. Herzberg believes that only job content can motivate workers. A healthy work environment, he argues, motivates workers and avoids worker dissatisfaction.[11]

A job's "satisfaction potential" includes six dimensions:

- variety—requires a variety of different skills;
- identity—permits workers to complete a "whole and identifiable piece of work";
- significance—impacts on the other people;
- autonomy—permits workers the freedom and discretion to schedule the work and determine the procedures for carrying it out;
- feedback—provides workers with immediate information regarding the effectiveness of their performance;
- opportunity—provides the opportunity for reasonable growth and recognition.[12]

Henry Farber's research studies indicate that the decline in demand for union representation can be accounted for almost entirely by an increase in the nonunion worker's job satisfaction. However, it is extremely important to note that once workers join the union, the union shares the blame with the employer for conditions that cause job dissatisfaction. Further, a 1980 study revealed that members' appreciation for their local union and its leadership is clearly linked to job satisfaction. Unfortunately, unions are not generally perceived as a vehicle for providing more challenging work that offers increased autonomy and responsibility.[13] If these findings are accurate, then unions clearly have a critical, vested interest in redesigning jobs to increase the job's "satisfaction potential." In particular, unions should place more emphasis on job content.

The equity theory, another expectancy model, indirectly relates satisfaction and dissatisfaction to motivation. The key concept in any employer-employee relationship involves equity based on the implied assumptions that each party has about the work arrangement. The employer expects loyalty, integrity, support for organizational objectives, cooperation with others, confidentiality, knowledge, skills, and abilities. On the other hand, the employee expects fair pay, good fringe benefits, pleasant and safe working conditions, fair treatment, respect, certain employee rights and privileges, recognition, advancement opportunities, and interesting and challenging work. Furthermore, employees measure equity in terms of not only how the organization treats them, but also how it treats other employees and even how other organizations treat their employees.

There is also a similar implied assumption between union leaders and union members. The union leader expects loyalty to the union, support for its objectives, participation in union activities, compliance with the union's constitution and bylaws, and cooperation with the officers and other members. The union member expects an effective and efficient operation, equity, competent and honest leadership, safety, security, community, recognition as an individual, respect, the opportunity for self-actualization, and, most important, the opportunity to participate in setting the union's objectives.

The equity theory is based on the assumption that a major factor in job motivation, performance, and satisfaction is the individual's evaluation of the equity or fairness of the reward received. Equity is defined as the ratio between the individual's efforts (KSAs) and the job rewards (pay, bonuses, promotion, etc.) compared to the rewards others are receiving for similar efforts. In equity theory, motivation depends on the individuals' subjective evaluation of the relationship between their effort/reward ratio and the effort/reward ratio of others in similar situations. Depending on whether they perceive an overpayment inequity or an underpayment inequity, they will increase or decrease their contributions to reestablish equity. Efforts can range from greater physical effort, to faithful attendance, while rewards can be anything from salary, to office size and location. Consequently, Management's primary objective is for all employees to see themselves as being treated equitably. When a worker's effort/reward ratio is not in harmony with that of other workers, performance suffers. Whenever an inequity exists, Management must first identify the source of the inequity and then revise the rules, policies, procedures and programs, as necessary, to minimize or eliminate the inequity.

The *composite-contingency motivation* model is a composite model because it combines the three primary theories of motivation. It is a contingency model because motivation is influenced by a number of internal and external variables. The composite-contingency motivation model (Figure 8.4) consists of four phases represented by four blocks. The environment block includes the external and internal variables that serve as stimuli. The individual block includes the individual's needs and motivation that encourage effort. The expectations block includes the worker's anticipation of success and rewards and perception of equity. The results block determines whether the outcomes are satisfying or dissatisfying. The reinforcement loop feeds information back to the individual regarding the outcome.

Figure 8.4
The Composite-Contingency Motivation Model

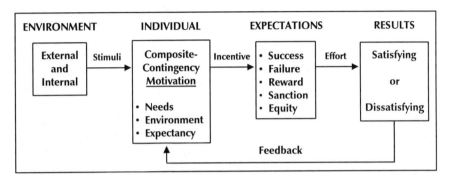

Based on research relating to this model, the following five factors appear to be most significant in determining personal effort and motivation:

- opportunities and constraints as the individual perceives them;
- individual's need for structure and motivation;
- reward perceived to be associated with any outcome;
- expectation of being successful;
- expectation of being rewarded if the goal is attained.[14]

Clearly, motivational theories and techniques can encourage high performance from union employees and greater participation by union members in union activities.

Teambuilding

The success of any organization is determined by how well people work together in teams. A team is a group of two or more people who interact with each other in such a way that each member influences every other member in a positive manner to achieve common objectives.[15] It is also a task-specific, permanent part of the organization structure with a high degree of autonomy in producing a product or providing a service. A team requires a continuing mission in which the specific tasks frequently change. If tasks do not change, there is no need for a team, and if there is no continuing mission, a task force is the appropriate structure. Teams, committees, and task forces all involve groups of people working together. A convenient distinction is that teams work together continuously, or at least more regularly than committees and task forces.

Teambuilding, getting people to participate, is a critical management skill. Kanter notes that change masters are also masters of the use of participation. Participation, she writes, is a means of involving and energizing the rank and file in team problem solving and performance. However, she points out, participation needs to be managed just as carefully as any other organization system, and it creates new problems demanding attention in the course of solving other problems. Teambuilding, Kanter observes, is easier when based on mutual respect, cooperation, open communication, and crosscutting ties.[16]

Drucker sees teams as being highly receptive to new ideas and innovative ways of doing things. He believes that teams also have great adaptability and are highly receptive to experimentation. Thus, he concludes, teams are the best means for overcoming functional insulation and parochialism. On the other hand, he notes, teams have poor stability, communication is often difficult, decision making is more complicated, and they are expensive. Drucker believes teams fail primarily because they do not impose on themselves the self-discipline and responsibility that are essential because of their high degree of freedom.[17]

In the future, teambuilding will be an even more important Management skill because knowledge workers will make up a greater percentage of the workforce. Since specialized knowledge is a piece of the whole, knowledge workers must work with other knowledge workers from other functions and disciplines to complete the task. Thus, Drucker sees an increasing need to manage the specialty to make sure that it contributes to the organizational objectives. In addition, he points out, the more advanced the knowledge worker, the more likely he or she will make his or her contribution as a member of a cross-functional team.[18]

Ray Marshall, former U.S. secretary of labor, sees teamwork in the workplace as critical to our nation's future economic success. He sees the United States confronted with two choices. One is to compete by lowering wages, and the other is to compete by improving productivity, quality, and wages. Thus, the choice is a low-wage strategy versus a high-wage strategy. The high-wage strategy, which Marshall calls a high-performance economy, is based on a high level of worker involvement and participation in joint Management teams.

Team leadership is essential to effective teambuilding. Directors train and develop individuals and teams. They also see that the work of the team is organized for high productivity and excellent quality. When directors do their job well, teams will be responsible, committed, objective-directed, and aligned in a finely tuned, high-performance organization.

Teambuilding for union leaders is much more complicated than for business executives. While business executives are primarily concerned with just building teams of employees, union leaders have three equal, separate, and distinct teambuilding roles. As union leaders, they must build teams of officers and members to promote reasonable and equitable social change. As union managers, they must build efficient, effective, high-performance teams of union employees. As union representatives, they must build teams of union workers to strengthen their position in the collective bargaining process and be more effective partners in shared-fate, participative-Management activities cohesiveness. Union leaders must combine these responsibilities to provide high-quality services cohesiveness to their members, employers, and community.

A team as a whole is always responsible for the task, and the individual member is always responsible for contributing his or her particular knowledge, skill, and abilities. Therefore, teams need clear and well-defined objectives to guide their work and to provide unbiased feedback to measure the performance of the team and each of its members. Consequently, the director's primary responsibility is to establish clarity—clarity of objectives and clarity regarding everybody's role, including his or her own. The director is also responsible for acquiring the necessary resources from the organization.

Team characteristics are membership, size, cohesiveness, rewards, development, reconciliation, design, and commitment.

Membership cohesiveness—The personality, needs, knowledge, skills, and abilities of the team's members affect the cohesiveness and productivity of the team. The most effective teams are made up of friendly, cooperative, informed, self-reliant, dependable, and responsible members.[19] Union directors must encourage participation by minimizing all obstacles to participation. Intimidated, uninformed, and untrained people are unproductive. The obstacles to teambuilding are covered later in this section. In the future, consultants, as knowledge workers with specialized expertise, will play an increasingly important role on the union Management team.

Size—Small teams are generally more effective than larger ones, because the larger the team, the more difficult the communications. However, there is no consensus on the best group size. One study sets it at four, while another study supports eleven. There are numerous examples of effective teams as large as twenty-five. In addition, team size is frequently compromised between the need to keep the team small in order to resolve conflict and the need to involve all affected organization members.

Cohesiveness—Five factors relate to team cohesiveness:

- size—small teams are more cohesive;
- success—to strengthen cohesiveness, while failure destroys it;
- stability—frequent turnover destroys cohesiveness, since time is required for group members to know and understand each other;
- status—high organizational status promotes cohesiveness and provides the necessary incentive for individuals to join the group. In the final analysis a team's status depends on its success in solving problems;
- common objectives—that all members can agree on encourage cohesiveness.

Rewards—People need to be recognized and compensated for their contributions to the team. Without a formal reward system people quickly lose enthusiasm. Thus, rewards strongly influence the extent to which people cooperate with each other. The issue of recognition and compensation must be resolved at the beginning of the teambuilding process.

Traditional rewards must be revised, and new rewards must be devised to encourage teamwork. First, rewards should be closely linked to broad organizational performance. Second, there should be a team-based pay structure that encourages total cross-training and teamwork. Third, there should be a gainsharing program that is tied to total organization performance and distributed in equal shares to all employees. Gainsharing reinforces team performance.[20] As union leaders, gainsharing could be an important tool when representing workers and, in some modified form, it could be useful for managing union employees.

Team development—All teams go through the following five-stage development cycle:

- the start-up stage focuses on training the team and handling the concerns of cautious supervisors;
- the confusion stage involves developing the process, which usually includes vocal opposition;
- the development stage, when internal leaders appear and teams grow in confidence;
- the identity stage, when fierce team allegiance could interfere with achieving larger organizational objectives;
- the maturation stage, when the team, committed to both team and organizational objectives, takes on new tasks, deals effectively with those outside as well as within the team, and refines the internal team process and support systems.[21]

Reconciliation—The essential feature of teambuilding is to reconcile the various and divergent interests of its members.

Design—The team process is designed to encourage mutual trust and the free flow of information and provide assurance that members will not be harmed.

Commitment—Top Management must make a full and firm commitment of time and resources to assure success. If teambuilding is not totally supported by top Management, it is doomed to failure or, at best, a life of mediocrity. They must create an infrastructure that assists in managing and implementing teambuilding efforts. The infrastructure is a set of management-owned and -operated support systems that exist to ensure the success of teams. In addition, top Management must create and communicate a mission so clear and inspiring that all participants fully understand and enthusiastically support it. This mission must be regularly reviewed and challenged to ensure its continuity across the organization.[22]

Control versus opportunity involves a delicate balancing act between Management control and team opportunity. There are no rules and formulas to substitute for sensitive judgment about the right trade-off in a particular situation. Teambuilding provides opportunities for people to step beyond their roles in primary jobs by getting involved in team problem-solving efforts and appears to work best when it has the following six elements:

- meaningful and manageable work with direct and verifiable results that can be provided to the members;
- an infrastructure that includes a supporting organizational structure that recognizes and reinforces team performance rather than individual performance, an education system that provides training and technical advice, an information system that offers information useful in making decisions, and a resource system that assures an adequate supply of tools and materials;
- distinct boundaries for action, clearly defined collective responsibilities, a realistic schedule, challenging team standards, and sufficient authority for the team to manage its own internal process;
- a clearly defined team authority, where the director retains responsibility for end results and outer behavior limits, but the team has full responsibility for the means of accomplishing the results;
- a mechanism for involving all stakeholders;
- a Management style that minimizes interventions, involves all stakeholders, encourages the team process, provides clear direction and timely feedback, and is based on fairness and trust.[23]

Participation works best where all parties involved in it are strong, since true cooperation cannot exist between parties of unequal power. When power is unequal, sooner or later the stronger party will assert its power, and all the best intentions and profound commitments to worker participation and cooperation programs will disappear. As a result, unions are critically important to the success of shared-fate, participative-management programs.

It is also very important that teambuilders allow people to decide whether or not they want to be involved, and allow them to define their own level of involvement. A viable option of not being involved is always necessary, since an unhappy individual can seriously undermine a team. Teambuilders must also manage expectations from the start and be politically sensitive to internal and external power shifts throughout the process.

Traps, gaps, and problems complicate and delay the development of the team. There are time, "big decision," and agenda traps. The time trap is concerned with time away from core jobs since team participation is always time-consuming. Accordingly, the time that team members invest in meetings and informing themselves must be justified. Moreover, people have different amounts of control over their time and, thus, greater or lesser opportunities to prepare and participate. Hence, organizations must approve team activities and authorize participants to take time for them. Time negotiation involves more than releasing team members from primary assignments to participate in team activities and properly allocating the cost of this time. Since production schedules must be maintained, nonparticipants are concerned about having to do the work for absent workers. Therefore, arrangements must be made to do the primary jobs in the absence of team members.

The "big decision" trap is concerned with the team's mission. The more distant, broad, and open-ended the mission of the team, the less likely it will achieve the desired results. In general, participants are not concerned about "big" issues. Studies show they are primarily interested in local issues involving their area of responsibility. As a result, successful teams are continually making improvements in their routine activities. Thus, it is extremely important to identify the real issues, and the best way to do this is to ask the team members.

The agenda trap is concerned with limiting the time allocated for agenda setting. While it is important that objectives are clear, concrete, and likely to produce solid results, teams tend to spend too much time setting an agenda. It is safe to assume that people want to be in a position to take action and bring about results. Thus, the team leader must assume the initiative for setting the basic direction.

Gaps are inequalities that destroy team participation and cohesiveness. Participation is more than observation and tacit approval of the efforts of other team members. People must feel they can make a contribution and be an integral part of the team. There are three kinds of gaps: hierarchy, information, and personal characteristics.

The hierarchy gap is caused by different levels in the organizational hierarchy of the team members, and studies indicate that status strongly influences the participation of others in team discussions. There is a natural tendency to give those with higher organizational status more discussion time, to give their opinions more weight, and to provide them a more privileged position in the team. This tendency to respect hierarchy is based on the emotions of fear and comfort—fear, because of the potential for later retaliation for challenging a person ranked higher in the hierarchy, and comfort, because it is simply easier to maintain familiar patterns of relationships and interaction than to experiment with the unfamiliar. In addition, the best participants, those who tend to dominate team discussions, turn out to be those who are already higher in the hierarchy and in the networks spawned by it. Thus, an exclusionary cycle develops characterized by the following: know-it-all clicks; body language between a few members; managed information; tasks or subjects outside responsibility and interest; fear of being criticized by the group; senior members who make newer members feel insecure. Equality can be achieved only with the full awareness of such gaps and a commitment of top Management to correct them. Meetings should focus on establishing a common team identity, and members must be encouraged to think about problems that prevent cooperation and to explore methods to improve relationships.

The information gap is the result of the lack of information. Effective participants are made, not born, and participation does not always equalize power. People in Management positions, such as officers, have an automatic information advantage and, thus, more power. Obviously, it takes information to contribute effectively to the discussion. As explained by the Johari grid, Figure 5.5, frustrating inequities quickly develop whenever an information gap is not filled. Consequently, top Management must provide all participants with all the necessary information to assure full and equal participation. Education is always necessary to create a sense of teamwork since effective team members require enhanced problem-solving skills and more open access to organizational information.

The personal characteristics gap is characterized by the individuality of the team members. Personal characteristics such as personality, communication and problem-solving skills, and interest in the task can play a major role in helping people become more connected to networks outside the team that gives them an advantage inside it. In addition, interpersonal attractions among team members can lead to subgroups and influential communication networks that provide an advantage in discussions. Furthermore, some participants have a distinct advantage over others because of their job or position in the organization. For example, specific skills involved in stating opinions, developing arguments, and reaching consensus are closely associated with Management positions and, thus, are unequally distributed within an organization. In addition, routine involvement in the decision-making process as part of the job also teaches people to state organizational objectives. Thus, teambuilders must implement training programs to minimize the advantages some participants have because of their personal characteristics.

The problem gap includes such common teambuilding problems as continuity, "suboptimization," political, "not invented here," and unrealistic expectations. Continuity problems are concerned with continuity. Teams can have a life of their own, but membership needs constant renewal. As renewal cycles become institutionalized, the entire teambuilding process becomes easier. New participants can build upon the experiences of former participants. Obviously, unplanned turnover can be a serious problem because as experienced people leave, new people enter. Turnover requires a team to constantly repeat activities, revise previous decisions, and continually change its agenda. This problem can be minimized by "fixing" some decisions so that they are removed from constant team negotiations. Fixed decisions are constraints issued by Management, past team decisions, and/or commitments to be honored that facilitate the functioning of the team.

"Suboptimization" problems result from teams' working together too well and closing themselves off from the rest of the organization. They become too much involved in their own objectives and activities and consequently lose sight of the organizational objectives. This internalization is known as suboptimization because the team functions at a less than optimal level. Team leaders need to be constantly aware that the primary reason for their existence is to advance the core objectives of the organization.

Political problems are caused by the different needs and interests of team members, which serve as the origins of team politics. How much differing needs and interests politicize a team depends on how the team is originally set up. For example, cooperation and reduced politicking are more likely when team members are participating as individuals and not as representatives of special interests, because they are free of the pressure of their outside affiliations.

Teams can also become politicized when there are previously existing tensions between members that have not been resolved before the team is formed. This is common in Labor-Management relations. If no attempt has been made to create a more integrative system, to resolve tensions, and to improve communication before the meeting, hostility may increase rather than decrease. To create a team out of adversaries, careful groundwork must be done before the parties begin joint problem solving.

Political problems also arise when other teams feel they have a stake in the problem or task. Accordingly, at the very beginning, it is necessary to identify all parties with a legitimate stake in the issue and decide how they will be involved. Frequently, directors feel their security threatened and do not want to give up power.

There is nothing inherently "democratic" about team decisions and, thus, autocracy and manipulated democracy could be another source of political problems. Management usually delegates decision and command authority that is task-derived and task-focused. Basically, the majority rule is limited to Management assigned-tasks or areas of responsibility. Furthermore, teams can be taken over by a few dominant people. Thus, the "tyranny" of peers, with pressures for conformity and sanctions for deviance, could easily replace the "tyranny" of managers. For union leaders, the political problems could vary substantially for Management teams, leadership teams, and representative teams.

"Not invented here" problems are the result of a team's reluctance to adopt outsiders' solutions or ideas. This is referred to as "Not invented here" (NIH) problems, and they prevent the diffusion of ideas and solutions throughout the organization. The realities of organizational life and its constraints mean that some people are going to be the recipients of solutions and programs developed by other teams. Since power accrues to idea generators rather than program administrators, other teams' ideas are frequently rejected. Resentment and jealously are other reasons for rejecting others' ideas. NIH problems can be minimized by coordinating the activities of the various teams and by including people from outside the particular area of interest.

Expectation problems exist because too many people expect too much of the team process. Teams, by involving employees and members, can help an organization stay ahead of change, but they will not solve all the organization's problems or create a perfect organization. Even successful team-building programs can be disappointing to employees, members, and officers. Some officers see them as a quick fix that will improve morale, increase productivity, and simplify management. Members and employees see them as an opportunity to seize more control of their lives and a means of empowerment. Expectation problems can be alleviated by establishing realistic objectives and communicating clearly the expected outcomes of the teambuilding process. Realistic objectives and better communication can narrow the expectation gap, but they will not eliminate it.[24]

Clearly, teambuilding is not easy, there are traps, gaps, and problems and, thus, good leadership is essential. It requires top Management involvement and guidance, changes in directors' and supervisory attitudes and practices, members trained in conflict resolution, and problem identification and problem-solving techniques. It also requires the recognition of rank-and-file members and union employees as unique individuals and partners in a shared-fate environment. Even though teambuilding is complicated and expensive, teams are extremely valuable because they continually improve the organization in a myriad of ways. They also are highly receptive to new ideas and innovative ways of doing things.

High-performance union directors, in their three roles as leaders, representatives, and managers are responsible for getting things done, and the best way to get things done is through other people. Thus, directors, as leaders, are best measured by performance. Transforming leaders engage followers in such a way as to raise each other to higher levels of motivation and morality. They are subordinate and people-oriented and utilize the full range of motivational concepts and techniques to encourage high performance by employees, members, and officers. They also are especially sensitive to their members' and employees' esteem and self-actualization needs and build teams that respond to rapid change and continually improve their union organization in innumerable ways.

HIGH-PERFORMANCE UNION CONTROLLERS

Control is universal to nature and pervasive in management. Control is at work whenever humans take corrective action, even when they are not aware of it. Thus, control is any process that guides activity toward some predetermined objective. Control involves measuring, and what is measured shapes and influences the behavior of the organization. Osborne and Gaebler note, "Organizations that measure the results of their work—even if they do not link funding or rewards to those results—find the information transforms them." If you cannot measure success, you cannot reward it, and if you cannot reward it, you are probably rewarding failure. If you cannot measure success, you cannot learn from it. If you cannot measure failure, you cannot correct it. Furthermore, if you can demonstrate results, you can gain support for them.[25]

Measurement is a key to high performance. Without information on results, decisions are usually made on political considerations. Too often unions spend blindly, not even knowing what they are buying. Measuring results gives union officers the information they need to make informed decisions on major issues.

Control is a critical management function because the best-prepared plans without controls have little chance for success, while poorly prepared plans with effective controls will probably succeed. Controls make plans effective, establish practical constraints on all activities, make organizations effective and efficient, provide feedback on status, and aid in decision making. Excellent organizations balance central direction—tight controls—with maximum individual autonomy driven by the nine dominant union values—loose controls.

Control is the process managers use to assure that actual activities conform to planned activities. In the planning process, basic objectives and the means of attaining them are established. In the control process, progress toward these objectives is measured so that corrective action can be taken if necessary.[26] Control is the monitoring and modification of organizational activity and resource utilization to ensure that predetermined standards are met and desired objectives are attained.

Controls

- make plans effective;
- establish constraints on organizational activities;
- make organizations effective;
- make organizations efficient;
- provide feedback on status;
- aid in decision making.[27]

Organization means control. An organization is an ordered structure of individual human interactions to encourage a certain amount of conformity and integration of diverse activities in pursuit of predetermined objectives. Plans, policies, and standards are the basic elements of control. Since organizational plans are highly interrelated and integrated, while methods of control cannot be integrated into one system, Management has the problem of balancing the various controls in terms of total organizational effectiveness.

The transforming process (Figure 8.5) shows how every organization takes inputs, processes them, and provides outputs of products and services. Clearly, since the basics of every organization are inputs, internal processes, and outputs, all three must be controlled. Each one consists of elements that must be measured to determine their status and their contributions to the objective.

The controller, frequently referred to as the comptroller, measures the progress toward an objective, evaluates the situation, and then takes necessary corrective action to achieve or exceed the objective. Measuring involves determining through formal and informal reports how much progress has been made toward achieving the objectives. Evaluating involves identifying the cause of major deviations from planned performance. Correcting involves taking necessary action to reverse an unfavorable trend or take advantage of an unforeseen opportunity. Consequently, the controller must have knowledge of standards and cost control policies and methods so that preestablished standards and performance can be compared.[28]

Figure 8.5
The Transforming Process

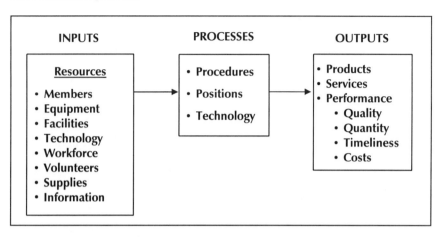

Change, complexity, and mistakes are three factors, common to all organizations, that create the need for control. Change, as we have seen, is a natural part of all organizations. Products, services, officers, departments, industries, and occupations are continuously changing. The control process helps managers detect changes that are affecting their organizations. Complexity is a common characteristic of today's organizations that requires a more participative and more responsive control system. Mistakes are part of everyday organizational life and must be caught before they become critical. Since delegation does not relieve managers from responsibility to their own superiors, they must establish a control process to determine if their subordinates are accomplishing the tasks delegated to them.[29]

The Control Process

A typical, four-step control process (Figure 8.6) sets objectives and establishes standards for measuring performance, measures actual performance, compares actual performance to the objectives and standards to identify deviations and, if necessary, takes corrective action.

The first step sets objectives and establishes standards for measuring performance. Standards provide a way of stating what should be accomplished, and the choice of a standard influences the control process. Standards must be stated in meaningful terms, designed with, and acceptable to, the people involved, and accurate. The controller must be able to distinguish between unimportant variations and variations requiring corrective action, because control of all deviations includes trivia, which detract from important matters.

Figure 8.6
The Control Process

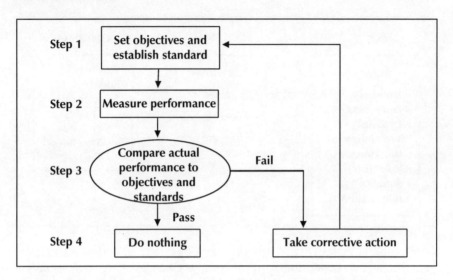

Establishing performance standards typically involves comparing present performance to past performance. The effectiveness of a control system depends on the prompt reporting of results to the person who has the power to produce change. All measurement is accurate only to some limited degree; thus, the degree of accuracy of the measurement depends on the needs of the specific application. Increased accuracy usually increases cost and frequently makes control unnecessarily expensive. The degree of control is also dependent on the situation and the people involved. The task of the controller is to find the proper balance. It is important to remember that inadequate control wastes resources, but excessive control can do even greater harm by stifling and inhibiting individual initiative. Effective control can be achieved only if key results areas can be identified, and close attention is directed to correction at those points.[30]

In the final analysis, the success of a control system is, in large measure, determined by the extent to which controls have been incorporated into the daily routines and expectations of the people affected by it. The meaning that they give a control system, in terms of their own outlook, is as critical as the technical design of the system. No matter how technically sound the standards are, the people controlled will not be supportive unless the standards fit their individual and group expectations.

The second step measures actual performance. A fundamental element of control is the ability to measure actual performance, and the frequency of measurement is dependent on the activity being measured. The timing of the measurement is also critical since the most common mistake is to allow too long a period of time to pass between performance and measurement.

The third step compares actual performance to objectives and standards to identify deviations. Whenever performance is not achieving the objectives, corrective action is necessary. If the standard matches the objective, there is the opportunity to transfer the success into encouragement and rewards. Deviations need to be interpreted in regard to their impact. Some deviations could be minor, requiring no corrective action, while other types of deviation could reach crisis scale, demanding an immediate and total commitment to resolving the issue.

The purpose of comparing actual performance with planned performance is not only to determine when corrective action is necessary but to enable the manager to predict future results. Ratios, averages, and indices are tools to enable the manager to focus on significant relationships. Typical standards are attendance records, production records, quality records, safety records, and so on.

The fourth step takes corrective action, if necessary. When activities stray from their target, an analysis is necessary to determine what type of corrective action is necessary. Corrective action involves changing one or more aspects of an organization's operations, or it may involve a change in the original standards or even revising the objective. Since organizational constraints often limit what a manager can do, the emphasis should be on ways to bring performance up to standard, rather than establishing blame.

High-performance control systems are always

- consistent with the style of Management;
- simple and understandable;
- flexible and self-adjusting;
- fair and objective;
- timely;
- revised periodically to ensure flexibility;
- positive, never punitive;
- consistent with the organizational environment;
- at the lowest-level unit that has a common objective and, thus, will not fight for resources within itself.

In addition, they

- meet the needs of the organization;
- involve everyone affected by them;
- focus on features of the organization structure and activities that are most significant;
- emphasize both long-term and short-term results;
- support the organization culture and the chain of command;
- establish clear lines of responsibility;
- separate the "measurer" from the "doer."

Future control processes will emphasize information sharing, uniqueness, and freedom. In a shared-fate environment, controls should encourage sharing information so knowledge workers have access to all relevant information. In an age of dynamic change and growing complexity, controls should encourage unique responses to unprecedented events. Finally, in this new American workplace, controls should encourage mangers to give workers the freedom to do their jobs.[31]

Types of Controls

The four basic types of controls are steering, screening, regulatory, and postaction. Figure 8.7 shows the relationship of these controls to the production process and provides the information flows necessary to take corrective action.

Figure 8.7
The Four Types of Control and the Transforming Process

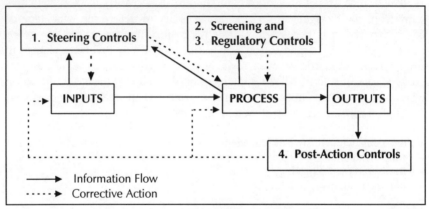

Source: Based on James A. F. Stoner, *Management* (Englewood Cliffs, NJ: Prentice-Hall, 1978), 573. Used with permission of Prentice-Hall Europe.

Steering controls involve establishing checkpoints or milestones as interim measures of progress toward the completion of the project to detect deviations from some standards or objectives. Scheduling or resource utilization problems can be corrected at each checkpoint before unrepairable damage is done. Steering controls are referred to as "concurrent," "in process," or "corrective action" controls. Typical steering controls are Management direction, measurements of progress, accomplishment of checkpoints, and short-term feedback.

Screening controls are standards that must be met if a proposed action is to be authorized. These are also known as "go/no go," "yes/no," or "preventive" controls. Screening controls are the most popular type of control because they provide a means of correcting the situation while the program is still viable. In fact, for unions, it is probably the most frequently used type of control. Typical screening controls are purchasing, job, and product specifications; budget limits; wage and salary scales; and specific item authorizations.

Regulatory controls promote uniformity and coordination in organizational activities. They relate to both strategic and operational planning and serve as constraints that guide and direct the organization. Typical regulatory controls are procedures, policies, rules, laws, job descriptions, scope of authority, organization charts, budget limitations, forms of departmentalization, and chain of command.

Postaction controls, or performance controls, measure the results of a completed action. They involve the reassessment and evaluation of what occurred in the past in order to improve future effectiveness. Typical postaction controls are measurement of key results areas that were important to attaining the objectives. Postaction controls are also used for rewarding and encouraging employees.[32]

The following is a more detailed list of the various types of controls:

- organizational structure controls include organizational charts, policy manuals, work flow chart rules, and so on;
- personnel controls include training programs, evaluation and promotion practices, hiring and separation procedures, job descriptions, and so on;
- authorization controls include preapproval for all transactions, budgets, approval review, and so on;
- performance controls include budgets, variance reports, performance reports, and so on;
- accounting system controls include chart of accounts, general-fund and line-item budget reports, internal and independent audits, general ledger, and so on;
- asset custody controls include periodic inventories and inventory control applications;
- Management controls include supervisory reviews and operational audits;
- operating controls includes procedure manuals and performance standards.[33]

Budget Systems

The foundation of any control process is the budgeting systems. The basic objectives of budgeting are

- to provide a mechanism for allocating scarce resources;
- to initiate a dialogue to ensure that organizational consensus is reached on specific objectives;
- to establish a framework to identify problems.

An effective budget system must involve top Management to resolve conflict and to provide support and overall direction. It must also identify key milestones and completion dates, so an early detection of variance from the plan can take place. An important benefit of the budgeting is the education of users and providers. The budget system provides periodic reports that highlight actual performance and plan variance reports and exception reports.

As noted in Chapter 4, the internal-customer model is Management's primary tool for improving customer satisfaction. Therefore, unions need to implement mission-driven, internal-customer budget systems with a practical charge-out system. The services provided by support and administrative departments, such as accounting, records management, legal, education, research, and information departments, need to be charged out to "customers" such as industry, occupation, organizing, and other line departments. In addition, the services of administrative service centers (ASCs) must be charged out to their clients.

Allocated, performance-unit cost centers encourage honesty in user requests. Inevitably, however, the charge-out system introduces a series of conflicts and friction because much of the system is arbitrary. Thus, there is almost always an immediate debate as to what is an appropriate cost and the comparison of internal costs to those provided by an outside service organization. Charge-out systems that involve complex formulas that include all costs tend to discourage innovation. This is unacceptable to most users because costs are artificially high, unintelligible, unpredictable, and very unstable. In most cases, it is unnecessary to charge 100 percent of the costs to the user. In addition, most successful charge-out systems are not rigorously administered.

Charge-out systems should encourage use of the available services and encourage the service provider to be effective and efficient. An effective and efficient charge-out system

- is understandable to the user;
- is perceived to be fair and reasonable by everyone involved;
- separates provider efficiency from user utilization;
- permits 20–25 percent of the charge-out to be allocated to organizational overhead.

As previously noted, unions, being nonprofit organizations, have unique control problems, since they do not have a "the bottom line"—profits. Osborne and Gaebler, authors of *Reinventing Government*, like most union executives, are critical of typical business-budget systems, so many of their ideas and observations on controlling entrepreneurial government organizations will be especially helpful to union managers.

A typical budget lists dozens of separate accounts called line items for the purpose of preventing bad management, but Osborne and Gaebler contend that budgets also make good management impossible. Consequently, instead of typical line-item budget systems, they recommend "mission-driven" budgets that are general-fund budgets that eliminate line-item entries and allow departments to keep what they do not spend. Each department's budget is calculated according to a formula that starts with last year's amount and is increased for inflation, normal growth, and new programs. Operational managers still use line-item budgets to control expenditures, but senior Management does not review or approve them. Mission-driven budgets empower organizations to pursue their missions unencumbered by rigid spending categories, such as line items. Mission-driven budgets, also known as expenditure-control budgets and objective-driven budgets, are the opposite of rule-driven budgets.

Mission-driven budgets

- give every employee and member an incentive to save money;
- free up resources to test new ideas;
- give managers the autonomy they need to respond to changing circumstances;
- create a predictable environment;
- simplify the budget process enormously;
- free top union officers to concentrate on the really important issues.

Obstacles to mission-driven budgets are

- a "We've always done it this way" mind-set;
- senior Management and officers resent the loss of line item control;
- a lack of trust between senior and middle managers.

Performance Controls

Performance controls are employee incentive-pay plans tied to measures of individual and/or team performance. Almost 29 percent of the firms in a 1996 Watson Wyatt survey reported using performance pay plans for hourly and non-Management professionals—three times more than a decade ago. These plans account for the fastest growing portion of the typical paycheck and account for about 5 percent of total pay.[34]

Osborne and Gaebler strongly endorse results-oriented management as the primary means of assuring accountability and performance. Results-oriented management establishes a set of objectives, condition indicators, and performance standards. Objectives were previously explained. Condition indicators give information on the present situation that needs correction or improvement, such as absentee rate, grievances per department, market pay scales, and so on. Performance indicators are specific measures of service quality, such as membership satisfaction, number of complaints, and voting turnout. Osborne and Gaebler observed that, typically, an organization begins with crude performance standards that trigger conflict and discontent. This pressure results in better and more acceptable measures. This cycle repeats itself, continually improving the measures. Their conclusion is that a poor start is better than no start. All organizations make mistakes, but over time high-performance organizations correct them. The information provided by performance standards allows organizations to reward high performers, use it as a Management tool to improve operations, and tie spending to results. Good measurement systems for nonprofit organizations can take years to develop.

Osborne and Gaebler noted three major distinctions that help facilitate the development of high-performance control systems. First, there is vast difference between measuring process—outputs—and measuring results—outcomes. Controllers naturally measure the volume of their output, that is, the number of apprentices graduated, surveys completed, training manuals developed, elections won or lost, the number of new members, the amount of wage increases negotiated, and so on. However, outputs do not guarantee outcomes. Controllers rarely think of outcomes—the impact the activities have on the "customers" they were created to serve. For example, when the union wins a high percentage of grievances, the output is desirable. However, the output is not as desirable as reducing the conflict that causes the grievances—the outcome.

Even though outcome measures are preferable, process measures are always necessary to help Management improve the organization by identifying problem areas. Further, some outcomes are very difficult to measure or will not be seen for many years. Thus, it is frequently necessary to select measures that appear to be reliable alternatives for the ultimate outcome.

Second, there is a vast difference between measuring efficiency and effectiveness. Efficiency is a measure of product cost, while effectiveness is a measure of product quality . Efficiency tells how much a specified output costs, while effectiveness tells if the investment is worthwhile. It is difficult to justify doing something very efficiently if it is not worth doing. Both efficiency and effectiveness are important, but a balanced relationship is essential. The activity should be worth doing, and it should be done at the least cost. Two prime Management responsibilities are maximizing efficiency and maximizing effectiveness.

Third, there are important differences between "program outcomes" and broader "strategy outcomes." The measure of a program outcome is not as important as a strategy outcome. Suppose, for example, the apprentice training program is graduating more and better-trained apprentices than ever before, but there are no jobs available. Here, the training program outcome is successful, but the placement strategy outcome is disastrous. Clearly, it is essential to measure both program outcomes and strategy outcomes.

Osborne and Gaebler have eight other suggestions for building high-performance control systems:

- Perform both quantitative and qualitative analysis. It is noted in Chapter 4 that excellent organizations almost always use qualitative, as opposed to quantitative, measures. However, there are times when quantitative measures will be extremely helpful. Therefore, it is frequently necessary to combine quantitative measurement with qualitative measurement.
- Watch out for creaming. Creaming is the art of selecting people and projects that are very likely to succeed.
- Anticipate powerful resistance. Measuring efficiency and effectiveness can be extremely threatening, especially to people who doubt their ability or lack trust and confidence in the process.
- Involve members, employees, and other stakeholders in developing the correct measures. Everyone affected by the measurement process must be involved in defining appropriate standards.

- Subject performance measures to annual review and modifications. Measures are never perfect, and change is constant and, thus, it is necessary to refine and modify performance measures often. Periodic, independent audits of performance measurements are helpful. However, it is very important to be aware that measures need some stability in order to compare performance from one year to the next.
- Use a reasonable number of measures. Too few measures may exclude important objectives, while too many measures dilute the effectiveness of the process. Providers can be overburdened with paperwork, and managers can be overwhelmed by detail. The right balance can usually be reached if everyone affected by the measurement process is involved.
- Watch out for perverse incentives. Perverse incentives encourage program outcomes that conflict with policy outcomes.
- Keep the measurement function in a politically independent, impartial office. Since peoples' futures rely on performance data, they must trust that data's objectivity. Consequently, it is important that an independent department be responsible for providing the necessary information.[35]

Osborne and Gaebler emphasize maximizing the use of performance data. However, most union managers are not used to having or using performance information, especially for future purposes. Unions have traditionally resisted performance measurements because workers frequently have been victimized by poorly designed, arbitrary, and subjective standards. Poorly designed standards are the cause of constant conflict and, thus, the source of many complaints. When unions do measure, they usually measure inputs and very seldom measure results. Thus, unions must develop systems and provide rewards to encourage the use of performance measurement systems. Executive information service (EIS) software and other software applications are now available to help control all organizational functions.[36]

Peter Drucker's wisdom is a fitting conclusion for this section. Drucker cautions that control is a tool of managers and must never become their master or an impediment to their work. He states that the purpose of control is to make the process go smoothly, properly, and according to high standards. He sees a three-element control process. The first control element questions whether the control system maintains the process within a permissible range of deviation with the minimum effort.

His second control element concerns the basic characteristics of controls. Since controls have to be preset, there has to be a decision about the desired performance and about the permissible deviation from the norm. Control, Drucker stresses, should be by "exception," where only significant deviation triggers the control. As long as the process operates within the preset standards, it is under control and does not require any action.

Drucker's third control element is feedback from the work done. Feedback is the process of adjusting future actions based on information about past performance. It involves the interdependence of one part of the system with another part. The work itself, he argues, has to provide the information. He points out that effective control systems designate the key results area at which control is built-in. They identify the point in the system where there is sufficient information to know whether corrective action is needed and where corrective action can be most effective.

In brief, Drucker's control process

- sets goals and values, neither of which can be objective or neutral;
- focuses on results;
- includes both measurable and nonmeasurable events.

Drucker believes that an organization's ultimate control is its system of rewards and sanctions and its values and prohibitions. Since organizations comprise people, each with his or her own ambitions, ideas, and needs, they have to satisfy the ambitions and needs of their members, as individuals, through organizational rewards and sanctions and incentives and deterrents.[37]

Since most union managers tend to microcontrol, they need to focus on the results rather than the process. Generally, union managers use prescriptions and requirements, rather than the results, for achieving objectives. Too much prescriptiveness and too many requirements stifle innovation and constrain flexibility. Planning for performance standards should be a "bottom up" program that develops measurements and standards from the "customer's" perspective. Unions need to identify and recommend standards for performance that meet the "customer's" expectations. Their primary objective is to measure the degree to which they meet the "customer's" expectations.

SUMMARY

Union directors are leaders and teambuilders responsible for implementing the approved plans for achieving their unit's objectives and the organization's mission. Union controllers measure the progress toward an objective, evaluate the situation, and, if necessary, take corrective action to achieve or exceed the objective.

High-Performance Union Directors

Union directors clarify expectations, communicate objectives, motivate people to take action, and maintain high-level performance. This section focuses on leadership, motivation, and teambuilding.

Leadership

First and foremost, effective directors must be good leaders. The essence of the leader-follower relationship is the interaction of persons with different levels of motivations and power potential, in pursuit of a common purpose. This leader-follower interaction takes two fundamentally different forms. A transactional leader contacts others with the purpose of an exchange of valued things. A transforming leader builds on an individual's need for meaning, and that creates an institutional purpose. A grand leadership model closely links the aspirations and expectations of both leaders and followers based on hard and detailed data about the followers. Successful leaders follow a four-step formula and possess ten common traits.

High-performance directors

- recognize that the genius of leadership lies in the manner in which leaders see and act on their own and their followers' values and motivations;
- are transforming, hands-on leaders;
- have a democratic leadership style.

Motivation

A director's output is the output of his or her organization, which depends on the skills and motivation of the people that make up the organization. Thus, a director's most important task is to elicit high-level performance from his or her subordinates. Since motivation encourages high performance by providing incentives, this section summarizes the needs, environmental, expectancy, and composite-contingency motivational theories.

High-performance union directors

- recognize that people are an organization's most valuable asset;
- emphasize the esteem and self-actualization needs of their members and employees;
- are more concerned with changing the environment than the individual;
- recognize the increasing importance of noneconomic, intrinsic rewards;
- recognize the importance of increasing their members' and employees' job satisfaction;
- assure that all members and employees see themselves as being treated equitably;
- utilize the full range of motivational theories and techniques to encourage high-level performance from their employees and greater participation by members in union activities;
- design organizational strategies and structures that enable both employees and members to realize their full potential.

Teambuilding

Teams are groups of two or more people who interact with each other in such a way that each member influences every other member in a positive manner to achieve common objectives. The success of any organization is determined by how well people work together in teams. Thus, teambuilding is a critical Management skill. This section also covers team leadership, team characteristics, Management control versus team opportunity, traps, gaps, and problems.

High-performance union directors

- train and develop individuals and teams;
- organize teams for high productivity and excellent quality;
- are primarily responsible for establishing clarity and providing necessary resources;
- minimize obstacles to participation;
- establish cohesive, small teams;
- reward and compensate people for their contributions to the team;
- reconcile the various and divergent interests of team members;
- build teams based on mutual trust, the free flow of information, and member security;
- skillfully balance Management control and team opportunity;
- assure a balance of power among all team members;
- avoid traps, gaps, and problems;
- change traditional middle Management and supervisory attitudes and practices to support teambuilding;
- train team members in conflict resolution and problem-identifying and problem-solving techniques;
- recognize union members and employees as unique individuals and partners in a shared-fate environment;
- provide opportunities for people to step beyond their roles in core jobs by getting them involved in team problem-solving efforts.

High-performance union teams

- have clear and well-defined objectives to guide their work, and there is unbiased feedback to measure the performance of the team and each of its members;
- have top Management support.

High-Performance Union Controllers

Control is a critical management function, since the best-prepared plans without controls have little chance for success, while poorly prepared plans with effective controls will probably succeed. What is measured shapes and influences the behavior of the organization. Control is the process managers use to assure that actual activities conform to planned activities. Controls make plans effective, establish practical constraints on all activities, make organizations effective and efficient, provide feedback on status, and aid in decision making.

The Control Process

A typical four-step control process involves for setting objectives and performance standards, measuring actual performance, comparing actual performance to objectives and standards, identifying deviations, and taking corrective action.

High-performance union control systems are

- consistent with the style of Management and the organizational environment;
- simple and understandable;
- flexible and self-adjusting;
- fair and objective;
- timely;
- revised periodically to ensure flexibility;
- positive, never punitive;
- applied at the lowest-level unit that has a common objective and, thus, will not fight for resources within itself.

In addition, they

- meet the needs of the organization;
- involve everyone affected by them;
- focus on features of the organization structure and activities that are most significant;
- emphasize both long-term and short-term results;
- support the organization culture and chain of command;
- establish clear lines of responsibility;
- separate the "measurer" from the "doer";
- emphasize information sharing, uniqueness, and freedom.

Types of Controls

The four basic types of controls are steering, screening, regulatory, and postaction. High-performance union controllers select and apply the four basic types of controls to achieve objectives.

Budget Systems

The foundation of any control process is the budgeting system, and the basic objectives of budgeting are to provide a mechanism for allocating scarce resources, initiating dialogues to ensure that organizational consensus is reached on specific objectives, and identifying problems. A charge-out system is essential in an internal-customer-driven budget system, and mission-driven budgets are another critically important component of an effective nonprofit control system. Mission-driven budgets are the opposite of rule-driven budgets.

High-performance union budget systems

- involve top union Management to provide support and resolve conflict;
- use mission-driven, internal-customer budgets with practical performance-unit, charge-out systems.

Performance Controls

Performance controls are employee incentive-pay plans tied to measures of individual and/or team performance. Results-oriented management is the primary means of assuring accountability and performance. Results-oriented management establishes a set of objectives, condition indicators, and performance standards.

High-performance union control systems

- focus on results rather than process;
- balance the relationship between effectiveness and efficiency;
- distinguish between "strategy outcomes" and "program outcomes";
- perform both quantitative and quantity analysis;
- watch out for creaming;
- anticipate powerful resistance;
- involve all stakeholders;
- annually review and modify performance measures;
- use a reasonable number of measures;
- watch out for perverse incentives;
- keep the control process politically independent;
- establish a permissible range of deviation where only significant deviation triggers corrective action;
- control only key results areas.

The AFL-CIO Institute for Managing Labor Organizations should encourage research and develop materials and training programs to help union leaders become more effective teambuilders and controllers.

NOTES

1. James MacGregor Burns, *Leadership* (New York: Harper & Row, 1978), 18–27.

2. Robert Black and Jane Srygley Mouton, *The Managerial Grid* (Houston, TX: Gulf, 1978), 11.

3. Howard M. Carlisle, *Management: Concepts, Methods, and Applications* (Chicago: Science Research Associates, 1982), 368.

4. Andrew S. Grove, *High Output Management* (New York: Randon House, 1983), 158.

5. James A. F. Stoner, *Management* (Englewood Cliffs, NJ: Prentice-Hall, 1978), 407–408.

6. Carlisle, *Management*, 369–373.

7. Neal Herrick, *Joint Management and Employee Participation* (San Francisco: Jossey-Bass, 1990), 166.

8. Carlisle, *Management*, 373–377.

9. Stoner, *Management*, 425.

10. Thomas I. Chacko, "Member Participation in Union Activities: Perceptions of Union Practices, Performance, and Satisfaction," *Journal of Labor Research* 6, no. 4, Fall 1985, 372.

11. Carlisle, *Management*, 386–387.

12. *Pryor Report* 3, no. 11, "Measuring a Job's Motivating Potential," (Clemson, SC: Fred Pryor, July 1987), 11.

13. Gordon et al., *Journal of Applied Psychology*, Aug. 1990, 492, 496.

14. Carlisle, *Management*, 379–380.

15. Herrick, *Joint Management*, 190.

16. Rosabeth Moss Kanter, *The Change Masters* (New York: Simon & Schuster, 1983), 241–243.

17. Peter F. Drucker, *Management Tasks, Responsibilities, Practices* (New York: Harper & Row, 1985), 567–568.

18. Ibid., 570.

19. Herrick, *Joint Management*, 190.

20. Robert J. Doyle, "Caution: Self-Directed Work Teams," *HRMagazine*, June 1992, 153.

21. Stephen S. McIntosh, "Help for the Self-Directed Work Team," *HRMagazine*, Sept. 1991, 9–10. Review of *Self-Directed Work Teams: The New American Challenge* by Jack D. Osburn et al.

22. Leslie L. Kossoff, "Total Quality or Total Chaos?," *HRMagazine*, Apr. 1993, 134.

23. Stephen S. McIntosh, "Some Teams Work, This one Doesn't," *HRMagazine*, July 1991, 9–10. Review of *Groups That Work (and Those That Don't) Creating Conditions for Effective Teamwork* by J. Richard Hackman.

24. Kanter, *The Change Masters*, 243–277.

25. David Osborne and Ted Gaebler, *Reinventing Government* (New York: Plume Books, 1993), 146–155.

26. Stoner, *Management*, 566.

27. Carlisle, *Management*, 282–284.

28. Harold Kerzner, *Project Management* (New York: Van Nostrand Reinhold, 1989), 234–235.

29. Stoner, *Management*, 569.

30. Ibid., 567–568.

31. Tom Post, "Firing Up for the Future," *Success*, Feb. 1989, 56.

32. Carlisle, *Management*, 283–284.

33. *Viewpoints*, "Assessing Your Control Risks," Thomas Havey Co., Sept. 1992.

34. Steven Pearlstein, "The Quiet Revolution: Linking Pay to the Bottom Line," *Washington Post*, Trendlines, 21 Nov. 1996.

35. Osborne and Gaebler, *Reinventing*, 349–359.

36. "Total Quality Management," *Washington Post*, 6 June 1993.

37. Drucker, *Management*, 218–220.

Selected Bibliography

AFL-CIO Committee on the Evolution of Work. (1983). *The Future Of Work.* Washington, DC: AFL-CIO.
———. (1985). *The Changing Situation of Workers and Their Unions.* Washington, DC: AFL-CIO.
———. (1994). *The New American Workplace: A Labor Perspective.* Washington, DC: AFL-CIO.
Ansoff, H. Igor. (1988). *The New Corporate Strategy.* New York, NY: John Wiley & Sons.
Being Heard Strategic Communications Report and Recommendations. (1994). Prepared for the AFL-CIO by Greer, Margolis, Mitchell, Burns, & Associates, Inc.
Belman, Dale, Morely Gunderson, and Douglas Hyatt, eds. (1996). *Public Sector Employment in a Time of Transition.* Madison, WI: Industrial Relations Research Association Series.
Bittle, Lester R. (1972). *The Nine Keys of Management.* New York: McGraw-Hill, Inc.
Burns, James MacGregor. (1978). *Leadership.* New York: Harper & Row, Publishers, Inc.
Buskirk, Richard H. (1974). *Modern Management & Machiavelli.* New York: Meridan.
Carlisle, Howard M. (1982). *Management: Concepts, Methods, and Applications.* Chicago: Science Research Associates.
Carver, John. (1990). *Boards That Make A Difference.* San Francisco: Jossey-Bass.
Coates, Joseph F. (1986). *Issues Management.* Mt. Airy, MD: Lomond.
Coates, Joseph F., and Jennifer Jarratt. (1989). *What Futurists Believe.* Mt. Airy, MD: Lomond.
David, Fred R. (1991). *Strategic Management.* New York: Macmillan.
Defense Systems Management College. (1986) *Risk Management Concepts and Guidance.* Developed under contract by the Analytic Sciences Corporation (TASC). Fort Belvoir, VA.
Douglas, Mary, and Aaron Wildavsky. (1983) *Risk and Culture.* Berkeley: University of California Press.

Drucker, Peter F. (1967). *The Effective Executive*. New York: Harper & Row.

———. (1985). *Management Tasks, Responsibilities, Practices*. New York, NY: Harper & Row.

———. (1990). *Managing the Nonprofit Organization*. New York, NY: Harper & Collins.

Dunlop, John. (1990). *The Management of Labor Unions*. Lexington, MA: Lexington Books.

Farb, Peter. (1973). *Word Play; What Happens When People Talk*. New York: Alfred A. Knopf.

Ferman, Luis A. et al., eds. (1990). *New Developments in Worker Training: A Legacy for the 1990s*. Madison, WI: Industrial Relations Research Association Series.

Fischhoff, Baruck. et al. *Acceptable Risk*. New York: Cambridge University Press.

Garrity, Robert K. (1989). *The Twentieth Century: An Epic of America and World Events*. Thousand Oaks, CA: K-G Books.

Geoghegan, Thomas. (1991). *Which Side Are You On?* New York: Farrar, Straus, & Giroux.

Gordon, Judith R. (1991). *Organizational Behavior*. Boston: Allyn and Bacon.

Gore, Andrew S. (1983). *High Output Management*. New York: Random House.

Gracian, Baltasar. (1992). *The Art of Worldly Wisdom*. Translated by Christopher Maurer. New York: Doubleday.

Hammer, Michael, and James Champy. (1993). *Reengineering the Corporation*. New York: Harper-Collins.

Haynes, W. Warren. (1964). *Management Analysis, Concepts and Cases*. Englewood Cliffs, NJ: Prentice-Hall.

Heirs, Ben, with Peter Farrell. (1987). *The Professional Decision Thinker*. New York: Dodd, Mead.

Herrick, Neal. (1990). *Joint Management and Employee Participation*. San Francisco: Jossey-Bass.

Hill, Percy H. et al. (1986). *Making Decisions*. Lanham, MD: University Press of America.

Hirsch, E. D., Jr. (1987). *Cultural Literacy*. Boston: Houghton Mifflin.

Hoffer, Eric. (1951). *The True Believer*. New York: Harper & Row.

———. (1955). *The Passionate State of Mind*. New York: Harper & Row.

———. (1963). *The Ordeal of Change*. New York: Harper & Row.

———. (1967). *The Temper of Our Times*. New York: Harper & Row.

Jones, Manley Howe. (1957). *Executive Decision Making*. Homewood, IL: Richard D. Iewin.

Kanter, Rosabeth Moss. (1983). *The Change Masters*. New York: Simon & Schuster.

Kaufman, Bruce E., and Morris M. Kleiner, eds. (1993). *Employee Representation Alternatives and Future Directions*. Madison, WI: Industrial Relations Research Association Series.

Kerzner, Harold. (1989). *Project Management a System Approach to Planning, Scheduling and Controlling*. New York: Van Nostrand Reinhold.

Keyes, Ralph. (1985). *Chancing It*. Boston: Little, Brown.

Kleiner, Morris M. et al. (1987) *Human Resources and the Performance of the Firm*. Madison, WI: Industrial Relations Research Association Series.

Kubr, Milan. (1988). *Management Consulting: A Guide to The Profession*. Geneva, Switzerland: International Labour Organization.

————. (1993). *How to Select and Use Consultants*. Geneva, Switzerland: International Labour Office.

Lewin, David, Olivia S. Mitchell, and Peter D. Sherer. eds. (1992). *Research Frontiers in Industrial Relations and Human Resources*. Madison, WI: Industrial Relations Research Association Series.

Lipset, Seymour, Martin, Martin Trow, and James Coleman. (1962). *Union Democracy*. Garden City, NY: Anchor Books, Doubleday.

Maclean, Douglas. (1986). *Values at Risk*. Totowa, NJ: Rowman and Allenhead.

McFarlan, F. Warren, and James L. McKenney. (1983). *Corporate Information Systems Management*. Homewood, IL: Richard D. Irwin.

McKelvey, Jean T., ed. (1977). *The Duty of Fair Representation*. Ithaca, NY: ILR.

Osborne, David, and Ted Gaebler. (1993). *Reinventing Government*. Reading, MA: Addison-Wesley.

Parkhurst, William. (1988). *The Eloquent Executive*. New York: Times Books.

Peters, Thomas J., and Robert H. Waterman, Jr. (1982). *In Search of Excellence*. New York: Warner Books.

Rawls John. (1972). *A Theory of Justice*. Cambridge: Belknap Press of Harvard University Press.

Reich, Robert B. (1991). *The Work of Nations*. New York: Alfred A. Knopf.

Shostak, Arthur B. (1991). *Robust Unionism*. Ithaca, NY: ILR Press.

Stoner, James A. F. (1978). *Management*. Englewood Cliffs, NJ: Prentice-Hall.

Stratton, Kay and Robert B. Brown. (1988). "Strategic Planning in U.S. Labor Unions." Industrial Relations Research Association Series, Proceedings of the Forty-First Annual Meeting, 28–30 December 1988.

Strauss, George, Daniel G. Gallagher, and Jack Fiorito. eds. (1991). *The State of the Unions*. Madison, WI: Industrial Relations Research Association Series.

Tong, Rosemarie. (1986). *Ethics in Policy Analysis*. Englewood Cliffs, NJ: Prentice-Hall.

Voos, Paula B., ed. (1994). *Contemporary Collective Bargaining in the Private Sector*. Madison, WI: Industrial Relations Research Association Series.

Wallihan, James. (1985). *Union Government and Organization*. Washington, DC: BNA.

Walter, Susan, and Pat Choate. (1984). *Thinking Strategically*. Washington, DC: Council of State Planning Agencies.

Ziegenfuss, James T., Jr. (1988). *Organizational Troubleshooters*. San Francisco: Jossey-Bass.

Index

Numbers in bold indicate first and second level headings

About the Author

THOMAS A. HANNIGAN has been a member of the International Brotherhood of Electrical Workers, Local 134, for more than 40 years. He started as an apprentice and moved up to journeyman electrician, steward, foreman, and, at the international union level, to Director of the Research and Education Department to Executive Assistant to the International Secretary. He served on various commissions under Presidents Johnson and Nixon, culminating when President Carter appointed him to the U.S. Metric Board. He is currently a member of the Industrial Relations Research Association and the Society for Human Resource Management. He has lectured at Notre Dame University, the U.S. Naval Academy, the Industrial College of the Armed Forces, and the U.S. Senior Executive Service.

ISBN 1-56720-102-4

90000>

EAN

9 781567 201024

HARDCOVER BAR CODE